# The Mapmaker's Wife

# The Mapmaker's Wife

*A True Tale of Love, Murder and Survival in the Amazon*

## Robert Whitaker

## Doubleday

LONDON · NEW YORK · TORONTO · SYDNEY · AUCKLAND

TRANSWORLD PUBLISHERS
61–63 Uxbridge Road, London W5 5SA
a division of The Random House Group Ltd

RANDOM HOUSE AUSTRALIA (PTY) LTD
20 Alfred Street, Milsons Point, Sydney,
New South Wales 2061, Australia

RANDOM HOUSE NEW ZEALAND LTD
18 Poland Road, Glenfield, Auckland 10, New Zealand

RANDOM HOUSE SOUTH AFRICA (PTY) LTD
Endulini, 5a Jubilee Road, Parktown 2193, South Africa

Published 2004 by Doubleday
a division of Transworld Publishers

A catalogue record for this book is available from the British Library.
ISBNs 0385 60520X (cased)
0385 605218 (tpb)

Typeset in Granjon

Printed in Great Britain
by Mackays of Chatham plc, Chatham, Kent

1 3 5 7 9 10 8 6 4 2

Papers used by Transworld Publishers are natural, recyclable products made from wood grown
in sustainable forests. The manufacturing processes conform to the environmental regulations
of the country of origin.

*To my wife, Andrea,*
*who shared with me our first adventure in Ecuador*

*and*

*To Ignacio Alvarez,*
*who long ago taught me to love all things Spanish*

THIS IS CONSECRATED to the memory of Isabel Godin des Odonais, which can never be too honored, who alone and abandoned, traversed so courageously the vast expanse of the American continent buoyed up by her greatness of spirit and a martyr to her duty.

—Charles Bonaparte,
nineteenth-century naturalist,
upon naming a South American
field bird *Champelix godina*

# Contents

| | *Preface* | xi |
|---|---|---|
| 1 | A Sunday in 1769 | 1 |
| 2 | Not Quite Round | 7 |
| 3 | A Daughter of Peru | 31 |
| 4 | The Mapmakers | 47 |
| 5 | Voyage to Quito | 65 |
| 6 | Measuring the Baseline | 93 |
| 7 | High-Altitude Science | 109 |
| 8 | Death in the Afternoon | 135 |
| 9 | Marriage in Quito | 151 |
| 10 | Down the Amazon | 169 |
| 11 | A Continent Apart | 205 |

# Contents

12  Lost on the Bobonaza                    231

13  Into the Jungle                          247

14  Deliverance                              269

15  Saint Amand                              283


Characters                                   297

Notes                                        303

Bibliography                                 329

Acknowledgments                              339

Index                                        343

# Preface

**M**ORE THAN TWENTY-FIVE years ago, I fell in love with Ecuador. I had recently graduated from college, and I lived for a time in a remote village called Las Manchas on Ecuador's coast. My girlfriend and I built a bamboo hut on stilts on the outskirts of the village, next to a river emptying into the Pacific, and hoped that we could stay there forever.

We couldn't, of course—the real world got in the way—but I always longed to go back. Researching this book provided me with that opportunity, and I quickly fell in love all over again with that mesmerizing country and its wonderful people.

In many ways, the Charles-Marie de La Condamine expedition—which provides the backdrop for this story of Isabel Godin's adventure in the Amazon—occupies a central place in South American history, akin to the exploration of North America by Meriwether Lewis and William Clark. Over the course of eight years (1736–1744), La Condamine and eleven others—nine Frenchmen and two Spaniards—collectively wandered far and wide across the continent, studying plants and minerals, climbing to altitudes in the Andes never before reached by Europeans, mapping the Amazon River, and, most important of all, precisely measuring the distance of one degree of latitude at the equator. This last effort was undertaken to answer questions about the earth's precise shape and to resolve a heated debate—between Newtonians and Cartesians—over the physics that governed the universe. Along the way, several of the expedition members died, one was murdered, and another—Jean Godin—married a Peruvian woman, Isabel Gramesón. Theirs became a legendary story of love and survival.

For reasons that are difficult to understand, this story has never gotten its due in history books. For the most part, the story of the La Condamine expedition has been relegated to chapter status in books on the exploration of South America, and as that brief story has been told and retold, the true history of the La Condamine expedition has become somewhat lost and muddied. Dialogue now and then has been imagined, events separated by years have been folded together for dramatic purposes, and a few incidents have been invented out of whole cloth. Lore has replaced history, so to speak, and when it comes to Isabel Godin, the basic chapter-length story that has been told over the past two centuries is simply mistaken in its most critical details.

The source material that writers have always relied upon for Isabel's story is a 1773 letter written by her husband Jean Godin, and while that letter is invaluable, he did not have access to information gathered by Peruvian authorities of witnesses to the event. That cache of documents fleshes out her story in a most vivid and surprising way.

To write this book, I relied on a variety of original sources. Journals by four members of the expedition, La Condamine, Pierre Bouguer, and the two Spaniards, Antonio de Ulloa and Jorge Juan, provide vivid eyewitness accounts of their eight years in South America. In some instances, I obtained eighteenth-century English translations of their work. In others, I had French documents translated into English. I also found much useful information in

## Modern-day Ecuador

various eighteenth-century articles published by the French Academy of Sciences in its yearly journal, *Histoire et memoires de l'Académie Royale des Sciences.*

The story of Jean and Isabel Godin is also well documented, even if much of the material lay forgotten in obscure journals. Jean Godin's correspondence is one such source. In addition to his 1773 letter to La Condamine, he wrote frequently to friends and to King Louis XV's ministers while living in French Guiana from 1750 to 1773. Much of this material was published in 1896 by a French historian, Henri Froidevaux, in the *Journal de la Société des Américanistes de Paris.* The testimonies gathered by Peruvian authorities in their 1770 investigation of the "Isabel Godin tragedy" were published in 1970 in an Ecuadorian journal, *Archivo Nacional de Historia.* The translations of those documents are mine.

I am also indebted to historians in Spain, France, and Ecuador who have done archival research on the expedition. In particular, I relied on research by an Ecuadorian scholar, Carlos Ortiz Arellano, for biographical information about Isabel Godin's early life and her family. It was through his writings, moreover, that I was alerted to the historical documents published in Ecuador's *Archivo Nacional de Historia.*

Finally, in order to flesh out this history, I retraced Isabel Godin's journey in the upper Amazon, and did so in October, the month that she began her journey. In that manner, I hoped to obtain a better sense of the landscape and of the fears that this wilderness can provoke. I went by bicycle from her hometown of Riobamba to Puyo at the base of the Andes, and then by dugout canoe from Canelos to Andoas. That experience was memorable in many ways, and it was one that left me ever more in awe of Isabel Godin.

—*Robert Whitaker*

# The Mapmaker's Wife

# CHAPTER ONE

# A Sunday in 1769

Today the Ecuadorian village of Cajabamba, which is about 110 miles south of Quito, is a place of little note. The Andean town stretches for a mile or so along the Pan American Highway, and most of the activity in the village centers on the bus stop, where vendors are lined up selling a mix of fruit, corn-on-the-cob, soup, and roasted meats. Tourists passing this way, if armed with a particularly good guidebook, might pause just long enough to scan a hillside on the north side of town, searching for a scar left by the great earthquake of 1797, which sent a flow of mud down upon the adobe homes below and killed thousands. At that time, this was a very different place. More than 16,000 people lived here, and Riobamba—as it was then called—was one of the most graceful cities in colonial Peru, home to musicians, artists, and wealthy landowners. But after the earthquake, the survivors picked up and rebuilt their town thirteen miles to the northeast, and old Riobamba gradually faded from memory. All that physically remains of the prosperous colonial city are a few ruins on the west side of Cajabamba.

However, there is one other faint echo of the past that can be found in Cajabamba. From the center of town, next to where the buses idle and the vendors linger, one can look up a long street heading east up a hill and spot a small statue. It sits in front of a school, a gold-painted bust of a rather stern-looking woman. The monument is in disrepair—the stone base is marred by graffiti, the gold paint is chipped and flaked, and the inscription is not quite readable—and few people in Cajabamba can say who the lady looking out over their town is or why she might have deserved a statue. However, in the late eighteenth century, the story of Isabel Godin became so well known that it left all of Europe spellbound. The statue was erected at the site of her colonial home, and thus it would have been from here, on the morning of October 1, 1769, that she began her most remarkable journey.

On that day, which was a Sunday, the dusty streets of Riobamba began to stir at an unusually early hour. Most mornings the town awoke slowly, the villagers waiting for the equatorial sun to chase away the nighttime chill. But this day was different. From the moment that dawn broke, people began coming out of their adobe homes, and soon many were lining up along the street that led north out of town. The wealthier women had even dressed up for the occasion, picking out their finest silk clothing to wear, and were gathered in small groups, whispering in disbelief at what was about to pass.

Isabel Godin was heading off into the Amazon.

Everyone understood her reason for going. She hoped to rejoin her husband, Jean, who was living on the northern coast of South America, in French Guiana. He had been a member of a French scientific expedition that had come to the Viceroyalty of Peru in 1736, Jean and the others hiking up and down the Andes for nearly eight years in search of an answer to a question so abstruse that few of the local people could grasp why they had come. Even so, the villagers of Riobamba had welcomed the French scientists into their midst, more so than any other community in the viceroyalty, and after the expedition had come to an end, Isabel and Jean had lived for a time—and happily so—in Riobamba. But then, through the twists and turns of fate and the cruel politics of the time, they had become separated, Jean stranded in French Guiana and unable to return to the Spanish colony. They had now been apart for twenty years. But travel from the Andes across the Amazon? No woman had ever dared to make such a trek.

Indeed, this was a journey that only a few men had ever made. When the most famous son of the town, Pedro Maldonado, had contemplated such a journey twenty-five years earlier, his family— as a friend of his later wrote—"had sought to detain him by any means." Maldonado's colleagues warned him that traveling this "unknown and dangerous route" was "imprudent and reckless," and that they personally viewed such a journey with "panicked ter- ror." Missionaries who traveled through the upper Amazon helped fuel such fear, for inevitably they returned with tales of how hard and perilous such travel could be.

The trip that lay ahead of Isabel stretched more than 3,000 miles. Even if all went well, it would take her six months. The route that she would follow east out of Riobamba would skirt around towering Mount Tungurahua, a volcano known to spit fire and rocks into the sky. The path would then disappear into a deep canyon and tumble quickly out of the Andes into a gloomy rain forest filled with the nerve-wracking cries of howler monkeys. From there, she would have to travel by dugout canoe down the turbulent headwaters of the Amazon, passing through a jungle that was home to clouds of insects and populated by any number of poisonous snakes and wild beasts, including the much feared American "tiger," which was believed to have quite an appetite for human flesh. Other hazards, wrote one eighteenth-century explor- er who had gone this route, included "naked savages" who "eat their prisoners."

In the center of town, the scene was growing ever more chaotic. Isabel had hired thirty-one Indian porters to transport her goods on the first leg of the journey, overland to the Rio Bobonaza, and they were busy packing a long line of mules. Isabel's traveling party had grown, too. Her two brothers had decided to come along to assure her safety, and one had decided—in a burst of questionable judgment—to bring along his eldest son, figuring that this would provide an opportunity to take him to Europe, where he could get a better education. Rumors of her impending trek had also spread far beyond Riobamba and had brought two strangers to her door, a French doctor and his traveling companion. They had been making their way along the Peruvian coast and now saw a trip across the Amazon as a more intriguing way to return to France. Both groups were bringing along servants as well: Isabel and her two brothers had two maids and a Negro slave, while the French doctor had one personal attendant, bringing the total number in Isabel's party to forty-one.

Isabel had been advised to travel as lightly as possible—advice that she found difficult to heed. There was the gear that they needed for the journey—blankets, ponchos, and food—and her many possessions. She was, after all, now *moving* to France. Fancy dresses, skirts, shawls, gold-buckled shoes, lace-trimmed underwear, and silver-studded belts were just a start. Next came the silver bowls, the fine china, the gold rosaries, the earrings set with emeralds, and various fancy linens. One reed basket after another was filled to the brim, the mules braying as cinches were tightened and the baskets heaved onto their backs.

Yet amid this confusion and bustle, Isabel appeared the picture of elegance and charm. She had stepped from her house that morning looking as though she were planning an evening at a lively dance. She wore a light-colored dress that billowed out from her waist, dainty cotton shoes, several silver bracelets, and two gold necklaces. Her appearance reflected who she was: a Riobamban woman who had lived all of her adult life in this village, rarely traveling far from home and enjoying the luxuries that came with being part of the elite class in colonial Peru. She was forty-one years old, a little plump, and the first streaks of white could be seen in her coal-black hair. She, like the other women of Riobamba, had simply dressed up for the occasion.

At last, the train of pack mules began to move. The procession of animals and men headed slowly down the town's main street, kicking up so much dust that Isabel's friends, waving to her as she went by, held scarves to their mouths. The mules brayed, Isabel's two brothers and several of the others rode horses, and Isabel drew up the rear. She was carried aloft in a sedan chair, the Indian porters having been given orders to jostle her as little as possible.

---

# CHAPTER TWO

# Not Quite Round

THE CHAIN OF EVENTS that led Isabel Godin to that moment in 1769, when she set off on her trek into the Amazon, had begun more than thirty-five years earlier, in a place far from her Peruvian home. At that time, a debate was raging in European scientific circles, one that was roiling the august halls of the French Academy of Sciences. The English were squaring off with the French, young scientists in the academy were battling their mentors, and tempers were such that when Voltaire jumped into the fray, with his customary stinging wit and on the side of the English, his book was summarily burned and he was forced to flee Paris. The question at hand was a profound one: What was the *precise* size and shape of the earth? And even more important, what did that shape reveal about the laws of gravitation and planetary motion that governed the universe?

Although the argument may have turned rancorous, the fact that this question had become the most pressing scientific topic of the day, one savored by the educated public in Paris and London, represented a coming-of-age for the Enlightenment. The roots of this transforming movement dated back more than a century to the writings of the English philosopher Francis Bacon and the French mathematician René Descartes. In his *Discourse on Method,* Descartes argued that in order to know the world, it was necessary to doubt all accepted wisdom. That was a heretical idea in 1637, for it meant questioning Christian doctrines about the natural world. Once the mind was emptied of such beliefs, Descartes wrote, insight could arise from "an unclouded and attentive mind, which springs from the light of reason." Seventeenth-century intellectuals adopted this faith in reason as their operating manifesto, even though it brought them into conflict with religious authorities. This approach produced a steady flow of achievements in astronomy, mathematics, and mapmaking, and as it did so, the literate public in France and England developed a keen interest in science, which, in the early eighteenth century, blossomed into the Enlightenment.

Paris, a city with a population of 500,000 in 1734, was at the epicenter of this revolution in thought. Upper-class men and women regularly gathered in sitting rooms to discuss art, philosophy, and science. Periodicals carried announcements of public lectures on these topics, which drew standing-room-only crowds. Lending libraries were created and stocked with books on science. As a historian of eighteenth-century France wrote, "Science was the true passion of the century at all literate levels of society, in every urban center of France, and even among the progressively minded gentleman-farmers."

The debate over the size and shape of the earth, which erupted in full force in the 1720s, resonated in particular with the French public. As the members of the French Academy of Sciences proudly wrote, this question had a long history and was so elemental that the intellectual progress of human civilization could be charted by following the steps that societies had made in solving it.

Scholars in ancient Greece and other early civilizations believed that the earth was flat, which is how it appears to the untutored eye. The idea that the earth might be a sphere, freely floating in space, was first advanced in the sixth century B.C. by the Greek philosopher Pythagoras. Aristotle subsequently provided evidence for this notion. The height of the sun, he noted, changed as one traveled north or south. And that could only be so, he pointed out, if one were traveling along a curve that altered one's line of sight. He estimated that the earth's circumference was 400,000 stades (about 40,000 miles).

Around 235 B.C., the Greek scholar Eratosthenes, who was head of the royal library in Alexandria, came up with a clever idea for actually calculating the earth's size. He had heard that there was a well in the town of Syene where the sun cast no shadow at noon on the summer solstice. That meant that the sun must be directly overhead at that moment. Alexandria was thought to be located directly north of Syene, and in Alexandria, at noon on the summer solstice, the sun cast a shadow equal to one-fiftieth of a circle (7.2 degrees). The distance between the two cities was thus one-fiftieth of the earth's circumference. Eratosthenes estimated the cities to be 5,000 stades apart—camel caravans traveling 100 stades a day took fifty days to travel from one city to the other—and thus he concluded that the earth's circumference was 250,000 stades.

His was obviously a rough calculation. He could not be certain that Alexandria was located directly north of Syene, and his estimate of the distance between the two cities was little better than a guess. However, Eratosthenes had come up with a sound theoretical method for determining the earth's size. First, measure the distance between two points along a north-south line, which is known as a meridian.* Next, measure the angle to the sun from each of the two points, which reveals how far apart those two points are in degrees. That is all the data needed to determine the earth's size. Posidonius applied these principles in the first century B.C. and concluded that the earth's circumference was 240,000 stades, a figure

---

* A meridian is any imaginary north-south line encircling the globe and passing through the poles.

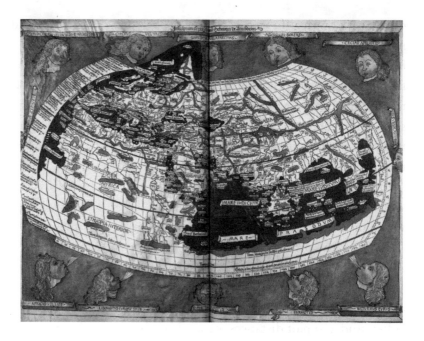

**Ptolemy's map of the world.**
*By permission of the British Library.*

that the Greek geographer Strabo later revised to 180,000 stades (about 18,000 miles).

During the second century B.C., the Greek astronomer Hipparchus conceived of a method for mapping the earth. A globe could be divided into 360 degrees along its breadth and length, creating a grid of latitude and longitude lines. Lines of latitude would encircle the globe parallel to the equator, while lines of longitude would encircle the globe through the poles. Every place on earth could be located at the intersection of two lines. While Hipparchus's idea was wonderfully elegant, it had its practical limitations. Angular measurements of the sun's apparent position in the sky—how high it was above the horizon at a specific time and date—could be used to determine the latitude, or north-south position, of any point on the globe. Figuring out longitude was much more difficult. Hipparchus understood how, in theory, it could be done. The Greeks believed that the sun revolved around the earth once every twenty-four hours. Thus, the sun, in its westward march across the sky, crossed fifteen degrees of longitude every hour, or one degree every four minutes. To measure longitude, then, it would be necessary to compare *time* in two places at once. If the sun in one city was reaching its highest point in the sky at the same time that, in a city to the west, it was still four minutes shy of that position, then those two cities were located one degree of longitude apart. But how could such simultaneous measurements be made in the absence of an accurate portable clock? The Greeks kept time with sundials and hourglasses filled with sand, neither of which measured time with sufficient precision.

Even so, the principles for mapping cities and landmasses on a spherical globe were now understood, and in the second century A.D. Claudius Ptolemy used them to create a world atlas. He relied on the reports of travelers to locate cities by latitude and a guessed-at longitude; to plot distances, he used Strabo's revised estimate of Posidonius's calculations of the earth's circumference. His decision to trust Strabo rather than Posidonius was a fateful one: Many centuries later, it would dramatically alter world history.

As the Roman Empire fell in the fifth century A.D. and Christianity took hold, Ptolemy's map and much of the knowledge underlying it was lost to Europe. Early Christian writers warned of the dangers of being too curious and scoffed at the notion that the earth was a sphere. In the sixth century, a monk in Alexandria, Cosmas Indicopleustes, drew the first Christian map. He took his inspiration from Saint Paul's declaration that the Tabernacle, a tent used as a portable house of worship, was a model of the world. His drawing showed the earth to be a conelike mountain inside a rectangular box that looked like a trunk. Other Christian maps of the Middle Ages depicted an earth in the shape of Christ's body (the rivers of the world were his veins), or as a flat disc with Jerusalem at the center. Such maps were often illustrated with scenes from the Bible and ancient fables, which many people took to be literally

**A medieval Christian map with Jerusalem at the center of the world.**
*By permission of the British Library.*

true. The medieval world was one in which dolphins leapt over the mainsails of ships, flying crocodiles had breath so foul it could kill, and African ants were as big as mastiffs. Travelers to foreign lands were likely to encounter horse-footed men, men with only one leg but a foot large enough to be used as a parasol, and men with drooping ears that covered their bodies, eliminating the need for clothing.

The arrival of the compass in Mediterranean lands in the twelfth century brought about the demise of Christian flat-earth beliefs.

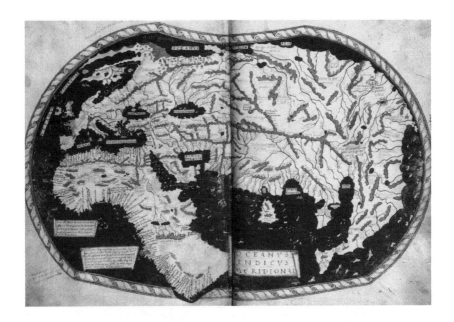

**Based on maps like this one by Henricus Martellus in 1488, it seemed**
**feasible to reach Asia by sailing west from Europe.**
*By permission of the British Library.*

This navigational device triggered an explosion in maritime exploration, and soon European sailors were drawing up sea charts with
compass lines, maps that fit not at all with the medieval ones drawn
to reflect religious teachings. In 1472, a printing of Ptolemy's map
appeared in Europe, putting longitude and latitude lines back onto
the world's atlas.

Europe's rediscovery of Ptolemy's work raised an intriguing question: Would it be possible to sail west from Europe and reach the Far
East, with its lucrative spice and silk trade, in a reasonable time?
Ptolemy, relying on Strabo, had pegged the earth's circumference at
around 18,000 miles, and fifteenth-century maps did not differ greatly from that figure. If that were true, Christopher Columbus reasoned, then it should be only 2,400 nautical miles from the Canary
Islands to Japan. When he struck land at about that distance, he naturally assumed the islands were near the Asian continent.

Once it became clear that Columbus had stumbled upon a New

World, the question of the earth's size became of paramount importance. The world was clearly bigger than anyone had thought, but how much bigger? All of the European powers were sending out trading ships to distant lands and the best cartographers of the day were scrambling to draw new maps, and yet the earth's size was not even roughly known. "Plato, Aristotle, and the old philosophers made progress, and Ptolemy added a great deal more," wrote Jean Fernel, physician to the king of France. "Yet, were one of them to return today, he would find geography changed beyond recognition. A new globe has been given to us by the navigators of our time." In 1525, Fernel attempted to measure its size, reviving a scientific quest that had been neglected for more than 1,500 years. To measure one degree of latitude, Fernel traveled in his coach from Paris to Amiens and used the wheels of his coach as an odometer. He counted 17,024 revolutions of the wheel during the journey and then multiplied this number by the wheel's circumference to determine the distance between the two cities, which were roughly located on a north-south meridian. After using a quadrant to determine the latitude of each city, he concluded that a degree of arc was sixty-three miles.*

The limitations of his method were evident. The road he traveled went up and down hills and certainly did not follow a perfectly straight line. A few years later, a Dutch mathematician, Gemma Frisius, proposed a more scientific method for measuring land distances—triangulation. His idea took advantage of the powers of trigonometry. An initial baseline of several miles could be measured; this line would serve as the first side of the first triangle. The angles from the baseline's two endpoints to a distant third point could then be determined. After these measurements, the surveyors would know both the length of one side of the triangle and all of its angles, and with that information in hand, they could mathematically calculate the lengths of the triangle's other two sides. By

---

* He determined that a degree was sixty-eight Italian miles, which was roughly equivalent to sixty-three English miles.

repeating this process a number of times, longer distances could be measured with a fair degree of precision.*

Nearly a century later, the Dutch astronomer Willebrord Snell finally put Frisius's idea to work. In 1615, he marked off thirty-three interconnecting triangles across the frozen meadows separating Alkmaar from Bergen op Zoom, a distance of eighty miles. He then found that these two points were 1.19 degrees apart in latitude, and thus he concluded that one degree of arc was sixty-seven miles. Soon a London mathematician, Richard Norwood, improved on Snell's effort by using a surveyor's chain to measure the baseline more precisely (the critical first step in the triangulation process). In 1635, he reported that a degree of arc was 69.5 miles. Next, an Italian group weighed in with a finding that suggested Norwood's calculation was too small—the earth's circumference was larger still by another 10 percent. The science of geodesy—the study of the earth's size and shape—was coming into its own as a recognized discipline, even if scientists were not coming up with quite the same answers.

The daunting problem of determining longitude, which had been at the top of every king's wish list since the New World had been discovered, was also coming close to being solved. The Greeks had realized that determining longitude would require comparing local times at two different places at the same moment, and in 1616, Italian astronomer Galileo Galelei came up with a proposal for doing just that. Jupiter's satellites, he discovered, could be used as a celestial timepiece. Galileo, who had been training a telescope on Jupiter every night for six years, had painstakingly composed tables charting the orbits of its four moons, which would rhythmically disappear on one side of the planet and then reappear on the other. Because this movement could be predicted from his charts, the

---

* In this process, a side from the first triangle—its length having been mathematically calculated—serves as a side of the second one. As a result, only the first baseline in the grid needs to be physically measured. All of the other distances can be determined mathematically based on the angles of the triangles.

eclipse of the moons could serve as a celestial signal that would enable observers in two different places to check local times at precisely the same instant. Galileo's tables could provide the local time at his laboratory for an observed eclipse, and observers elsewhere could calculate how far east or west they were of Galileo's laboratory based on the difference in their local time from Galileo's. Every four minutes of difference in local time would equal one degree of difference in longitude.

Galileo's idea was not immediately recognized for the brilliant solution that it was. In 1598, King Philip III of Spain had offered a huge reward to the "discoverer of longitude," a prize that had drawn a flood of crank ideas, causing Galileo's proposal, sent to the Spanish monarch in 1616, to initially fall on deaf ears. By that time, the king and his court had lost faith that the problem was ever going to be solved. In 1632, a frustrated Galileo brought his idea to the Dutch, who took another decade to fully embrace it. But even then, there remained a secondary problem that needed to be solved before his method could be put to good use: How could observers accurately determine local times at night, when the moons of Jupiter would be visible? Local time could be set by close observation of the sun, but even the best mechanical watches of the early sixteenth century lost or gained fifteen minutes every twenty-four hours. In 1657, Dutch mathematician Christiaan Huygens developed the needed timepiece—a pendulum clock. His wondrous invention relied on gravity to beat out time, each swing of the pendulum precisely ticking off one second.

Nearly 2,000 years after Eratosthenes had first sought to measure the earth, the stage was set for cartography to be transformed from an art into a science, a challenge that King Louis XIV of France, in 1666, agreed to take on.


THE FRENCH ACADEMY OF SCIENCES, which held its first meeting on December 22, 1666, was the brainchild of Jean-Baptiste Colbert, the king's minister of finance. He convinced Louis XIV

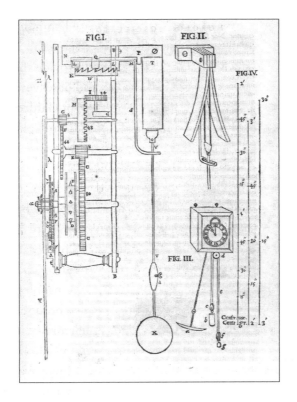

**Christiaan Huygens's diagram of his pendulum clock.**
*By permission of the British Library.*

that gathering scientists together into an academy and providing them with salaries and funds for their experiments would bring both glory and commercial benefits to the Crown. The academy could be expected to produce improvements in mapmaking and navigation that would give France an advantage in trading and warfare.

With the king's blessing, Colbert extended his recruitment efforts beyond France. In an age when European monarchs were constantly waging war, fighting over distant territories and trade routes, Colbert boldly made the French Academy of Sciences an international group, recruiting astronomers, mathematicians, and geographers from Germany, Italy, and Holland. He hired Huygens, a Dutchman, to help direct it and gave him a princely salary of 6,000 livres. He plucked Italian astronomer Gian Domenico Cassini, whose fame rested on his study of Jupiter's moons, away from the University of Bologna with a similarly rich offer. Cassini moved his family into a grand observatory that the academy was building outside Paris, an arrangement that so pleased him he changed his name to Jean-Dominique Cassini in honor of his adopted country.

The academy made drawing an accurate map of France its first priority. To begin this task, the academy asked French astronomer Jean Picard to newly determine the earth's circumference. Picard used varnished wooden rods to carefully stake out a seven-mile baseline between Paris and Fontainebleau, and he employed a quadrant equipped with two telescopes to lay out a precise grid of thirteen triangles from Paris to Amiens. He utilized both solar and celestial observations to determine the latitudes of the endpoints on his north-south meridian, and after two years of painstaking labor, he reported that a degree of arc was 57,060 *toises* (a French unit of measurement), or 69.1 miles.

Galileo's idea of using Jupiter's moons as a celestial timepiece to determine the longitude of various places could now be put to the

Jean Picard's measurement of a degree of latitude.
*By permission of the British Library.*

test. This effort was led by Cassini, and after nearly a decade of work, the academy unveiled a startling new map of France. Some cities had moved more than 100 miles, and the country's coastline had shifted 1.5 degrees closer to Paris. Along its southern border, the coastline had jumped thirty-five miles to the north. France had noticeably shrunk, prompting King Louis XIV, upon being shown the map on May 1, 1682, to lament that the academy's work "has cost me a major portion of my realm."

First France, then the world. Data began pouring into the Paris observatory from astronomers throughout Europe, who utilized Cassini's tables of Jupiter's moons and newly made pendulum clocks to make their observations. Jesuit missionaries fanning out to the Far East were outfitted with instruments and trained by the academy so that they too could send in longitude and latitude data. Cassini turned all this information into a huge world map, twenty-

**The Paris Observatory.**
*By permission of the British Library.*

four feet in diameter, that mesmerized those who saw it. The boundaries between European kingdoms had been redrawn, the Mediterranean coastline had a new shape, and the distant continent of Asia was snapping into focus.

At the turn of the century, Cassini and his son Jacques initiated yet another grand project, one that involved building on Picard's earlier triangulation work. Picard had measured a distance along a north-south meridian in the vicinity of Paris. The Cassinis decided that they would extend this triangulation across all of France. By doing so, they would further refine the academy's measurement of the earth's circumference, and they would also be able to address a nagging question about the earth's shape: Was it a perfect sphere?

Ever since Galileo's time, astronomers focusing their telescopes on Jupiter had noticed that it was flattened at the poles. That observation led to speculation that perhaps the earth was similarly shaped, and then reports began coming into the academy about the strange behavior of the pendulum clock at diverse locations. In 1672, the academy had sent Jean Richer to Cayenne, on the northern coast of South America, where he had found that a pendulum clock that was accurate in Paris lost two minutes, twenty-eight seconds each day. In order to make the clock keep accurate time in Cayenne, Richer had needed to shorten the pendulum by one-twelfth of an inch. Although gravity was not yet understood, Richer's experiment indicated that its force was not equal at all points on the globe, suggesting that something was indeed amiss with the earth's shape. And if the earth was not a perfect sphere, then the length of one degree of latitude—as one moved north or south along a meridian line—should change ever so slightly.

The Cassinis began their work in the south of France, where they found a degree of arc to be 57,097 toises (69.2 miles). This was thirty-seven toises—237 feet—longer than Picard's arc in Paris. Although far from conclusive, "the success of this work gave us room to conjecture that the degrees of the meridian increase as they approach the equator; whence it results that the earth is prolonged toward the poles," Jacques Cassini wrote. Over the next eighteen years, the academy extended its triangulation across eight degrees of latitude, a distance of more than 550 miles. This work proceeded fitfully, interrupted by the War of the Spanish Succession and Jean Cassini's death in 1712, but it produced data consistent with the first observations made in the south. A degree of arc in the north of France was only 56,960 toises, nearly 140 toises shorter than an arc in the southern part of the country. Each degree of latitude apparently increased by fifteen toises or so as one moved toward the equator, and the conclusion to be drawn from this was clear. The earth, Jacques Cassini flatly declared in a 1718 presentation to the academy, was a "prolate spheroid"—elongated at the poles and cinched in at the equator.*

Cassini's speech marked a triumphant end to a fifty-year effort. France had been mapped, the world had become better known, and the subtleties of the earth's shape had been revealed. This was an achievement that gave Jacques Cassini and the academy reason to be proud. "Nothing in our research appears more dignified than to find out the size and shape of the earth, and nothing seems quite as difficult an undertaking," Cassini wrote. The knowledge that had at last been gained would contribute to "the perfection of Geography and Navigation, sciences that are most useful to society."

There was only one fly in this sea of French pride: Isaac Newton.

INVESTIGATIONS INTO THE EARTH'S size and shape invariably raised questions about the physical forces that governed the universe. The great conceptual leap of the Greeks in the sixth century B.C. was not just recognizing that the earth was a globe but coming to believe that it was a globe freely floating in space. Nicholas Copernicus's declaration in 1543 that the earth and other planets orbited around the sun, while seen by the Catholic church as the worst sort of heresy, set the great minds of Europe to pondering how this could be: What kept the planets in their orbits? In 1609, German astronomer Johannes Kepler, observing that planets traveled about the sun in elliptical orbits, speculated that the sun "emits from itself through the extent of the Universe" an attractive power that held the planets in its grasp. Kepler theorized that the sun sent out straight lines of force, like spokes on a wheel, and that as the sun rotated on its axis, these lines of force pushed the planets along.

* In other words, the distance from the center of the earth to a pole would be greater than the distance from the earth's center to the equator.

Religious persecution prevented Galileo from directly addressing this question, but he still managed to make his thoughts known. In 1633, he was forced by the Inquisition in Rome, upon threat of torture, to recant the Copernican doctrine. Afterward, he did not dare write openly about planetary orbits. However, in his 1638 book *Discourses on Two Sciences,* he described how a body in motion travels in a straight line unless a force acts upon it and changes its course. Alert readers understood the implication: The earth and other planets would fly off into space unless there was a force—presumably emitted by the sun—that caused them to travel along curved paths.

The greatest French thinker of this period was Descartes, who applied the philosophy he articulated in *Discourse on Method* to the movement of planets. God, he reasoned, had set the universe in motion, much as one might wind up a clock. But once in motion, the universe operated according to a mechanistic design. Descartes reasoned that space could not exist without material, and thus even if it were empty of heavier matter, like water or air, it remained filled with invisible particles. In essence, space was to be seen as a fluid-filled medium; thus fluid dynamics could explain the forces of the universe. Descartes theorized that streams of particles swirled around the sun like water in a whirlpool, carrying along the planets, with the rings of particles nearest the sun swirling the fastest. The reason that the swirling particles did not fly away from the sun in a straight line was that there were similar vortices around all the other stars, each great vortex crowding into the next, and it was this pressure from the other stars' vortices that kept the system in balance.

Descartes set forth his cosmology in *Principles of Philosophy,* published in 1644. Although religious authorities in France did not react well to it—his writings were placed on the country's Index of Prohibited Books in 1663—the members of the French Academy of Sciences did. Descartes had provided a mechanistic explanation for the workings of the universe, and in *Principles of Philosophy*, he had even explained how a fluid-filled space transmitted light. It all made

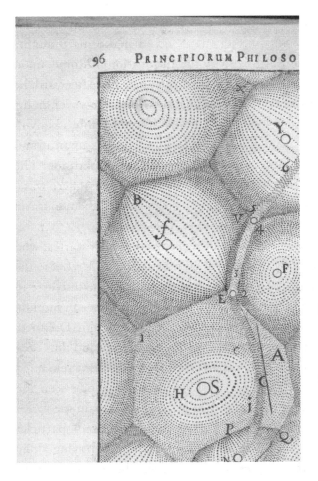

96    PRINCIPIORUM PHILOSO

The Cartesian
vortices.
The circle in the
center of each
vortex represents
a sun.
*From René Descartes,*
Principles of
Philosophy *(1644).*
*Edgar Fahs Smith
Collection, University
of Pennsylvania
Library*

sense, and it was a worldview that guided the academy members in their own investigations into the nature of the universe. Huygens, for instance, applied Cartesian physics to the problem of gravity, writing that the rotating ether thrusts those standing on the surface of the earth toward its center. In 1686, the academy's secretary, Bernard Le Bovier de Fontenelle, published a popular book on astronomy titled *Entretiens sur la pluralité des mondes* that was essentially a primer on Cartesian physics, and it not only survived the king's censorship but became a best-seller. Descartes and his swirling vortices were one of the crowning achievements of seventeenth-century French science.

Across the English Channel, Sir Isaac Newton was in partial agreement with Descartes: He too believed that science should search for a mechanical explanation of the universe. However, his inquiries and mathematical brilliance led him to a different model, one that followed Kepler's notion of "attraction at a distance." By his twenty-fourth birthday, in 1666, Newton had deduced a mathematical formula for gravity. The attraction between two bodies, he concluded, is directly proportional to the product of their masses and indirectly proportional to the square of the distance between their centers. Thus the tug of gravity at the earth's surface is sixty-four times stronger than it is at a place eight times further from the earth's center. However, when Newton applied his theory to the moon's movements, the numbers did not quite add up. At that time, English sea charts—whose authors were apparently unaware of the arc measurements made by Snell and Norwood fifty years earlier—stated that one degree of latitude was only sixty miles, and if that were so, the earth was too small to exert a sufficient gravitational pull to keep the moon in its orbit. This led the baffled Newton, a historian later wrote, "to entertain a notion that together with the force of gravity there might be a mixture of that force which the moon would have if it was carried along in a vortex." In other words, perhaps Descartes was partly right.

Newton's doubts about his theory of gravity disappeared in 1682 after he came upon Picard's updated estimate for the size of the earth. Once he plugged in 24,714 miles for the earth's circumference, his formula for gravity worked almost perfectly. "How these Attractions (between bodies) may be perform'd, I do not here consider," he wrote in his masterpiece, *Principia*. "What I call Attraction may be perform'd by impulse, or by some other means unknown to me. I use that Word here to signify only in general any force by which bodies tend towards one another, whatsoever be the Cause."

In *Principia,* Newton specifically attacked Descartes's vortex theory, pointing the French to their own experiments as proof that Descartes was wrong. The fact that Richer's pendulum clock beat slower in Cayenne was evidence that gravitational pull at the equator was less than it was in Paris, which in turn was evidence that the earth bulged at the equator—the clock was further away from the earth's center. And the reason the earth bulged at the equator was because it rotated on its axis, which created a stronger centrifugal force at the equator than at the poles.* The same physics, Newton argued, had turned Jupiter into a similar oblate shape. In Book III of *Principia,* Newton summed up his challenge to French beliefs, proclaiming—as Proposition 18, Theorem 16—that "the axes of the planets are less than the diameters drawn perpendicular to the axes." By his calculation, this ratio of axis to diameter should be 229 to 230.

At first, Newton's work did not cause much of a stir in France. England and France were constantly at war during this period, which diminished the exchange of scientific information, and the Newtonian ideas that did filter into Paris had to compete with a variety of other ponderings on the earth's shape. In 1691, Samuel Eisenschmidt, a famous astronomer from Strasbourg, concluded in his *Treatise of the Figure of the Earth* that the earth was a "spheroid prolonged toward the poles," similar to what the French believed. Thomas Burnet, an Englishman, published his *Sacred Theory of the Earth* shortly afterward, and he agreed with Eisenschmidt. Such differing theories subsequently served as a catalyst for the academy's measurement of a meridian throughout the whole of France, but that lengthy effort—as Cassini happily reported in 1718— proved that Newton was wrong.

Nor were the academy members swayed by the supporting bits of evidence that Newton had called upon. The fact that Jupiter was flattened at the poles was not seen as particularly relevant. The physics that governed the "supralunar" world—the heavens beyond the moon—were not believed to be the same as those that

* To calculate this effect, Newton imagined the centrifugal force exerted on a canal of fluid extending from the earth's center to a pole and on a similar canal from the earth's center to the equator. The canal extending to the equator would need to be longer and of greater weight in order to neutralize the increased centrifugal force on this column caused by the earth's rotation.

governed the sublunar world of the earth and its orbiting satellite. This distinction between supralunar and sublunar realms went all the way back to the Greeks. The academy members also had an explanation for Richer's pendulum experiment. Differences in temperature that led metal to shrink or expand were thought to be at fault. Either that, or poor work on Richer's part: "It is suspected that this resulted from some error in the observations," Cassini sniffed. Even more telling, Newton was at a loss to offer a mechanical explanation for how this force of gravity might work. The Cartesians had developed a rational, understandable explanation for the universe: a fluidlike ether that *pushed* on orbiting planets. All Newton had come up with was a mathematical formula, one that seemed to require the invisible hand of God, reaching across vast regions. The idea of attraction at such distances, Huygens wrote in a letter to Newton, was "absurd."

Indeed, if one wanted to know the shape of the earth, and one had to choose between the concrete measurements of the French and the obscure mathematics of an Englishman, how could anyone doubt which presented a stronger case? "It is obvious," Fontenelle declared, "that the current measurements, which are the refinement of Cassini's work, must be preferred to the result of geometrical theories based on a very small number of very simple assumptions, which are isolated from all the complications of physics and reality." Even the great Belgian mathematician, Johann Bernoulli, complained that Newton's theories relating to the shape of the earth were little better than "gibberish." "I tried to understand it," he wrote in a letter to one of his students. "I read and reread what he had to say concerning the subject, but I could not understand a thing. All I found was obscurity and impenetrability."

Yet Newtonian physics would not go away. In 1713, France, England, and Holland signed the Treaty of Utrecht, which brought an end to the War of the Spanish Succession and ushered in a thirty-year period of peace that encouraged the sharing of scientific ideas throughout Europe. Huguenots living in England helped speed this intellectual exchange. More than 200,000 French Protestants had fled France following a 1685 edict that deemed Protestantism heretical, and they busily published works in French that were designed to open up Catholic France to outside influences. In 1725, John Theophilus Desaguliers, a Huguenot refugee and experimental physicist, took up the Newtonian cause by publishing a blistering critique of Cassini's measurements in the *Philosophical Transactions* of the Royal Society of London. He dismissed Cassini's work as so sloppily done that it could not possibly raise questions about the elegant theories of Newton. Debate over the shape of the earth and Newtonian physics had moved to center stage in European science. It was the first topic discussed at the inaugural meeting of the Russian Academy of Sciences in 1725, and the argument there turned so vitriolic that in 1729 the minutes of the academy had to be expunged, lest the members be embarrassed by a record of their outbursts.

Dissension began to surface within the French Academy as well. The revolt against Cartesian doctrine was led by a young mathematician with a sharp tongue, Pierre-Louis Moreau de Maupertuis. He had visited London in the spring of 1728 and had returned convinced that Cartesian cosmology, with its swirling particles pushing the planets along, was not just wrong but *dumb*. The twice-weekly meetings of the French Academy of Sciences were ordinarily quite civil affairs, but Maupertuis, as one historian wrote, "badgered, intimidated, cajoled, coerced, and ridiculed the Cartesians in the Academy," gleefully attacking their mathematics as being tedious and incomprehensible. Although Maupertuis may have wounded the sensibilities of many, a number of the younger members were drawn to his side, including Alexis-Claude Clairaut, a child prodigy in math who had been elected to the academy at age eighteen. Maupertuis elaborated on Newtonian physics in a 1732 paper, "Discours sur les différentes figures des astres," and Clairaut followed with papers criticizing Cassini's measurements. It all led an infuriated Fontenelle to cry out in protest. Why did Maupertuis and his band of rebels want to "justify the English at the expense of the French?" he complained. "Who would have ever thought it necessary to pray to Heaven to preserve Frenchmen from a too favorable bias for an incomprehensible system, they who love clarity so dearly, and for a System originating in a foreign land, they who have been charged with loving only that which is their own?"

There was much at stake for Fontenelle, Cassini, and the rest of the academy's older members. Their life's work and the reputation of French science were at risk. The academy had long embraced Cartesian physics, all the way back to the mid-1600s when Descartes's writings were officially banned as heretical, and it was only now—in 1733—that the Jesuits were finally beginning to teach Descartes's doctrine. The academy had made measurement of the earth's size and shape a priority since it had first opened its doors, and it had spent a half-century on that effort, which had come to an apparently successful conclusion in 1718. The triumphs of the past would fall apart if Newton were right.

Voltaire was soon to discover just how touchy the country was on the subject. He had lived in England from 1726 to 1729, exiled from Paris for his usual needling of all things French, and there he had become an ardent disciple of Newton. He had written a series of letters on English society and Newtonian physics, which were published in England to good reviews. However, when a French version of his writings, titled *Lettres philosophiques,* appeared in Paris in 1734, authorities ordered that the book, "being scandalous, and offensive to religion, good morals and the respect owed to the State, should be burned by the executioner, at the foot of the great stairway." Pamphlets appeared charging Voltaire with defamation and degradation of his own people, a warrant was issued for his arrest, and he was forced to flee to Cirey in Champagne, where he holed up in the chateau of a beautiful woman, Madame Gabrielle-Émilie du Châtelet. "Apparently a poor Frenchman is not allowed to express his belief in the proven existence of a gravitational force, or of a vacuum in space, or that the earth is flat at the poles, and that Descartes' theory is absurd," he bitterly complained in a letter to Maupertuis. Cassini and the other old fogies in the academy, he added, had "this senseless and ridiculous phantom, the vortices, haunting their erudite heads."

The rancorous debate swept up everyone in the academy. As one eighteenth-century scholar wrote, it occupied the minds of the "most eminent geniuses of Europe." Pierre Bouguer, a mathematician who was the same age as Maupertuis, tried to carve out a middle ground by synthesizing Cartesian and Newtonian views. The earth, he argued, "cannot have any determinate shape, but instead it alternatively takes different shapes, representing extremes." His model, which relied on fluid mechanics, provided an explanation for why one set of observations would find an elongated earth and another a flattened one: The earth was constantly changing shapes. Meanwhile, Cassini once again measured a degree of latitude near Paris, and once again he came up with results indicating that the earth was a prolate spheroid. The Cartesians in the academy also had the pleasure of awarding a prize in 1734 to Bernoulli for an essay in which he devised a set of mathematical equations showing that swirling whirlpools would indeed cause the earth to be elongated at the poles. Bernoulli, whose reputation for brilliance was second to none in Europe, further pleased the older members of the academy by praising Cassini's measurements as "inconceivably exact" and dismissing the criticisms of Maupertuis, whom he had once tutored, as "sectarian" and "indiscreet."

Bernoulli's essay gave Cartesian cosmology a theoretical weight it had previously lacked. The academy's Cartesians could now point to both mathematical theory and experimental evidence to support their worldview. But so too could the Newtonians. They had Newton's law of gravity, his work on centrifugal forces, and Richer's experiment in Cayenne with the pendulum clocks. Great minds were lined up on both sides, and both sides realized, as Maupertuis declared in 1733, that a decisive experiment was needed to get at the "facts of the matter." In December of that year, the astronomer Louis Godin, a senior member of the French Academy, proposed one that everyone agreed would resolve the issue. The academy would send an expedition to the equator to measure a degree of arc. The difference between the degree of an arc there and one in France should be of a magnitude that would supersede any imprecision in the measurement itself. Was the earth, as the Newtonians would have it, shaped like a squashed orange? Or was it, as the Cartesians believed, prolonged at the poles and pulled in at the equator, its appearance—as some in the academy liked to quip—like that of a "pot-bellied man wearing a tight belt?"

The great scientific question of the day had been neatly defined. A team of ten French scientists would soon be on its way to the Viceroyalty of Peru, to the high Andean town of Quito. And there, it so happened, lived a young Catholic girl, Isabel Gramesón, who, in 1734, had just turned six years old.

# CHAPTER THREE

# A Daughter of Peru

MARÍA ISABEL DE JESUS GRAMESÓN was born on January 28, 1728, in Guayaquil, a port city 200 miles southwest of Quito. She was the second of four children, with two brothers and a younger sister, and she had the good fortune to be born to parents who enjoyed both wealth and political influence.

Isabel's mother, Josefa Pardo de Figueroa, came from a distinguished Spanish family, and she was a distant descendant of a Castilian king, Alfonso XI. Her colonial lineage was similarly impressive. Her ancestors had arrived in the Viceroyalty of Peru in the final years of the sixteenth century, which enabled her to proudly claim, with only a small degree of exaggeration, that she was one of the "daughters of the conquistadors." As a nineteenth-century historian wrote, Josefa Pardo was "equipped with a considerable fortune" and rightfully seen as "one of the most gracious women of the Spanish colonies." Two of her brothers were known throughout Peru. One, Pedro, was a bishop, and the other, José Augustín, was an accomplished writer who served a term as governor of the

Cuzco province and was anointed the Marqués de Valleumbroso—
an official title of nobility—by the Spanish Crown.

Josefa's marriage to Pedro Manuel Gramesón y Bruno in 1724
followed a common pattern for the time. Although the Pardos
were part of the colonial elite, they were still Creoles—people of
Spanish blood who had been born in the viceroyalty—and in eighteenth-century Peru, Creoles were rarely named to positions of
high rank in the government.* For nearly two centuries, Spain had
sent a steady stream of bureaucrats, drawn from the nobility or the
military, to govern its South American colony, and prosperous
Creoles, in order to maintain access to political power, had made a
habit of marrying their daughters to the arriving officials or to
Spaniards with good prospects for assuming a position of rank.
Twenty-one-year-old Pedro Manuel Gramesón, a military man
from Cadiz, Spain, had the latter credentials.

As his last name revealed, Gramesón was of French ancestry.
His father had been born in France but by routes unknown had
come to serve as a captain in the Spanish military regiment that
guarded King Philip V (who was also of French blood). Pedro followed his father into the military, and there he became acquainted
with a nobleman, José de Armendáriz, the Marqués de
Castelfuerte, who, in early 1724, was picked to be the viceroy of
Peru, the top political post in the colony. Gramesón sailed with
Armendáriz to the New World, and less than nine months later, he
married Josefa Pardo. Much like his friendship with the viceroy,
this was a union certain to serve him well. Wealthy Creole families
like the Pardos provided their daughters with dowries that included land, jewels, slaves, and thousands of pesos in silver coins.

The Gramesóns flourished in the years that followed. All of
their four children survived the childhood scourges that struck
down so many in colonial Peru, and Guayaquil provided both

---

* Although "Creole" is commonly used today to refer to people of mixed
blood, in eighteenth-century Peru it was used to describe people of white
blood born in the colony.

financial and military opportunities for Pedro. The port was a bustling town of 20,000, its economy fueled by import-export trade. Arriving boats dropped off such luxury European goods as wine, brandy, olive oil, and fine silk clothing, and departed with goods produced in coastal areas and in the Andean valleys—timber, cotton, woolen goods, bacon, hams, cheeses, and cocoa. Three forts defended the city, which had been sacked by marauding pirates in 1686 and 1709, and the "foreign company," composed of men like Pedro Gramesón who were natives of Spain, was reported to have "the most splendid appearance among the whole militia." Pedro quickly moved up in rank, and soon everyone who met him was certain to be informed that he was *General* Pedro Manuel Gramesón y Bruno.

Although Guayaquil was a prosperous city, its swampy environs made it a somewhat unpleasant place to live. Insects and rats were a constant torment. The ground, one eighteenth-century writer noted, was of a "spongy chalk," and "everywhere so level, that there is no declivity for carrying off the water, and therefore, on the first rain, it becomes one general slough." Many of the town's wealthier people viewed life in the Andes as preferable, and so, in 1733, when Armendáriz offered his old friend the chance to be the *corregidor*— or governor—of Otavalo, a township north of Quito, Gramesón jumped at the chance.

A corregidor was an all-purpose government official whose functions ranged from justice of the peace to police chief. He sat on town councils, known as *cabildos,* throughout his district and generally kept his finger in everyone's business. He also had an exclusive right to sell goods to *los Indios,* a monopoly in trade that could prove very lucrative. Pedro Gramesón fulfilled all the usual duties, and— according to a minor complaint that was filed against him—engaged in some trading that was supposed to be off limits to a corregidor. In 1734, he paid "300 loads of wheat" for a shipload of clothes from Castile, luxury goods that he then sold at a nice markup to his wealthy friends in Quito. As one of his peers remarked, Pedro Gramesón "didn't let pass by any business that was favorable."

These early years were kind to Isabel as well. She and her siblings enjoyed every privilege. Her parents doted on her, and she was tended to by an Indian maid. Those who met young Isabel, one of her relatives would later write, remarked that "she was quite precocious and had a very lively and willful character." But by the end of 1734, Isabel had reached the age when the life of a young girl in Peru underwent a profound change. The colonial elite whisked their six-year-old daughters off to convent schools, where they remained sequestered for the next six or seven years. There, they would be taught to be chaste and virtuous, and—at least in theory—to be a bit timid, too.

The schooling that lay ahead for Isabel reflected cultural values at the heart of Peruvian society, which had a history of a most dramatic sort. The place of women in eighteenth-century Peru arose from a past rooted in the Christian Reconquest of Spain and Spain's medieval world of knights.

Moors swept into Iberia in A.D. 711 and conquered most of it within seven years. However, they never gained a firm hold over the harsh plains northwest of Madrid. Soon Christian warriors, riding in from the Asturian mountains to the north and armed with swords, resettled the region. The society that formed here in the ninth and tenth centuries was a rough one. The thin soils would not easily support settled agricultural communities, where culture and education historically thrive. Instead, the terrain encouraged nomadic, pastoral pursuits, like the raising of sheep, which were tended to by rugged men on horseback. Warlords built castles perched on crags and organized legions of fighting men to protect their feudal estates.

During the tenth century, this warring society coalesced into the Kingdom of Castile, which quickly began eyeing the prosperous Moorish states to the south. Militant priests filled the young men of Castile with fervor for a crusade against the infidels, while Castilian kings egged them on with promises of earthly rewards—

those who fought and defeated the Moors would be rewarded with grants of land and titles of nobility. The warrior on horseback could hope to live off the wealth of the land, with the subjugated Moors and peasants supplying goods and tribute.

The first major Moorish city to fall was Toledo, in 1085. A decade later, the most famous Christian hero of the Middle Ages, Rodrigo Díaz de Vivar, known as El Cid, conquered Valencia and the surrounding environs. With each new victory, ballads were sung celebrating the feats of these triumphant knights, and soon Castile had come to cherish the notion of the *hidalgo,* a man of great courage and honor who lived for war, and who achieved wealth and nobility through his feats on the battlefield. The man who toiled the fields, who lived by the sweat of his labor, was a man who deserved to be a vassal. In 1248, Castile sacked Seville, near the southern coast, which left Granada as the only Moorish enclave in Iberia.

Although the Castilians may have reviled the Moors' religion, they nevertheless adopted many Moorish customs. They studied the Moors' architecture, their city-planning methods, and their commerce. The Castilians took to sitting on the floor and dressing in long flowing robes. Most notable of all, they adopted Moorish attitudes toward women. Arab poets employed fanciful metaphors to tell of a woman's beauty and of the romantic love that such beauty could evoke in a man, and soon these conventions appeared in Castilian ballads. A woman's eyes were "bright as the stars above," her teeth "white as pearls"—these were the features of a heavenly creature who made men swoon. At the same time, she was a temptress who needed to be removed from society. The Castilians, a historian later wrote, "kept their women sequestered like the Arabs. A *duenna* or elderly chaperon guarded the women of a household much as if they formed a harem."

After the fall of Seville, Christians, Arabs, and Jews lived side by side in Spain in relative tranquillity for two centuries, a pluralistic society unlike any other in Europe. Ferdinand III, who ruled over Castile in the thirteenth century, called himself the King of Three Religions. The reawakening of a crusade against the Moors began in 1469 with the marriage of Isabella, heiress to the throne of Castile, to Ferdinand, heir to the throne of Aragon, a Christian kingdom in the northeast corner of Iberia. Isabella was a zealous Catholic, and she was intent on purging her dominion of nonbelievers. In 1478, she and Ferdinand obtained a papal bull allowing them to establish an inquisition into heresy, which initially focused on identifying Jews who were "false converts" to Christianity. The first such "heretics" were burned at the stake in 1481, and a year later, Isabella and Ferdinand launched a full-scale effort to conquer Granada, which was still a Moorish stronghold. Unlike during the earlier era of conquest, in which private militias did most of the fighting, the monarchy now raised a public army to wage war. When Granada fell in 1492, Castilians hailed it as the "most distinguished and blessed day there has ever been in Spain."

The seven centuries of Reconquest, which had come to a triumphant end, had molded the Spanish character into a distinct type. Other European countries at this time were moving out of the Middle Ages and into a period of intellectual renaissance. The merchant and the scholar were the types that would lead France, England, Holland, and other societies into the Enlightenment. But in Spain, a militant Christianity had taken hold and produced a society that celebrated the soldier who fought the infidels and then lived off the spoils of his victory. And it was at that moment that all of Spain fell under the spell of "romances of chivalry," tales that reminded them of their great triumph over the Moors and instilled in them a yearning to do it again.

THE PRINTING PRESS appeared in Spain in 1473, and soon the verse narratives and ballads of an earlier time evolved into wildly inventive novels of errant knights who saved Christian kingdoms from pagan hordes. The first such tale, *Tirant lo Blanch,* was published in 1490, and over the next century, Spanish and Portuguese writers produced more than forty such narratives. The most popular of all the storied knights was Amadís de Gaula, who appeared

A Daughter of Peru

on the literary scene in 1508 and whose exploits—and those of his descendants—were subsequently celebrated in a dozen novels.

The Amadís romances, one twentieth-century scholar has observed, "mirrored with sufficient fidelity the Spanish gentleman's dream of himself." The plots were all much the same, Amadís and the other knights regularly marching off to magical lands of a sort that had once appeared on medieval Christian maps. The foreign countries were inhabited by dog-faced monsters, serpents that had human feet, and fighting Amazon women who lived in a land called California. There were giants, centaurs, lions, and dragons to be seen and mountains of gold and silver to be found. Amadís and the other knights of Christendom typically went into battle against great odds, a handful of men against armies of thousands. During the ensuing clashes, the knights, who were often wounded but rarely died, would attack with such ferocity that the ground would turn crimson, littered at every turn with the severed heads and limbs of the vanquished.

Although the knights were fearless and brutal in battle, they were of the most delicate sort when it came to matters of love. Knights in a faraway land were constantly heartsick over beautiful maidens back home, who were locked away in castles. So great was their mutual passion that should a knight return and appear at his maiden's window, her honor would be at great peril. How could she resist him? Yet the virtuous woman would find a way to remain in her chamber, offering her knight only a hand to kiss, for it was essential that she preserve her honor and remain a virgin until marriage. A similar chastity was not expected of the knight, however. He was quite adept at luring lower-class women into his bed, and in his travels abroad, he regularly took time out from his fighting to dally with the ladies. A knight, the writers made clear, was skilled at the art of seduction.

While the romances were fanciful in the extreme, they were presented to the public as historical novels, and readers often thought of them as true. As one sixteenth-century priest wrote, the books had to be factual, "for our rulers would not commit so great a crime as to allow falsehoods to be spread abroad." Authors exploited this naiveté by calling their romances "chronicles," often claiming that that they had simply rediscovered old handwritten texts recording past crusades. *Tirant lo Blanch* employed this device, as did the *Chronicle of Don Roderick,* which was sold as a "history" of the Moorish invasion of Spain.

This was the imaginative world that Spaniards inhabited in the early 1500s, and thus it was, their minds feverish with such fantasies, that they set off to conquer the New World.

THE SPANISH CONQUISTADORS came from the same class of men that had waged the Reconquest. Many were poor, hailing from the harsh plains of Castile. In the first twenty-five years after Columbus's 1492 voyage, they established control over Hispaniola and Cuba, explored most of the islands in the West Indies, and crossed over the Panama isthmus to the Pacific Ocean. And everywhere they went, they queried natives about where to find the mythical lands they had read about. Mexico was whispered to be such a place, and in 1518, those on an exploratory voyage from Cuba to Yucatán returned with thrilling news. "We went along the coast where we found a beautiful tower on a point said to be inhabited by women who live without men," reported a priest, Juan Diaz. "It is believed that they are a race of Amazons."

This report stirred the governor of Cuba, Diego Velázquez, to enter into a contract with Hernando Cortés for the conquest of Mexico. Velázquez warned Cortés to expect the fantastic, "because it is said that there are people with large, broad ears and others with faces like dogs." He also directed Cortés to find out "where and in what direction are the Amazons."

Cortés sailed from Cuba with 600 men, sixteen horses, thirteen muskets, and one cannon—a small contingent to conquer an empire. After landing on the coast at a site he christened Villa Rica de Vera Cruz, Cortés took a page from the tales of knighthood and burned all his ships but one, which he offered to anyone who wanted to turn back. "If there be any so craven as to shrink from sharing the dangers of our glorious enterprise," he told them, "let them go home, in God's name. They can tell there how they deserted their commander and their comrades, and patient wait till we return loaded with spoils of the Aztecs."

Cortés and his men were Amadís knights on the march. Their adventure soon unfolded like the plots in the novels they read. As they neared the central plateau of Mexico, Aztecs greeted them with glittering gifts from their ruler, Montezuma. The goods were meant as bribes—the Aztecs hoped that the Spaniards would take them and leave—but the treasures simply hastened Cortés's march. He demanded to see Montezuma, and on November 8, 1519, he and his men were escorted along a great causeway into the Aztec capital of Tenochtitlán, which was built, in the manner of a fairy tale, upon islands in Lake Texcoco. "We were amazed," marveled Bernal Díaz del Castillo, a soldier in Cortés's army, in his *True History of the Conquest of New Spain*. "We said that it was like the enchanted things related in the *Book of Amadís* because of the huge towers, temples and buildings rising from the water and all of masonry. Some of the soldiers even asked whether the things we saw were not a dream."

Within three years, the men of Castile had defeated the Aztecs, and while they were disappointed in the amount of gold and silver to be had, they took the place of the Aztecs as ruling overlords of Mexico. The legal method that the Spanish Crown had established for rewarding conquistadors was known as the *encomienda* system. A native village or group of villages would be "commended" to the care of an individual Spaniard, who was obligated to protect the inhabitants and bring in a priest to convert them to Catholicism. In return, the governing Spaniard, who was known as an *encomendero,* was authorized to collect a "tribute" from the Indians in the form of food, goods, clothing, and labor. Cortés became the master of 23,000 Indian families, while others in his army were awarded encomiendas of 2,000 households.

The conquest of Mexico inspired Spaniards to new heights of

fancy. While the Amazon women first spotted on the Yucatán coast had never materialized, their location was now better known. A tribe of women warriors, Cortés explained in a letter to King Charles V, was living on an island further west, where "at given times men from the mainland visit them; if they conceive, they keep the female children to which they give birth, but the males they throw away." There were also rumors circulating of an "otro Mexico" waiting to be discovered south of Panama, this one said to be even richer in gold and silver. The people there, the Spaniards believed, "eat and drink out of gold vessels."

In 1531, Francisco Pizarro, a soldier of fortune who was living as an encomendero in Panama, set out with 180 men and thirty-seven horses to conquer this empire to the south. He had the good fortune to arrive while the Incas were bogged down in a civil war. The Incas were a mountain people from the Cuzco region who had begun to conquer neighboring tribes in the middle of the four-teenth century. Over the next 150 years, they had extended their control over a territory that stretched more than 2,000 miles along the spine of the Andes, from Quito to the Maule River (in central Chile), with a total population of more than 10 million people. The Incas were skilled potters and weavers, and they had utilized advanced irrigation techniques to turn desert coastal areas into thriving agricultural regions. They had built more than 15,000 miles of roads. They also maintained warehouses of clothing, food, and weapons, and had a communication system, composed of relay runners, that could deliver a message from Cuzco to Quito, a dis-tance of 1,230 miles, in just eight days. But around 1525, the reign-ing Inca, Huayna Capac, died of smallpox (a plague that had begun to creep south from Panama), and two of his sons, Atahualpa and Huáscar, immediately began a fratricidal battle.

Atahualpa controlled the northern half of the empire, and so it was he who heard, in late 1532, of Spaniards advancing inland toward his army of 40,000 headquartered outside the Andean vil-lage of Cajamarca, where he was enjoying the hot springs. The small group of intruders did not inspire fear in Atahualpa, and he,

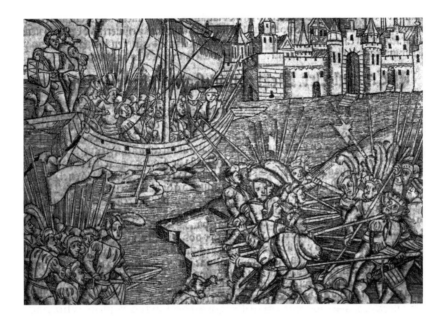

**A sixteenth-century illustration of the conquest of Peru.**
*From* Historia General de las Indias y Nuevo Mundo *(1554)*.
*Biblioteca Universidad, Barcelona, Spain. Bridgeman Art Library.*

like Montezuma, sent out emissaries bearing gifts—llamas, sheep, and woolens embroidered with gold and silver—and invited them to visit. Pizarro and his men peacefully entered Cajamarca on November 15, and the following day, Atahualpa was carried into the town square on a litter decorated with plumes of tropical birds and studded with plates of gold and silver. He was accompanied by 5,000 men and was expecting to dine with Pizarro, but instead, a Dominican priest, Vicente de Velvarde, stepped forward to read to him a formal document of conquest, known as the *Requierimiento*. The Spanish Crown, intent on believing that its conquest of the New World was a just and honorable enterprise, had drawn up this legal paper in 1513. All conquistadors were required to read it to natives before a notary and through an interpreter. It told of the history of the world starting with Adam and Eve, of man's fall and his redemption by Jesus Christ, and the grant of dominion over the New World given to the kings of Castile by the pope. It concluded by asking that aboriginal groups acknowledge their obligation to pay homage to the agents of the Spanish Crown, advising them that a gruesome fate would be theirs if they failed to submit. Friar Velvarde informed Atahualpa, "We protest that the deaths and losses which shall accrue from this are your fault."

Once the Requierimiento had been read, the conquistadors were absolved by the church for any actions they subsequently took. Natives found the reading of this document utterly bizarre, and Atahualpa responded by throwing down the Bible he had been handed. Pizarro's men took this as a signal to attack. They rushed into the plaza on horseback, shooting their muskets and hacking at panicked Incas with their swords. In the course of an hour, they killed more than 2,000 Incas without suffering a single death of their own. They also took Atahualpa prisoner. He agreed to pay Pizarro a ransom for his freedom, promising to fill a room twenty-two feet long and seventeen feet wide with gold piled nine feet high, and a smaller room twice over with silver. Over the next six months, his followers worked at doing just that, but before the rooms had been completely filled, the Spaniards grew restless and began melting the gold and silver treasures into ingots. Pizarro also reneged on his agreement and charged Atahualpa with a variety of crimes, including idolatry and adultery. After a short trial, he had Atahualpa strangled. A final tally of the spoils of conquest came to seven tons of twenty-two-carat gold and thirteen tons of pure silver. Even the lowliest infantryman accompanying Pizarro received forty-five pounds of gold and twice that weight in silver.

No Amadís author had ever dared to write such a script. The exploits of the literary knights paled beside those of Pizarro and his men at Cajamarca. Had not a handful of Castilians triumphed over an army of thousands without suffering a single death? Had not the square filled with the blood of the vanquished? Had not their own eyes seen a room filled with the most exquisite treasures of gold? Soon other such amazing events occurred. The Spanish conquered Cuzco on November 15, 1533, and there they found royal buildings covered with gold and virgins waiting in the temples. At

**Execution of the Inca
king Atahualpa.**
*By Felipe Huaman Poma
de Ayala. Biblioteca del
ICI, Madrid, Spain.
Bridgeman Art Library.*

Potosí, high in the Andes, they discovered veins of silver so immense that it seemed the mountain itself must be made of this treasure.

There was one final chapter in this knightly tale yet to come true: The discovery of the Amazons. Ever since the mythical warrior women had been sighted off the Yucatán coast, they had seemed to jump one step ahead of the advancing Spaniards. But much New World wilderness remained unexplored, and in 1541, Francisco's brother Gonzalo Pizarro departed from Quito in search of El Dorado, a rumored kingdom of great riches east of the Andes. He and his troop of 200 men quickly became bogged down in the jungle, but a splinter group from his party, led by Francisco de Orellana, forged ahead and traveled down the length of a great river, all the way to the Atlantic. During this voyage—or so they reported—they came upon the fierce women the Spanish had been

seeking for so long. Friar Gaspar de Carvajal chronicled the aston-
ishing sight:

> These women are very white and tall, and they have long and
> braided hair wound about their heads; they are very robust and
> go about naked, their privy parts covered. With bows and arrows
> in hand, they do as much fighting as ten Indian men. Indeed,
> there was one woman among them who shot an arrow a span
> deep into one of the brigantines, and others less deep, so that our
> boats looked liked porcupines.

The New World was a place where the fanciful plots and exotic
creatures of medieval romances had sprung to life. Barely twenty
years had passed since Cortés had departed from Cuba with his 600
men, and the conquest of two great indigenous empires was complete. The men of Castile could now get down to the business of liv-

**The warrior women of the Amazon.**
*Fotomas/Topham/The Image Works.*

ing in the manner of aristocrats and nobles, just as they had pictured themselves in their dreams.

THIS HISTORY, so literary and imaginative, was the mold that made Peru. The society was organized in ways that reflected the ambitions of an Amadís knight, and 200 years later, that remained the case. Spaniards and Creoles relied on Indians and slaves for labor, and the men turned to lower-class women—Indians, mulattos, mestizos, and slaves—for sexual conquest. This practice was so common, an eighteenth-century writer noted, that "it is considered a shame to live without a concubine." However, the Spanish men of Peru expected their own daughters and wives to remain "pure" and "honorable" and demanded that they live sheltered lives.

Elite women in Peru rarely ventured outside their homes unless accompanied by a servant. Inside the house, they were bound by customs that reflected Moorish influences. Rather than sit on chairs, the women would crouch on cushions. They would "spend almost whole days in this manner," one eighteenth-century writer noted, "without altering their posture, even to eat, for they are served apart, on little chests." Custom barred their participation in dinner conversations as well, partly because it was thought that whatever they had to say would be trivial. Wives were legally bound to obey their husbands, and the man's authority was such that he was allowed to hit her. As a Peruvian who had beaten his spouse told a tribunal in 1609, "If sometimes I had put my hands on her, it would have been with moderation and in the spirit of correcting some of her imperfections and trying to scare her a little, which is permissible to a husband according to the law."

The cloistering of upper-class girls in colonial Peru began when they reached six or seven years of age. Up until that age, they might be spoiled in every way imaginable. But then they were sent off to a convent school, an often traumatic event. The girls were not allowed to wander outside the cloister, and even their visitors had to be approved by the headmistress. The curriculum reflected soci-

A distinguished woman in Quito with her Negro slave.
*By Vicente Alban. Museo de America, Madrid, Spain.*
*Bridgeman Art Library.*

etal wishes that they be groomed to be dutiful wives: They were
taught homemaking skills such as sewing, embroidering, and cook-
ing, and every day they recited fifty Hail Mary's and studied the life
of the Virgin Mary, the nuns seeking to instill in them the virtues of
purity, humility, and charity.

There is no historical record of the name of the convent school
that Isabel Gramesón attended. But the schools were all much the
same, and it is easy to imagine the moment she entered the cloister
and the gates clanged shut behind her. She must have felt bewil-
dered and a little frightened. She had been plucked from her family, and now this austere place was to be her new home. Her future
seemed to stretch out before her in a predictable way, and yet fate
can be fickle: A band of French scientists would soon arrive in
Quito, and in the years ahead, that would lead her to think anew
about life's possibilities.

# CHAPTER FOUR

# The Mapmakers

Although the French Academy of Sciences had decided by late 1733 to send an expedition to the equator, it was not until May 15, 1735, that Louis Godin and nine others gathered at La Rochelle, ready to depart for the New World. The port that spring day was a frenzy of activity. There was box after box of luggage and scientific equipment to bring aboard the *Portefaix*, a naval frigate that would transport them across the Atlantic. The three academy members who were to lead the expedition—Louis Godin, Pierre Bouguer, and Charles-Marie de La Condamine—were quite different in temperament, which was reflected in how they were keeping busy. Godin, a large man, was chatting with the locals who had come to see them off. Bouguer, looking rather pale, was fretting over the handling of his instruments. La Condamine was energetically directing the loading of the boat—clearly, he was taking charge of the trip's logistics.

At thirty-one years of age, Godin was the youngest of the three, and yet, because he had proposed the voyage, he was its official leader. His resume was impressive even by academy standards. As a youth, he had done such brilliant work in mathematics and astronomy that he had been elected to the academy at the age of twenty-one. His colleagues there found him imaginative, ambitious, and tireless in his pursuit of knowledge, with a biting wit. "He knew how to intersperse humor into the most serious of matters," a colleague wrote years later. "He was sometimes accused of taking his vivacity too far, but it was never more than a passing thing for him." During his first years at the academy, Godin had edited an eleven-volume history of the institution, which had made him a member of its inner circle. He had also published papers on the aurora borealis, planetary orbits, and lunar eclipses.

In preparation for the mission, Godin had traveled to London to consult with Edmond Halley, England's best-known astronomer. There he hired an English artisan, George Graham, to construct several scientific instruments. Graham had provided the expedition with telescope-equipped quadrants for measuring angles, a zenith sector for celestial observations, and a seconds pendulum to gauge gravitational pull at the equator. Godin had also commissioned a French craftsman, Claude Langlois, to make an iron bar one toise in length, which would serve as the expedition's ruler. A toise was six Paris feet (6.39 English feet), and its exact length, as established in 1668, was that of an iron bar set in the foot of the stairs of the Grand Châtelet in Paris. All of these instruments had to be exquisitely calibrated, made more precisely than any that Graham or Langlois had built before. Otherwise, the margin of error in the French scientists' measurements—given that any bulging or flattening at the equator was not very pronounced—would render their findings meaningless.

These preparations had left Godin buoyed with optimism. Halley had voiced his enthusiasm for the mission, and Graham had been eager to lend his expertise. The willingness of the English to contribute to the expedition was evidence that this scientific excursion truly was, as the French Academy had so often claimed, "of interest to all nations." Godin expected that he would be gone from

**Pierre Bouguer.**
*By Jean-Baptiste Perroneau. Louvre, Paris, France.*
*Bridgeman Art Library.*

his wife and two children for three or four years at most, not an unreasonable time for an expedition that involved travel to such a distant place.

Unfortunately, Bouguer, thirty-seven years old, was not similarly enthused—or at least he did not want anyone to think he was. He had been quite clear with the academy: Because of his weak health and his hearty "dislike for sea voyages," he had told them, he had "no intention of taking part in such an enterprise." But other academy members had begged off, and Bouguer, once he had milked the situation for a dollop of flattery from his peers, had grudgingly agreed to go. And the mission, it was true, was certain to benefit from his scientific acumen. A child prodigy in math, he had been made a royal professor of hydrography at age fifteen. Over the next twenty years, he had written on such diverse topics as the best method for rigging sailing ships, the making of celestial observations at sea, and the use of a barometer to determine altitudes. He was both a perfectionist and a sourpuss, traits not uncommon to brilliant minds, and the academy, partly to convince him to join the expedition, had made him its "resident astronomer." This was a title that assured Bouguer the trip would be worth his while—if successful, the lion's share of the scientific credit would probably be his.

La Condamine, thirty-four, was in many ways the antithesis of Bouguer. Although he was not the equal of either Godin or Bouguer as a scientist, he was a fearless adventurer who loved nothing more than finding himself in a difficult spot in a foreign country. He came from a wealthy family with ties to the Bourbon monarchy; his father was a district tax collector. As a youth, he had been an indifferent student, and at age eighteen he had left the academic world in order to join the military, eager to fight in an ongoing campaign against Spain. There, he had become famous for his relentless curiosity. At the siege of Rosas in the Pyrenees, he had climbed a hill and set up a telescope to observe the battle, his scarlet coat making him such a visible target that enemy soldiers immediately blasted away. His fellow French soldiers had to beg him to come down, uncertain whether to applaud his bravery or to chide him for his recklessness.

Although La Condamine escaped that day, the war left him physically marked. Struck by smallpox during the campaign, the "extensive scarification of his face" made him horribly shy around women, observed his academy biographer, Jacques Delille. "It did not occur to him that he might be pleasing to anyone, and he was still naïve enough to think that one could do without being cared for." For a time after the war, La Condamine devoted all his energies to science, and in 1730 he was admitted to the academy as an assistant chemist. But ever the restless type, he grew bored with laboratory science and turned his attention to geography, a discipline that would give him an opportunity to travel. He sailed with a French naval fleet to the Barbary Coast, a trip that turned into a year-long tour of northern Africa and the Middle East. In Turkey, he was arrested for refusing to pay a bribe solicited by an official in the port of Bassa. He was so enraged that following his release, he traveled to Constantinople to demand an apology. He remained there for five months, hounding Turkish authorities until they finally admitted their mistake. Upon his return to France in 1732, he presented the academy with an engaging account of his trip, which, Delille wrote, "earned him the reputation of a competent mathematician, an observant traveler, and a good storyteller."

Neither Bouguer nor Godin had publicly taken sides in the debate over the earth's shape. Bouguer had tried to reconcile Newtonian and Cartesian views, while Godin had published a paper in 1733 describing how the distances between lines of latitude would vary depending on whether the earth was flattened or elongated at the poles. Either was possible from Godin's point of view. But La Condamine had jumped into the fray on the side of the rebels.

Charles-Marie de La Condamine.
*By Louis Carmontelle.*
*Musée Conde, Chantilly, France.*
*Lauros-Giraudon-Bridgeman*
*Art Library.*

Maupertuis and Clairaut counted him as an ally, and Voltaire had written him a fan letter, hailing him as "an apostle of Newton and Locke." In 1733, La Condamine had floated the idea of mounting an expedition to the equator to solve the debate, but since he was a friend of the scorned Maupertuis and a junior member of the academy, Cassini and the other Cartesians had ignored him. It took someone of Louis Godin's status to get the academy's leaders behind the idea. Once they were, La Condamine, more than any other member, lobbied to be named to the expedition. The academy, a colleague said, "sensed that his zeal and courage would serve the enterprise well."

La Condamine, who had spent much of the previous sixteen months organizing the voyage, was the first to arrive in La Rochelle, having come in mid-April. The other seven members of the expedition were expected to assist the academicians, except perhaps for Joseph de Jussieu, who had his own scientific duties. Jussieu's two brothers, Antoine and Bernard, were botanists and academy members, and they had requested that Joseph, a doctor at the medical school of Paris, be named the expedition's botanist, charged with gathering plants and seeds from the New World. Joseph, however, had a fragile temperament, and everyone knew that he would have to be treated gently. His peers in Paris often spoke about his "vivid imagination," which was a polite way of saying that at times he was haunted by demons and prone to horrible bouts of melancholy.

Most of the others in the crew were professionals as well. The surgeon Jean Senièrgues would attend to the team's medical needs, ready to bleed and purge at the first sign of sickness. Jean Verguin was a naval engineer and draftsman expected to draw maps. The watchmaker Hugo would be responsible for the care and maintenance of the scientific instruments, while Morainville, an engineer, would help build the observatories for their celestial measurements. The final two members of the expedition were younger men who would be general assistants: Couplet and Jean Godin des Odonais. Couplet was the nephew of the academy's treasurer, Nicolas Couplet, and it was rumored that his uncle had twisted an arm or two to get him on the expedition. As for Jean Godin, he was Louis's twenty-one-year-old cousin, and the minute he had heard about the expedition, he had hurried to Paris to volunteer.

The son of Amand Godin and Anne Fouquet, Jean was born on July 5, 1713, in Saint Amand, a village in the central region of France about 165 miles south of Paris. He was the seventh of eleven children, but only four of his siblings—two brothers and two sisters—survived past infancy. Jean's family was fairly prosperous. Amand was an attorney, and he also owned a property, Odonais, in the parish of Charenton, which provided Jean with the descriptive name—"des Odonais"—listed on the expedition's travel documents. The countryside around Saint Amand was quite beautiful, the river Cher flowing through the fertile fields, and Jean would spend hours walking here, lost in his thoughts. He was "born a traveler," a relative later wrote. "As a child, he dreamed of far-off places."

He would be paired with Couplet on the expedition. Their job would be to carry the survey chains and do the advance mapping that triangulation required. He and Couplet would be expected to travel ahead of the main group to identify the best geographical sites for establishing a triangulation point. Jean, as a nineteenth-century French historian noted, also planned to "study at their source some of the lesser-known languages of the New World." Upon his return to France, Jean hoped to publish a grammar on the New World idioms, establishing himself as an intellectual in his own right. He already felt the sting that comes from standing in the shadow of a famous relative, and—as his behavior on the expedition would later reveal—he wanted to be known as something more than just the cousin of a famous Parisian mathematician.

But on this day, those were half-formed ambitions. Jean had talked his way onto the voyage for the same reason that any young man would: He smelled adventure. He and the others would be the first group of foreigners to be allowed to travel to the interior of Peru, a colony that had stirred European curiosity for 200 years.

SPAIN HAD SOUGHT to keep the rest of Europe in the dark about its new lands almost from the moment of their discovery. By 1504, it had established a house of trade, the *Casa de Contratación,* to oversee all voyages to the New World. No one could ship goods or go there without the consent of the *Casa.* After Pizarro's conquest of the Incas revealed the mineral riches of South America, Spain formally decreed that no foreigner could enter its colonies. To put teeth into this law, Spain later declared that helping a foreigner enter Peru was a crime punishable by death.

As New World silver and gold flowed into Spain in the sixteenth century, France and the other European powers looked on with envy. What particularly galled them was that it was their uncouth neighbor to the south that had built this world empire. "By the abundant treasure of that country (Peru)," Sir Walter Raleigh complained, "the Spanish King vexeth all the Princes of Europe, and is become in a few years from a poor King of Castile the greatest monarch of this part of the world." French, English, and Dutch pirates regularly attacked Spanish ships in the colonial period, and occasionally they attacked Peruvian ports as well, which prompted Spain to further withdraw from the rest of Europe.

Ironically, it was a book by a Spanish priest, Bartolomé de Las Casas, that provided Europe with reason to season its envy with scorn. Until Las Casas published *A Short Account of the Destruction of the Indies* in 1542, the story of Spain's conquest had been written by chroniclers who had celebrated the conquistadors' feats as heroic, surpassing in glory even those of the Castilian knights of old. Bernal Díaz del Castillo glorified Cortés's triumph over the Aztecs in this way, and these early histories became known throughout Europe. But Las Casas, who went to the New World in 1502, saw things through a different prism. In his account, he likened the conquistadors to "Moorish barbarians" who, like "ravening wolves among gentle lambs," slaughtered Indians with abandon.

Hoping that his book would lead Spain to pass laws protecting the natives, Las Casas attacked all elements of the conquest. The encomienda system, he wrote, was "a moral pestilence which daily consumes these people." He said that the Requierimiento, the formal document of conquest, was so absurd that he did not know whether to laugh or cry. And in his book, he described one graphic episode after another of Indians being killed, raped, and enslaved. Francisco Pizarro and his men—according to the testimony of an eyewitness who had told his story to Las Casas—were the worst brutes of all:

> I testify that I saw with my own eyes Spaniards cutting off the hands, noses and ears of local people, both men and women, simply for the fun of it, and that this happened time and again in various places throughout the region. On several occasions I also saw them set dogs on the people, many being torn to pieces in this fashion, and they also burned down houses and even whole settlements, too numerous to count. It is also the case that they tore babes and sucklings from the mother's breast and played games with them, seeing who could throw them the farthest.

While much of what Las Casas wrote was true, historians have noted that he also employed exaggerated rhetoric—such as the tale of baby tossing—to make his point. Las Casas hoped that his polemical book would stir reform in the colonies, but it served primarily to bring a flood of international hatred down upon his country. *A Short Account of the Destruction of the Indies* was immediately translated into every major European language. The ghoulish engravings of a Protestant Flemish artist, Theodore de Bry, which accompanied the translations, deepened the image of Spanish cruelty. He drew scenes of pregnant Indian women being thrown into pits and impaled, of Indian babies being roasted alive, and of dogs tearing apart the severed limbs of those so slaughtered.

After the publication of Las Casas's book, Spain redoubled its efforts to build a wall that would separate it and its colonies from Europe. In 1551, the Spanish Inquisition published its first Index of Forbidden Books, which was designed to keep reformist writings—like those of Las Casas—out of print. Anyone who dared to challenge biblical teachings or the Spanish monarchy risked being branded a heretic and burned at the stake. Seven years later, Spain banned all foreign books in Spanish translations. Violators of these laws could be put to death. In 1559, Spaniards studying in other European countries were ordered to come home, and those who

**Theodore de Bry's depiction of the Spanish hunting Indians with dogs.**
*By permission of the British Library.*

returned from the colonies hoping to tell of their experiences were forbidden to publish a word.

As a result of this censorship, the rest of Europe learned little about Peru or the rest of South America. Rumors, gossip, and the scattered writings of a handful of foreign traders were the primary sources of information, and these reports often encouraged the imagination to run wild.

One of the earliest travelogues was written by an Italian slave trader, Francesco Carletti. He returned from Peru in 1594 with tales of an amazing wilderness, reporting, for instance, that frogs and toads of "frightening size" were found in such quantity in Cartagena that people there were uncertain whether "they rain[ed] down from the sky" or whether they were "born when the water falls and touches that arid land." Vampire bats liked to feast on a person's fingers and ears; chiggers bored into the feet and nibbled on the flesh until they grew fat; and in the forests, Carletti wrote, there were "mandril cats" so smart that, to cross a river, they linked "themselves together by their tails" and swung from trees on one side of the river to the other.

**Levinus Hulsius's depiction of Sir Walter Raleigh's
headless men in Guiana (1599).**
*By permission of the British Library.*

At this same time, the English explorer Sir Walter Raleigh
returned with a report on the Guianas, where he had gone to search
for El Dorado. This region, he said, was home to a fierce tribe of
headless men, known as the Ewaiponoma, who had "eyes in their
shoulders and their mouths in the middle of their breasts, and a
long train of hair growing between their shoulders." Sir Walter also
had met a man named Juan Martinez who claimed to have *lived* in
El Dorado for seven months. This fabled empire, Raleigh wrote,
was located around a salt lake 200 leagues (600 miles) in length and
was graced by a city of stone, named Manoa, so grand in size that it
"far exceeds any of the world, at least so much of it as is known to
the Spanish nation."

As a result of such writings, European cartographers depicted
colonial South America in ways that recalled medieval maps of old.
One map drawn in the sixteenth century featured a landscape filled

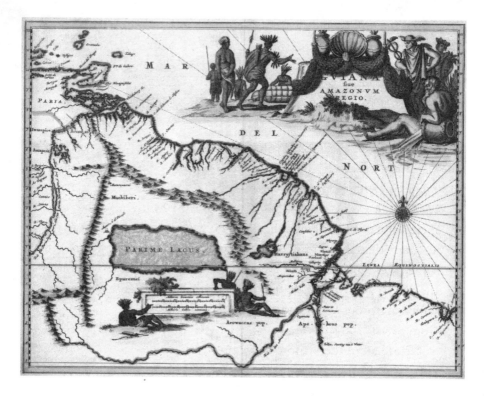

A seventeenth-century map depicting Lake Parima.
*By John Ogilby (1671). Rucker Agee Map Collection
of the Birmingham Alabama Public Library.*

with minotaurs, headless men with eyes in their chests, and bipedal creatures with ratlike heads. While many of these more fanciful items had disappeared from maps by the early 1700s when La Condamine and the others were preparing their voyage, El Dorado and the Amazon women were still present. The great lake described by Sir Walter Raleigh was called Lake Parima, and cartographers located it northeast of Río Negro as a body of water—on some maps—bigger than the Caspian Sea.

Accounts of Peruvian society, which were almost entirely based on life in the port cities of Lima, Guayaquil, and Cartagena, also left readers uncertain of where truth left off and exaggeration began. Peruvian merchants, Carletti wrote, piled treasures "of three and four hundred bars and ingots of silver" beneath their mattresses and spent "two hundred thousand escudos with greater security and ease than one of us buys a bit of salad." Even the "common people live much at their ease," reported a Frenchman, Acarete du Biscay, who slipped into the colony in 1658. "They always go dressed very fine, either in cloth of gold and silver, or in silk trimmed with gold and silver lace."

The elite in Peru, the visitors said, busied themselves with the pageantry of society. There were fancy balls to attend and a steady calendar of religious festivals, bullfights, and military parades. At such public events, they noted, the men were ever ready to defend their sense of knightly honor, quick to display daggers or swords to anyone "that should oppose their pleasures or offend them." In some cities in Peru, Biscay reported, sword pulling was so common that men "wear three or four buff-waistcoats one upon another, which are proof against the point of a sword, to secure themselves from private stabs."

Nearly all of the visitors were quite taken by Peruvian women, entranced in particular by the mestizos and mulattos who were mistresses to the rich. In Lima, reported Pedro de León Portocarrero, a Portuguese trader who lived there in the early 1600s, such women liked to "display themselves strolling about in public" and had a ravenous "desire to satisfy their carnal appetites." In 1714, the Frenchman Amadée Frezier similarly marveled at the lusty Peruvian women. They would sneak out from their homes at night under the cover of their veils for "immodest" purposes, he wrote, performing "the part which men do in France." At societal events, he added, they favored risqué dresses that left their "breasts and shoulders half naked," and they were pleased to field "proposals which a lover would not dare to make in France without incurring the indignation of a modest woman." When it came to "matters of love," Frezier concluded, Peruvians "yield to no nation."

Readers of such literature could conclude only one thing: In the New World, everything was upside down. As one traveler quipped, South America appeared to be a place "where the rivers ran inland and the women urinated standing up." The French explorers, however, were eager to sort out fact from fiction and planned to bring back "scientific" accounts of Peru. Existing travelogues, Bouguer declared, were from "persons who have never been induced to a strict examination of what they beheld."

THE POLITICS that had led up to this moment, when Spain was finally going to lift the veil that it had thrown over its colony, dated back to 1700, when the long reign of the Hapsburg kings had come to an end. The last Hapsburg king of Spain, Charles II, was a sickly and haunted man—many in Europe considered him an inbred imbecile—and as he lay dying, childless, he had selected Philip of Anjou to be his successor. Philip was the great-grandson of Philip IV of Spain and the grandson of France's Louis XIV, a Bourbon king. He had blood ties to both monarchies.

With a member of the Bourbon family on the Spanish throne, France seemed poised to gain coveted trading rights with Peru. It established a trading company, the Compagnie Royale de la Mer Pacifique, to carry out this commerce, and in 1701, Spain gave French ships permission to buy supplies in its colonial ports. However, the Council of the Indies, in Madrid, which governed colonial matters, privately seethed over this French influence, as did England and the Netherlands, which worried that the two Catholic countries were merging into a superpower. England and the Netherlands declared war, and when the War of the Spanish Succession finally came to an end in 1713 with the signing of the Treaty of Utrecht, Spain and France were forced to agree to keep their countries separate. Philip V renounced any right he might have to the French throne upon the death of Louis XIV, and England was granted a commercial monopoly over the African slave trade to the New World.

After that, Philip V governed in a way that pleased Spanish isolationists. He refused to grant the French full trading privileges with Spain's colonies, and shortly after Louis XIV died in 1715, the two countries even went to war. Philip's embrace of the old guard in Spain also led him to pump new life into the Spanish Inquisition. During his reign, the Inquisition held 782 autos-da-fé, at which thousands of heretics were punished. This revival of medieval ways prompted Benito Jerónimo Feijoo, a reform-minded Benedictine monk, to bitterly complain that "while abroad there is progress in physics, anatomy, botany, geography and natural history, we break each other's heads and drown our halls with howls."

Indeed, in spite of Philip's Bourbon bloodlines, the old dynamic still held sway in 1733, when the French Academy of Sciences decided to mount its expedition. The French wanted into Peru, and the Spanish wanted to keep them out. The mission, however, provided Louis XV with a sly way to break the stalemate.

There was no scientific reason that the French had to go precisely to the equator. A trip to their own colony, French Guiana, on the northern coast of South America, would get them close enough to zero degrees latitude to serve their purpose. Measuring an arc there would reveal whether a degree close to the equator was longer or shorter than one in France and thus reveal the earth's shape. And certainly it would have been easier and quicker to complete this task in a French colony. La Condamine had even argued—with a "sharp voice," Bouguer recalled—for going to Cayenne in French Guiana.* But La Condamine was naive about the political opportunity at hand, an opportunity that Count Jean-Frédéric Phélypeaux de Maurepas, minister of the marine, eagerly laid out for the king. A scientific expedition, he told Louis XV in early 1734, would be above suspicion and yet it would enable France, as a French historian later wrote, "to study the country and bring back a detailed description."

Properly briefed, Louis XV wrote his "dear uncle" on April 6, 1734, asking for permission for the French to travel to Peru. He assured Philip V that there was no reason for the Spanish to fret.

* The academy quickly rejected any thought of going to Africa, for it was considered to be populated by "savages."

His mapmakers would simply be making observations "which would be advantageous not only for the advancing of Science, but also very useful to commerce, by increasing the safety and ease of navigation." How could his uncle stand in the way of such progress?

Philip's response showed that he had indeed been hoodwinked, at least in regard to the science. On August 14, 1734, he granted passports to the ten French scientists. He did so, he wrote, because the French were desirous of making astronomical observations that had to "be made at the Equator itself. ... It is only on the coast of Peru that they may undertake [such observations] without undergoing great difficulties." Knowing the precise shape of the earth, he added, would be "useful for navigation in general, and in particular, for the navigation of my subjects." The French had successfully convinced Philip that the expedition would provide Spain with a practical benefit, even though such a claim was a stretch. While it was true that the expedition would enable cartographers to draw more precise maps, the improvement in accuracy would be modest—the French had already used updated triangulation techniques to develop a fairly reliable estimate of the earth's circumference. The expedition was designed to answer a more abstract question, one of physics and gravitational forces, but Spain was unlikely to open the door to its colonies for such an abstruse end. However, the advancement of cartography and of the science of navigation were practical ends that every eighteenth-century European monarch desired, and in a letter dated August 20, 1734, Philip promised the French savants every possible support. They could borrow funds from Peru's treasury, and he would advise his governors in Peru to "give them all of the assistance, favors and protection that they should require so that they may easily find housing, transportation, and mounts ... and pay the just and ordinary prices without any obstacle whatsoever." Philip, it seemed, was even going to protect the French from the price gouging that most travelers knew to expect.

The whole exchange was very cordial, an uncle replying in a most gracious manner to his "dear nephew." But Philip also had a few requests of his own. The French astronomers, he informed his nephew, would have to present their gear for close inspection upon arrival in Santo Domingo and at every other stop in their journey. This was necessary so that they could prove they were "above suspicion of any illegal commerce which might be deemed prejudicial to my Kingdoms." Nor would La Condamine and the others be allowed to go wherever they wanted in Peru. Their route to Quito was carefully proscribed, and once there, their travel was to be limited to those areas where the scientific work was to be done. Finally, Philip would assign two Spanish military officers to the expedition; they would "assist said Frenchmen in all of the observations they shall undertake."

In the political arena, everyone understood each other perfectly. The French could go to Peru, but the Spanish officers would keep a close eye on them to ensure that they did not poke their noses where they did not belong. On this expedition, science would be mixed with the gamesmanship of espionage.

BY THE MORNING of May 16, 1735, the *Portefaix* was ready to sail. The frigate's holds were crammed with the scientists' goods, La Condamine having checked off hundreds of items from a long inventory list. In addition to the quadrants and zenith sector, their scientific equipment included two telescopes, survey chains, watches with second hands, land and sea compasses, thermometers, a rain gauge, several barometers, a galvanometer, an instrument for measuring the blueness of the sky, and another for determining the boiling point of water. Each of the ten men had his own personal trunk, filled with numerous changes of clothes, toiletries, and powder bags for dressing wigs. They also were bringing along a library of books, surgical instruments, medicines, twelve shotguns, six swords, 225 books of gunpowder, nine barrels of brandy, and six packets of playing cards. Four servants would accompany them, and they planned to buy several slaves at their first stop in the West Indies.

They all knew there was much at stake. They were setting out to explore a continent and pursue a grand scientific quest. What was the earth's shape? Was Newton or Descartes right? What was the force that kept planets in their orbits? And how could one best know the world? Through concrete observations, as the French had done with their many measurements of an arc? Or through abstract mathematics?

As the *Portefaix* pulled away from the dock, they all stood on deck. For a moment, they looked back at the crowd that had come to see them off. There were the usual waves and shouts of good-bye, and then, in the morning fog, the wooden pier slid from view, and they turned their sights to the open expanse of ocean to the west. La Condamine, Louis Godin, Bouguer, Jean Godin, and the others—all felt excited. Their mission, the French had proudly proclaimed, was "the greatest expedition the world had ever known."

# CHAPTER FIVE

# Voyage to Quito

B Y EIGHTEENTH-CENTURY STANDARDS, the *Portefaix* provided La Condamine and the others with pleasant accommodations. Each of the three academy savants had a small private cabin, and while the others had to make do with tiny wooden bunks, they took comfort in knowing that the *Portefaix,* under the able hand of Captain Ricour, was sailing along at a speedy five knots an hour and would reach the West Indies in little more than a month. They ate a steady diet of salted meats, with La Condamine, Bouguer, and Louis Godin dining at the captain's table, and each night they all enjoyed a nip of the fine brandy they had brought along. Even the weather was cooperative, the moments when their ship was buffeted about by "large and long waves" interspersed with longer periods of calm.

They also stayed busy with a variety of tasks. From the moment they had put to sea, La Condamine and Bouguer had been compiling navigational logs and conducting experiments, with Jean Godin and the others assisting them. Much of their time was spent studying the utility of several newly invented navigational instruments, which had been awarded prizes by the French Academy of Sciences, including "Mr. Amonton's sea barometer, and the Marquis of Poleni's machine to measure the wake of a vessel." Poleni's invention was designed to improve on standard methods for calculating a ship's speed, which involved throwing overboard a weighted wooden disk attached to a rope with knots tied at equal distance along its length. By counting the number of knots that reeled out over a given period of time, sailors could get a rough measure of how fast the ship was moving. The problem was that this method did not account for the speed of the current. Poleni's machine was supposed to remedy this deficiency, but La Condamine's experiments were inconclusive on whether it accurately did so.

Another instrument that La Condamine and Bouguer tested was John Hadley's octant for determining latitude at sea. Mariners had long used the simple astrolabe to determine the altitude of the North Star or the sun, which in turn gave them an estimate of their latitude. Other devices, such as the cross-staff and sea quadrant, were employed for this purpose as well. The shortcoming with such instruments, as Bouguer had detailed in a 1729 paper titled "De la methode d'observer exactement sur mer la hauteur des astres," was that they were used by sailors standing on a heaving deck, which made it difficult to obtain a precise reading of the angular distance between the horizon and a celestial star. Hadley, a member of the Royal Society of London, had invented a novel solution for this problem. His octant employed two mirrors and a sighting telescope in such a manner that if the instrument vibrated for any reason, the instrument and the objects under observation, such as the horizon and the sun, would move as one. The observed angle between horizon and sun would thus remain the same. His invention, which he had presented to the Royal Society in 1731, was designed to "be of Use, where the Motion of the Objects, or any Circumstance occasioning an Unsteadiness in the common Instruments, renders the Observations difficult or uncertain." Louis Godin had brought the octant back from his instrument-gathering trip to London, and as the *Portefaix* sailed across the Atlantic, Bouguer and La Condamine tested its usefulness by measuring the height of the sun each day at noon. With the octant, they found that they could chart the movement of the sun so closely that they could identify the moment, to within fifteen seconds, when it reached its highest point. This, La Condamine noted, was "far beyond the usual limits, which previously did not allow for being certain of midday at sea by closer than two minutes." Hadley's invention apparently produced an eightfold improvement in accuracy. Captain Ricour could now be confident that his latitude measurements were accurate to within a couple of miles.

With their minds occupied in this way, the days passed quickly. Even Bouguer found that putting Hadley's octant to the test and the other experiments had helped him forget his natural "repugnance" for sea travel. The one unsettling moment of the voyage came when Jussieu, the expedition's botanist, was bitten by a dog that the mission's doctor, Senièrgues, had brought aboard. Although Jussieu was not badly hurt, Senièrgues decided that the dog needed to be killed. This so upset the sentimental Jussieu that he hid for days below deck in his bunk with the curtain drawn, refusing all entreaties to come out.

They arrived in Martinique in the West Indies late in the afternoon of June 22, 1735, docking at Fort Royal. They had traveled more than 4,000 miles in thirty-seven days, and now they delighted at the sight of the volcano Mount Pelée, its slopes thick with tropical vegetation. This was a gentle introduction to the New World, for Martinique could provide many of the amenities of home. Although Columbus had sighted the island in 1493, naming it Martinica in honor of Saint Martin, the Spanish had never settled it, leaving the door open for a French trading company to claim it in 1635. The French brought in slaves to work sugar plantations and rapidly pushed the native Carib Indians into the far corners of the island. As part of a 1660 treaty, the Caribs agreed to reside only on the Atlantic side, but that peace was short-lived, and soon the Caribs who were not killed in battle fled the island altogether.

La Condamine and the others stayed ten days on Martinique, buying supplies and lugging their barometer up the slopes of Mount Pelée to an altitude of "700 toises above sea level," where they found the cold, even in the tropics, "severe."* They were intent on using the barometer to measure altitude in the Andes, and in order to do so, they needed to improve their understanding of how the instrument could be used for this purpose. The barometer had been invented a century earlier by an Italian, Evangelista Torricelli, who had shown that weather-related changes in air pressure caused water in a thirty-five-foot-tall vacuum tube to rise or fall. By replacing water with mercury, which was fourteen times heavier, Torricelli was able to create a barometer less than three feet tall, a size that made his new invention portable. Wealthy people in the late seventeenth century proudly displayed this weather instrument in their homes. However, in 1648, France's Blaise Pascal observed that air pressure also dropped as one climbed in altitude. Mercury levels in a barometer dropped about one inch for every 1,000 feet gained, but this change in pressure was not precisely linear: The drop in the mercury level grew ever so slightly less pronounced as one climbed higher. What Bouguer hoped to do on this voyage was develop a logarithmic scale that would describe this variable change in air pressure, and Martinique provided an ideal laboratory to launch the effort. He and La Condamine took the barometer to different spots on Mount Pelée and, with the sea visible, they were able to "determine their heights geometrically." They then correlated their altitude to the barometric readings, a first step toward creating the desired logarithm.

Their next stop was Saint Domingue, a French territory on the island of Hispaniola. They departed from Martinique on July 4, with La Condamine recovering from a mild case of the "illness of Siam," or yellow fever. One of their guides in Martinique had come down with symptoms of the disease on July 2, and a day later La Condamine began exhibiting them as well. A dreaded sickness in

---

* Mount Pelée is 4,586 feet tall.

Voyage to Quito, 1735-1736

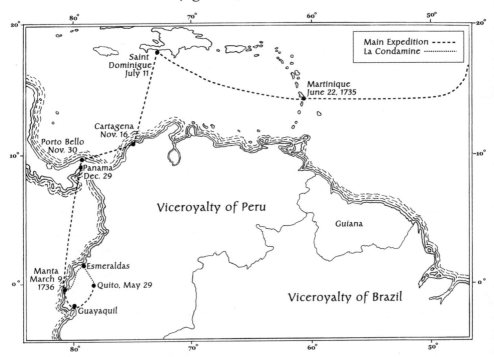

the New World, the illness of Siam's initial fever and vomiting often gave way to seizures, coma, and death. But Senièrgues and Jussieu treated La Condamine with "all haste," and he revived so quickly that he later recounted that he was "ill, bled, purged, cured and placed on board within 24 hours."

Hispaniola had been the first island colonized by Spain, and so it was a sore point with Spain that France had wrested control of its western third in 1697. French pirates had long hidden in the coves and bays on this part of the island, harassing Spanish shipping at every turn, and in 1697, with the decrepit King Charles II slowly dying in Madrid, Spain reluctantly signed the Treaty of Ryswick relinquishing the western region. The *Portefaix* anchored on July 11 at Fort Saint Louis, on the southern coast, and then sailed around a spit of land to Petit Goave. There the French visitors lodged in a small inn and waited for permission to proceed, a wait that quickly turned frustrating. The governor of the French colony wrote his counterpart in Santo Domingo, asking that he send a ship to take the French academicians to Cartagena, but the Spanish governor wrote back to say that he was unable, at the moment, to provide such transport.* Time was passing, and what unsettled the French academicians, even though they did not want to admit it, was that they knew they were in a race.

Shortly before they had departed from La Rochelle, Maupertuis had proposed to the academy that he lead a second arc-measuring mission, this one to Lapland. By sending expeditions to both Lapland and the equator, Maupertuis had argued, the academy could be assured a more definitive answer about the earth's shape. Rather than comparing the length of an arc at the equator to that of one in France, the academy would be able to compare arcs measured at the two extremes of the earth, which would greatly lessen the possibility that an imprecise measurement would lead to a misleading result. While this was good science, it was disturbing to those heading to Peru. The group that came back first, they knew, would most likely gain fame for having solved the great question.

As the French and Spanish diplomats exchanged letters, the French scientists occupied themselves as best they could. They determined the longitude and latitude of various forts and towns on the island, and Verguin drew several maps. La Condamine also hired a merchant to make two large tents with awnings, each a copy of the largest tent they had brought with them from La Rochelle. He was tending to a delicate matter, for if they had only one large tent, a question would arise over which of the three academicians would get it. By commissioning two more, he ensured that each would now have his own sleeping quarters. The others in the crew would share three smaller tents, befitting their lower status as assistants.

Even so, as the party lingered in Saint Domingue, tensions surfaced between Godin, Bouguer, and La Condamine. Each had his

---

* Although La Condamine is unclear on this point, apparently the *Portefaix* had not been authorized to sail to a Spanish port.

own ideas about how the expedition should be run, and to make matters worse, Godin, with idle time on his hands, took up with a local woman. Gregarious as always, he delighted in strutting about town with her, which did not endear him to the local populace, and he showered her with gifts. This upset La Condamine and Bouguer, for it meant he was piddling away the expedition's cash. The three exchanged sharp words on more than one occasion, causing Godin to remind everyone that *he* was both the senior member of the academy and the expedition's leader. By early October, even the mild-mannered Jussieu was irritated with Godin, deriding him in a letter home as a "youngbeard without experience."

Six hundred miles away, two young Spanish military officers in Cartagena—Antonio de Ulloa and Jorge Juan y Santacilia—were similarly growing impatient, wondering if the "French academicians" they were supposed to keep an eye on would ever arrive.

AT FIRST GLANCE, Ulloa and Juan did not appear to be very well suited for the task at hand. They were so young—Ulloa was nineteen and Juan twenty-two—that it seemed certain they would be easily intimidated by the French savants, who were not only older but of much higher status. Yet, as would become evident in the months ahead, King Philip V had chosen wisely. Both Ulloa and Juan were well educated, firm in their resolve, and intellectually curious.

Ulloa, a native of Seville, was the son of a well-known economist, Bernardo de Ulloa. As a child, Antonio was small and sickly, and his father constantly worried that he would never amount to much. When Ulloa turned thirteen, his father decided that the only education that could save his son from mediocrity was harsh experience, and so he asked the commander of Spain's trans-Atlantic fleet, Manuel Pintado, to take him on as a cabin boy. This was an unusual position for a wellborn boy, and yet no schooling could have offered Ulloa more. The experience both steeled his character and fired his imagination. In 1733, he entered the Spanish naval academy, the Royal Academy of Midshipmen, where he became a member of an elite company, the Guardias Marinas. There he was taught mathematics, astronomy, and navigation.

Juan's early childhood had also been difficult. Born into a noble family in Valencia, he was orphaned at age three, at which time he went to live with an uncle. He was tutored at home until he was twelve; then he was sent to a boarding school in Malta, where he showed such an aptitude for mathematics that the other students nicknamed him Euclid. At age sixteen, he decided upon a naval career, and like Ulloa, was admitted into the Guardias Marinas. King Philip V promoted them both to the rank of lieutenant for the mission to Peru.

They had reached Cartagena on July 9, 1735, having had the good fortune to travel from Spain in the company of the new viceroy of Peru, José de Mendoza, the Marqués de Villagarcía. Although they were eager for the French to arrive, they had plenty to do. In addition to chaperoning the French visitors, Ulloa and Juan had been asked by Philip V to prepare a thorough report on Peru, and they had taken this responsibility to heart, filling their notebooks with engaging accounts of Cartagena's history and daily life.

The bay of Cartagena had been discovered by Spaniards in 1502, and its geography made it ideal for a military port. From the sea, ships could reach the city only by sailing through a narrow straight, which in 1735 was guarded by two forts. Even so, pirates and other foreigners had attacked Cartagena numerous times in its 200-year history. Its worst moment had come in 1586, Ulloa and Juan noted, when the Englishman Sir Francis Drake had set the town on fire and extracted a ransom of 120,000 silver ducats from its inhabitants.

As was the Spanish custom, the streets of Cartagena were laid out in a grid, with a *plaza mayor* in the center, where the administrative buildings, including the Court of the Inquisition, could be found. Well-to-do whites lived in fine houses with wooden balconies, and their homes, Ulloa and Juan observed, were "splendidly furnished." During the midday heat, the women of these homes could usually be found "sitting in their hammocks and swinging themselves for air," and everyone, men and women, stopped for a brandy each morning at eleven. Nature and commerce provided a daily feast for their dinner tables. The wealthy of Cartagena dined on rice, grains, fish, meats from animals of every kind—cows, hogs, geese, deer, and rabbits—and a cornucopia of New World fruits, such as pineapples, guavas, papayas, guanabanas, and zapotes. Chocolates filled their cravings for sweets, and nearly everyone, including the women, enjoyed a good smoke.

But these pleasures were reserved for the well-to-do. The other inhabitants of Cartagena, Ulloa and Juan noted, "are indigent, and reduced to mean and hard labour for subsistence." There was a leper colony in the town, and many of the poor—mostly mestizos and freed Negroes—resided in miserable straw huts, where they lived "little different from beasts, cultivating, in a very small spot, such vegetables as are at hand, and subsisting on the sale of them." The street markets where such produce was sold had a distinct African tone, the Negro women wearing "only a small piece of cotton stuff about their waist" and caring for their infants in a way that amazed the two Spaniards:

> Those who have children sucking at their breast, which is the case of the generality, carry them on their shoulders, in order to have their arms at liberty; and when the infants are hungry, they give them the breast either under the arm or over the shoulders, without taking them from their backs. This will perhaps appear incredible; but their breasts, being left to grow without any pressure on them, often hang down to their very waist, and are not therefore difficult to turn over their shoulders for the convenience of the infant.

As was true throughout Peru, the bringing together of three races—whites, Negroes, and indigenous groups—had produced a multihued population in Cartagena, and the colonial city went to great lengths to identify the amount of "impure blood," whether

**Daily life in Cartagena.**
*From Jorge Juan and Antonio de Ulloa,* Relación histórica del viage a la
América Meridional *(1749).*

black or Indian, that tainted those who were not 100 percent white. The result was a very complicated caste system. When a white mated with a Negro, Ulloa and Juan reported, the child was deemed a mulatto, and it took several generations of marrying back into white families for the mulatto blood to be washed out. The offspring of a mulatto and a white was deemed to be a *terceron,* and if a terceron married a white, their children were considered *quarterones.* A mix of quarteron and white produced a *quinteron,* and the child of a quinteron and a white was considered to have made it all the way back to being a "Spaniard, free from all taint of the Negro race." When a Negro married an Indian, their offspring were known as *sambos,* and when a quarteron married a terceron or a mulatto, their children were called *salto atras,* or "retrogrades, because, instead of advancing towards being whites, they have gone backwards towards the Negro race." This was a racial ladder of many steps, and everyone knew where he or she stood on it, "so jealous of the order of their tribe or cast that if, through inadvertence, you call them by a degree lower than what they actually are, they are highly offended, never suffering themselves to be deprived of so valuable a gift of fortune."

Ulloa and Juan observed the wildlife of Cartagena with equal diligence. There were tigers, foxes, armadillos, lizards, monkeys, and colorful snakes to be described. At dusk, vampire bats flew in such great numbers that they covered the sky and made their way into homes, where "if they happen to find the foot of any one bare, they insinuate their tooth into a vein, with all the art of the most expert surgeon, sucking the blood till they are satiated." The two Spaniards identified "four principle kinds" of mosquitoes that tormented the inhabitants of Cartagena, described the life cycle of a parasitic worm called the *cobrilla* that was about the "size of a coarse sewing thread," and dwelled at great length upon the *nigua,* a flea that would pester them for the rest of their days in Peru. This insect liked to bury itself in "the legs, the soles of the feet or toes" and make its nest there, depositing its eggs and eating the host's flesh for sustenance, all of which caused a "fiery itching." Removing the insect and its nest often caused extreme pain, because sometimes "they penetrate even to the bone, and the pain, even after the foot is cleared of them, lasts till the flesh has filled up the cavities they had made." To ward off infection, the wounds were "filled either with tobacco ashes, chewed tobacco, or snuff."

Cartagena was only the first stop on their journey, but already Ulloa and Juan were proving to be keen observers and able writers, busily compiling notes for the first chapter of a travelogue that would, upon its publication in 1748, become a best-seller throughout Europe.

It was not until early November that the French academicians obtained permission to depart for Cartagena. The governor of Santo Domingo, unable to provide them with a ship, at last allowed them to sail in a French vessel, the *Vautour,* captained by a Mr. Hericourt. On November 16, the two groups finally met, and while the French were initially a bit resentful of this intrusion into their expedition, the friendliness of the two Spaniards quickly put every-one at ease, La Condamine remarking that "the knowledge and the personal merit of these two officers showed the high level of the guards of the Spanish Navy." With everyone together now, they debated the best way to proceed. Several in the group favored head-ing overland to Quito, a journey that would involve poling up the Magdalena River for 400 miles and then proceeding on mules through the Andes for another 500 miles. "Ordinary travelers" took nearly four months to make this trek, and La Condamine was adamantly opposed to this route. Their equipment and delicate instruments would all have to be repacked, and with the large amount of baggage they carried, the journey could be expected to take much longer than usual. All this, he said, would cause "great fatigue, time and expense." The forceful La Condamine won this argument—indeed, he rarely lost such battles—and on November 24, they all boarded the *Vautour* for Porto Bello, where they would disembark in order to cross the Isthmus of Panama. Their group numbered twenty-six: Ulloa and Juan had two servants and the French now had twelve, the governor of Saint Domingue having provided them with five or six slaves.

Porto Bello was well known throughout the Spanish Empire as a dreadful place to visit. It was a hub for the Peruvian export trade, the market open forty days each year. All of the goods exported from Quito and points south in Peru came through this port, hav-ing been shipped up along the Pacific coast to Panama City and then packed across the isthmus by mule. The mule train would reach Porto Bello at the same time as a convoy of trading ships from Spain, the *Galeones*, arrived bearing luxury items to be imported into Peru. Tents filled with merchandise crowded the *plaza mayor* and slaves were sold; with so many traders in town, rent for a single house for the six weeks could fetch "four, five, six thousand crowns," Ulloa and Juan reported. But the swampy port was also a hotbed of disease. Low mountains surrounded the town, blocking winds that might have refreshed the air or blown away the mosquitoes, and rain pounded down incessantly. The illness of

Siam and "fever," soon to become identified as malaria, often claimed the lives of half the crew of a visiting ship, earning Porto Bello the nickname "the tomb of Spaniards."

As the *Vautour* neared the port on November 29, it encountered a storm that stirred all their misgivings. Gale winds tossed the ship about so fiercely that it was unable to enter the harbor, and the men had to wait until the following day to go ashore. Jussieu arrived with a fever, and several others fell sick during the next several days. Local bureaucrats also took to heart King Philip's order that their baggage be closely inventoried. "These verifications were so precise," La Condamine complained, "that we were unable to prevent the customs officials from discovering a metal mirror which formed part of a catoptrical telescope, which we feared the humidity in the air of Porto Bello might damage." A scorpion's sting deepened La Condamine's foul mood. He treated the bite with a poultice of his own making, which, he reported, relieved the pain so well that it could replace "all of the ridiculous and disgusting remedies used in the country."

The men were stranded in Porto Bello for nearly a month. The route across the isthmus to Panama City had been made impassable by rain—La Condamine called it "the worst road in the world." Their only alternative was to travel up the Chagres River, and that required waiting for the governor of Panama to send them riverboats. They spent the time doing what experiments and good deeds they could. After Jussieu recovered from his fever, he provided medical care to the local populace; Godin and Bouguer measured the length of the seconds pendulum; and Ulloa, Juan, and Verguin mapped the town. But most days were gray and damp, so gloomy that even the two Spaniards concluded that the town was "cursed by nature." The incessant croaking of frogs kept them awake all night, and in the morning, if it had rained, the streets would be so blanketed with toads that the men could barely walk "without treading on them."

The vessels that arrived for them on December 22 were flat-bottomed barges known as *chatas*. Each had a cabin at its stern for the comfort of passengers, and a crew of "eighteen to twenty robust Negroes" manning the oars. The forty-three-mile trip up the Chagres turned out to be an unexpected joy. For the first two days, the flow of the river was such that they could proceed by rowing, but then the river's speed quickened and its depth lessened, so they poled their way along. The surrounding wilderness, Ulloa wrote, was so glorious that "the most fertile imagination of a painter can never equal the magnificence of the rural landscapes here drawn by the pencil of Nature." Alligators sunned themselves on the riverbank, turtles floated by on drifting tree limbs, and everywhere they looked they could see the colorful plumage of peacocks, turtledoves, and herons. Monkeys diverse in size and color swung from every tree, and each night, the boat's crew would gather food from the forest for their supper, plucking pineapples from trees and hunting pheasants and peacocks. Monkey was also served, and this meal, Ulloa confessed, initially made some of the group uneasy:

> When dead, [the monkeys] are scalded in order to take off the hair, whence the skin is contracted by the heat, and when thoroughly cleaned, looks perfectly white, and very greatly resembles a child of about two or three years of age, when crying. This resemblance is shocking to humanity, yet the scarcity of food in many parts of America renders the flesh of these creatures valuable, and not only the Negroes, but the Creoles and Europeans themselves, make no scruple of eating it.

As they ascended the Chagres, La Condamine mapped its winding route, and Jussieu, at every possible occasion, urged them to stop so that he could gather plant specimens. It took them five days to reach Cruces, a small village at the head of the river, and from there it was a short fifteen miles by mule to Panama City, where they arrived late in the afternoon on December 29. Here they spent the next seven weeks making arrangements for a boat to take them south to Peru, and except for the fact that La Condamine, Bouguer, and Godin continued to quarrel over money and plans for measur-

**Along the Chagres River.**
*From Jorge Juan and Antonio de Ulloa,* Relación histórica del viage
a la América Meridional *(1749).*

ing the arc, the respite was welcome. All of the French members of
the expedition studied Spanish, and the three academics performed
various investigations "of the thermometer, the barometer, and
variations of the magnetic needle," La Condamine reported.
Jussieu explored the local vegetation, going out alone on walks each
day with a bag on his back to gather botanical specimens. "I see that
this trip," he wrote in a letter to his brothers on February 15, 1736,
"which shall after all have but one (stated) purpose, will in fact collect knowledge of geographic, historical, mathematical, astronomical, botanical, medicinal, surgical and anatomical subjects, etc. As
we go along we collect instructive reports, which shall make up a
comprehensive and fascinating body of work."

Meanwhile, Jean Godin, Couplet, Verguin, and the other assistants, when not helping the academics with their studies, enjoyed
being tourists. They sampled oysters and other regional delicacies,
like iguana seasoned with red pepper and lime juice, a recipe that
unfortunately failed to hide the "nauseous smell" of the reptile's

white meat. Several times they stood along the shore and watched Negro slaves dive for pearls in the bay. Ten or twenty of them would go out in a boat at a time, and with a rope tied around their waists, they would jump overboard with small weights to accelerate their sinking. They dove to depths approaching fifty feet, Ulloa discovered, and in order to make the most of each descent, the divers would put an oyster under the left arm, one in each hand, "and sometimes another in their mouth," before rising to breathe. They went down time and again until their daily quota was filled, and all the while they had to be on the alert for sharks, octopuses, and huge stingrays that haunted the bay. The boat's officer also kept an eye out for these marauders and would tug on the ropes at the first sight of one, but this scheme, Ulloa lamented, was often "ineffectual" in protecting the divers. More than one slave had lost an arm or a leg or his life to a shark, and several—or so Ulloa was told—had been killed by giant rays, a "fish," it was said, that "wraps its fins round a man, or any other animal, that happens to come within its reach, and immediately squeezes it to death."

They sailed from Panama City on February 22, having chartered the *San Cristóbal* for the 800-mile voyage down the coast. They were eager to be in Peru, and yet their plans for precisely how they would proceed when they arrived were still quite unsettled. The ongoing feud between the three academicians was now focused on whether they should attempt to do their arc measurements along the coast, which Bouguer and La Condamine favored, or in the Andes, as Godin desired. The *San Cristóbal* crossed the equator on March 8, and a day later, it dropped anchor in the bay of Manta. The expedition members should have been overjoyed—the snow-capped Andes were now visible in the distance—but the tension between the three leaders was so palpable that Senièrgues, in a letter to Bernard and Antoine de Jussieu, worried that the expedition was blowing apart:

> Tomorrow we are to see if the terrain will be adequate for the measurement of a base. Mr. Godin does not agree and intends to

leave for Guayaquil and from there go directly to Quito. Mr. de La Condamine already announced in front of everyone that if no one wanted to stay he would remain alone. If he feels this strongly about it, Mr. Bouguer will no doubt remain with him. Mr. Godin has not been speaking to them for some time now. They fight like cats and dogs and attack each other's observations. It is not possible that they will remain together for the rest of this trip.

To investigate the coast, they traveled to Monte Christi, a small village about eight miles inland. They were put up by the locals in bamboo huts raised on stilts, La Condamine awaking that first night to the unsettling sight of a snake dangling overhead. After the expedition surveyed the surrounding terrain, Bouguer, on March 12, wrote a formal memorandum to Godin. If they were to do their survey work here, he argued, it would save them the time and expense of transporting their gear from Guayaquil to Quito, which would require hiring more than 100 mules. It would also be "easier to provide for the subsistence of our company" along the coast, he wrote. Nor should it matter that King Philip was expecting them to do their work around Quito. Spain would be well served by their staying here: "I can even dare to add that it is within [the king's] interest that our operations be carried out in the indicated place ... because, in fact, we cannot conclude our work near the sea without drawing up a map which Navigators shall find invaluable."

Although there might have been much to recommend Bouguer's proposal, Godin did not want to discuss it. He was the leader of this expedition, Spain was expecting them to do their work around Quito, and that was that. Besides, Ulloa and Juan had explored the terrain, and they did not see the same opportunity that Bouguer did. The landscape around Manta, they wrote, was "extremely mountainous and almost covered with prodigious trees," which made "any geometrical operations ... impractical there."

The leaders of the group were at loggerheads, and yet at the last moment, they resolved the matter in a way that at least held open the possibility of a later reconciliation. On March 13, everyone but La Condamine and Bouguer—and their personal servants—boarded the *San Cristóbal,* which was newly supplied with food and water. They would continue along the coast to Guayaquil and then travel inland north to Quito. La Condamine and Bouguer, having lost this particular battle, would conduct some experiments along the coast and then make their way to Quito. The bitterness of the moment, they all hoped, could be forgotten once they had some time apart, and not even Ulloa and Juan stopped to think about what else La Condamine and Bouguer might be accomplishing by staying behind. The two French academicians had barely stepped into Peru, and yet, once the *San Cristóbal* set sail, they had already freed themselves from their Spanish minders, a precedent for traveling about the colony with independence.

In anticipation of a lunar eclipse on March 26, La Condamine and Bouguer quickly built a makeshift observatory on the outskirts of Monte Christi. The event would provide them with a celestial timepiece, one much easier to use than Jupiter's satellites, enabling them to fix the longitude "of all this coast, the most westerly of South America." Skies were clear that night and both were elated to have made such "an extremely important observation," Bouguer wrote. They now knew that Monte Christi was fourteen leagues west of the meridian at Panama City, and that the nearby Cape of Saint Lorenzo was four leagues further west. When these data reached France, they enabled cartographers to draw the South American continent with much greater accuracy than ever before.

Over the next few weeks, La Condamine and Bouguer made their way north along the coast, traveling by horse along the beach. They stopped in several villages—Puerto Viejo, Charapoto, and Canow—and learned about the local folklore. Centuries ago, they were told, the people living in this region had worshipped "an emerald the size of an ostrich egg," which was kept in a temple. When the Spanish arrived, the natives had hidden the precious stone, and they had remained mum about it ever since. Their silence, Bouguer observed, was wise, for if the Spanish had ever been able to find the source of the emeralds, the Indians would have immediately been put to work digging for more, a toil "of labour painful to excess, which they alone would bear the weight, and with but little portion of the profits."

In early April, La Condamine and Bouguer set up camp along the Rio Jama, just a few miles south of the equator. Here Bouguer spent several weeks studying the refractory properties of the atmosphere, which he had been investigating ever since reaching Petit Goave. He planned to make similar studies once he reached Quito, enabling him to answer a critical question: Was refraction—which altered the apparent position of stars—more or less pronounced at higher altitudes? This difference would have to be factored into their arc-measuring calculations. The bitter feelings of Manta had definitely subsided, and on April 23, Bouguer decided that it was time to turn back. He had finished his refraction studies, and the rigors of traveling along the coast had worn him out. He found the heat oppressive, the insects a "plague," and he had even grown tired of the birds in the forest, which, to his ear, produced a "discordant stunning noise." He would hurry on to Guayaquil and try to catch Godin and the others.

La Condamine, however, was eager to continue north. While Bouguer had been at his Rio Jama camp, La Condamine had spent five days fixing the point where the equator crossed the coast. This was at "Palmar, where I carved on the most prominent boulder an inscription for the benefit of Sailors," he wrote in his journal. "I should have perhaps included a warning to not stop at that place; the persecution one undergoes night and day from mosquitoes and the different species of flies unknown in Europe is beyond any exaggeration." He was happy to be on his own, with only a servant by his side, and it mattered little to him that at every step of the way, he had to fight legions of mosquitoes and drag along a bulky quadrant and telescope. These were inconveniences that any adventurer could expect.

.  .  .

AFTER ARRIVING in Guayaquil on March 26, Godin and the others were unable to depart at once for Quito, the constant rains making travel overland impossible. So much rain fell in April that the river overflowed its banks, driving "snakes, poisonous vipers and scorpions" into the houses where they were staying, Ulloa and Juan complained. The streets turned so muddy that people had to walk from the porch of one house to the next over planks set down as bridges between them. Waterlogged rats scurried about everywhere, marching through ceiling rafters at night with such a loud step that it was difficult to sleep.

On May 3, they thankfully escaped from Guayaquil aboard a chata, heading up the Guayaquil River to Caracol, a distance of about eighty miles. Indians living along this stretch of water, Ulloa and Juan noted, skillfully hunted fish with spears and harpoons. In smaller creeks, the Indians would chop up a plant root, called *barbasco,* mix it with bait, and toss the mixture into the water. The herbal concoction would knock out the fish, which would then float to the surface, enabling the Indians to scoop them up with nets. Alligators, some nearly fifteen feet long, lined the banks, and those that had tasted human flesh before were rumored to be "inflamed with an insatiable desire of repeating the same delicious repast." But insects were the worst menace:

> The tortures we received on the river from the moschitos were beyond imagination. We had provided ourselves with moschito cloths, but to very little purpose. The whole day we were in continual motion to keep them off, but at night our torments were excessive. Our gloves were indeed some defense to our hands, but our faces were entirely exposed, nor were our clothes a sufficient defense for the rest of our bodies, for their stings, penetrating through the cloth, caused a very painful and fiery itching. ... At day-break, we could not without concern look upon each other. Our faces were swelled, and our hands covered with painful tumours, which sufficiently indicated the condition of the other parts of our bodies exposed to the attacks of those insects.

**La Condamine marks the equator.**

*From Charles-Marie de La Condamine,* Journal du voyage fait par
ordre du roi à l'équateur *(1751).*

**A balsa raft in the Bay of Guayaquil.**

*From Jorge Juan and Antonio de Ulloa,* Relación histórica del viage a la
América Meridional *(1749).*

After eight such miserable days, they transferred their baggage at Caracol to the backs of seventy mules and immediately found themselves mired in a bog. The mules "at every step sunk almost up to their bellies," and when they finally reached the Ojibar River, only twelve miles from Caracol, they had to spend the night in a village with the unhappy name of Puerto de Moschitos. Jean Godin and a few others, in an effort to find relief from the insects, "stripped themselves and went into the river, keeping only their heads above water, but the face, being the only part exposed, was immediately covered with them, so that those who had recourse to this expedient, were soon forced to deliver up their whole bodies to these tormenting creatures."

They now began their climb into the mountains, and while they had the pleasure of passing many beautiful waterfalls, some more than 300 feet high, the path was so narrow that as they rode on the mules, they frequently banged "against the trees and rocks," giving them a collection of bruises to go with their multitude of insect bites. They also had to cross swaying bridges strung high over cascading rivers:

> The bridges [are] made with cords, bark of trees, or lianas. These lianas, netted together, form an aerial gallery, which is suspended from two large cables of similar materials, the extremities of which are fastened to branches of trees on opposite banks. Collectively the whole of these singular bridges resembles a fisher's net, or rather an Indian hammock, extending from one to the other side of the river. As the meshes of this net are very wide, and would suffer the foot to go between them, a sort of flooring is superimposed, consisting of branches and shrubs. It will readily be conceived, that the weight of this network, but especially that of the passenger, must give a considerable curve to the bridge, and when, in addition, one reflects that the traveler passing it is exposed to great oscillations, to which it is incident, particularly when the wind is high, and he reaches near the middle, this kind

**Huts on the Guayaquil River.**
*From Jorge Juan and Antonio de Ulloa,* Relación histórica del viage
a la América Meridional *(1749).*

of bridge, which is oftentimes thirty fathoms long, [it] must needs
have something frightful in its aspect. The natives, however, who
are far from being naturally intrepid, pass such bridges on the
trot, with their loads on their shoulders, together with the saddles
of the mules, which cross the river by swimming, and laugh at
the timidity of the traveller who hesitates to venture [across].

Even more frightening, they discovered that their lives were
now dependent on their mules' having good judgment and a steady
step. The muddy trail was filled with holes, "near three quarters of
a yard deep, in which the mules put their fore and hind feet, so that
sometimes they draw their bellies and riders' legs along the ground.
Should the creature happen to put his foot between two of these
holes, or not place it right, the rider falls, and, if on the side of the
precipice, inevitably perishes." They spent two or three days in this
manner, at times inching along ledges that looked out over "deep
abysses," which, Ulloa and Juan confessed, filled their "minds with
terror." They reached an altitude of more than 10,000 feet, having

ascended the western cordillera of the Andes,* and then, in the early afternoon of May 18, they crossed over a mountain pass called Pucara. Now they began their descent into the valley below, the slopes so steep and muddy that the mules slid down on their bellies, with their forelegs stretched out, moving with the "swiftness of a meteor." All that the startled riders—Ulloa, Juan, Louis Godin, Jussieu, Senièrgues, Hugo, Morainville, Verguin, Couplet, and Jean Godin—could do was hang on for dear life.

They spotted the village of Guaranda just before sunset. A sorry-looking bunch of travelers, the lot of them bruised, muddied, and exhausted, they felt overwhelmed with relief when the corregidor of the town came out to greet them. A priest then appeared, leading a parade of Indians boys waving flags, dancing, and singing, and as the expedition entered the town, bells were rung, "and every house resounded with the noise of trumpets, tabors and pipes." When they expressed their surprise, they were informed that such a reception was not at all unusual, but was given to all who entered the town. It was Guaranda's way of "paying congratulations" to those who had survived the perilous journey from Guayaquil.

They now had to travel north for 120 miles to reach Quito. They left Guaranda on May 21, skirted around the flanks of snow-capped Mount Chimborazo, a volcano more than 20,000 feet tall, and spent that first night in a stone cave called Rumi Machai. Over the course of the next week, they stumbled across the ruins of an Inca palace, awoke several mornings in huts covered with ice, crossed several deep chasms formed by earthquakes, and then, on May 29, at dusk, they rode into Quito. There they were greeted with every civility by the president of the Quito Audiencia,† Dionesio de Alsedo y Herrera, their journey of twelve months having finally come to an end.

* The Andes in this part of South America consists of two mountain ranges, or cordilleras, separated by a valley twenty-five to thirty-five miles wide.

† The Viceroyalty of Peru was divided up into a number of administrative districts known as *audiencias*. The Audiencia de Quito governed a territory about five times the present size of Ecuador, stretching from the Pacific to the Amazon.

. . .

BOUGUER AND LA CONDAMINE fared even worse in their travels. Bouguer, after leaving La Condamine at the Rio Jama, had suffered a miserable journey down the coast to Guayaquil, the trail so swampy that even mounted on a horse, he was often up to his knees in water. He reached Guayaquil three days after the others had departed, and he then followed in their wake all the way to Quito. His travel, however, was slowed by his poor health, and he did not arrive until June 10.

At first, La Condamine's trip had not been too unpleasant. After he and Bouguer split up, he had traveled north in a sea canoe, hugging the shoreline and stopping to determine the longitude of landmarks along the coast, such as the Cape of San Francisco. He was filling out the map that he and Bouguer had begun in Manta, and he continued his sea travels for more than 120 miles, until he reached Esmeraldas, a town populated primarily by free Negroes, the descendants of slaves who had escaped from a nearby shipwreck fifty years earlier. There he had the good fortune to meet the governor of the province, Pedro Maldonado, who had heard from administrators in Quito about the French mission. Maldonado was about the same age as La Condamine, and he shared his enthusiasm for exploration and science. A lasting friendship was born, and Maldonado told La Condamine of his plans to build a road from Esmeraldas to Quito—a route, he said, that La Condamine could now take.

The first leg of this 140-mile trip was up the Esmeraldas River. The river was so named because the conquistadors had come upon natives mining gems from its banks, and La Condamine, ever the indefatigable scientist, mapped its every turn. After that, he plunged into the jungle. Maldonado's vision for a road to Quito was just that—a dream for the future—and La Condamine had to bushwhack his way through the forest. His Indian guides cut their way through the brush with axes, La Condamine carrying his compass and thermometer in his hands, "more often than not on foot rather than horseback." It rained every afternoon, La Condamine dragging "along several instruments and a large quadrant, which two Indians had a hard time carrying." The dense foliage slowed their progress, and yet La Condamine turned even this to his advantage, collecting "in this vast jungle a large number of singular plants and seeds," which he looked forward to giving to Jussieu upon his arrival in Quito. His mood turned sour only after he was abandoned by his guides. He had but one horse to help him carry his goods, which consisted of a hammock, a suitcase of clothes, and his treasured instruments, which he was loathe to leave behind.* He was also nearly out of food: "I remained for eight days in this jungle. Powder and other provisions became scarce. I subsisted on bananas and other native fruits. I suffered a fever which I treated by a diet, which was recommended to me by reason and ordered by necessity."

He emerged from this solitude by "following the crest of a mountain," coming upon a narrow path much like the one that Godin and the others had followed into the Andes from Guayaquil. The trail passed waterfalls and crossed ravines "carved by torrents of melting snow," and La Condamine, like the others, found the liana bridges nerve-racking. Halfway up the Andes, he came upon several Indian villages—Niguas, Tambillo, and Guatea—where the natives, known as *Los Colorados*, colored themselves with red paint. In the last of these, he obtained new guides and mules. Because he had no money left, he was forced to leave behind his suitcase and quadrant as a guarantee that someone would return and pay for these services. Los Colorados led him to Nono, a village high in the Andes, where a Franciscan monk supplied him with all that he needed for the rest of his journey. La Condamine made his way ever higher into the mountains, stopping at times to catch his breath. The path scooted around the northern flank of boulder-strewn Mount Pichincha, a volcano that topped 15,700 feet. As he

---

* La Condamine writes of being alone once the guides abandoned him. It is most likely, however, that he was still accompanied by a personal servant.

reached the highest point on the trail, the clouds lifted, and suddenly he could see for miles:

I was seized by a sense of wonder at the appearance of a large valley of five to six leagues wide, interspersed with streams which joined together to form a river. I saw as far as my sight could see cultivated lands, divided into plains and prairies, green spaces, villages and towns surrounded by bushes and gardens. The city of Quito, far off, was at the end of this beautiful view. I felt as if I had been transported to the most beautiful of provinces in France, and as I descended I felt the imperceptible change in climate by going from extreme cold to the temperature of the most beautiful days in May.

His journey had come to an end. It was June 4, 1736, and now La Condamine and the others could begin the daunting task of measuring a degree of latitude in this rugged terrain.

# CHAPTER SIX

# Measuring the Baseline

Q UITO IS BUILT ON the lower slopes of Mount Pichincha, a volcano that has often rained ashes down on the homes below. The landscape is also cut by two deep ravines carrying waters tumbling down from Pichincha, which, in the 1700s, was covered with snow and ice. Such topography makes it an unlikely place for a city, and yet, as the members of the French expedition quickly sensed, there was something special, even spiritual, about this spot. Upon his arrival, Bouguer called it a "tropical paradise," and at every step they were confronted with evidence of its long history. Barefoot Indians trotted through the city, the men dressed in white cotton pants and a black cotton poncho, and they greatly outnumbered those of Spanish blood.

As far back as the fifth century A.D., Indians had come to this spot to trade goods, with gold, silver, and pearls the treasured items of the day. The people in this region came to be known as the Quitus. In the eleventh century, a tribe living along the coast, the Caras, ascended the Esmeraldas River into the valley, intermarrying with the Quitus, and collectively the two groups came to be known as the Shyri Nation. Two centuries later, the Shyris intermarried with the Puruhás to the south, forming the peaceful Kingdom of Quitu. The people worshipped the sun and built an observatory to study the solstices.

Around 1470, the Incas, led by the great warrior Tupac Yupanqui, began their conquest of this kingdom, capturing the city of Quitu in 1492. They brought with them a language, Quechua, which they made the common tongue of the realm, and for the next thirty-five years, during the reign of Huayna Capac, the Inca Empire prospered, with Quito its northern capital. Huayna Capac died in 1525, and after his son Atahualpa was killed by Pizarro at Cajamarca in 1533, one of Pizarro's men, Sebastián de Benalcázar, marched north to lay claim to Quito. He entered Quito in December 1534, with 150 horsemen and an infantry of eighty, but found it deserted and in ruins. Rumiñahui, a local Indian chieftain who had remained loyal to the Incas, had torched the city rather than hand it over to the Spaniards.

Benalcázar founded the new village of San Francisco de Quito atop the ashes of the old. As was their custom, the Spaniards plotted out a blueprint for their city, locating the *plaza mayor* close to the old Indian marketplace. In 1563, Spain made Quito the capital of the Audiencia de Quito, a jurisdictional district that stretched more than 1,500 miles north to south and 500 miles east to west. As a capital, Quito was home to all the fixtures of colonial government—an administrative palace, a judicial court, and a royal treasury. By the early eighteenth century, it could also boast of three colleges and a hospital (founded in the sixteenth century), and it was famous throughout Peru for its elaborate cathedrals.

The people of Quito had been waiting for the arrival of the French expedition for months, for Philip V's letter, in which he urged his representatives to treat the visitors well, had reached them on September 10, 1735 (thirteen months after it was written). No one had been quite sure what to expect—after all, the city had never hosted a group of foreigners before, and these men were said

# The Viceroyalty of Peru in 1650

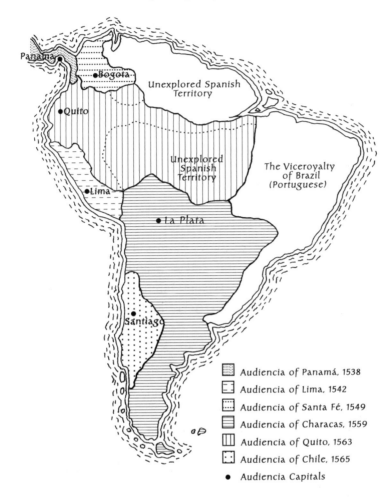

Panama
Bogota
Unexplored Spanish Territory
Quito
Unexplored Spanish Territory
The Viceroyalty of Brazil (Portuguese)
Lima
La Plata
Santiago

▦ Audiencia of Panamá, 1538
▢ Audiencia of Lima, 1542
⋯ Audiencia of Santa Fé, 1549
▤ Audiencia of Characas, 1559
▥ Audiencia of Quito, 1563
⋮ Audiencia of Chile, 1565
• Audiencia Capitals

to be the great minds of Europe—so when Godin and the others arrived on May 29, 1736, with their long train of mules bearing a load of strange instruments, the streets were lined with spectators. The audiencia president, Dionesio de Alsedo y Herrera, put them up in the royal palace and greeted them with a written proclamation, grandly announcing that the two nations were uniting for the "transcendental matters of science." For three days, Alsedo hosted one dinner and ceremony after another for the visitors, with the wealthy and powerful coming from miles to attend. Members of the town council, the judges of the audiencia court, church officials, and wealthy merchants all came to introduce themselves, and everyone, Ulloa and Juan wrote, "seemed to vie with each other in their civilities towards us."

Bouguer and La Condamine missed this grand welcome. Godin and the others, while waiting for them to arrive, joyfully explored this city of 30,000 and its environs. Quito, they believed, was the "highest situated" city in the world, its inhabitants—Bouguer would later write—"breathing an air more rarefied by one third than other men." All found the weather a delight, the city warmed by its proximity to the equator but cooled by its altitude, a combination that created a "perpetual spring." The valley to the south was a sea of green and gold. Cattle grazed on grassy plots while Indians worked the plowed fields, the mild climate allowing one field to be sown while, on the same day, the one next to it was harvested. Orchards dripped with apples, pears, and peaches, and the entire valley was ringed by snow-capped volcanoes. There was Mount Cotopaxi to marvel at, as well as Antisana, Cayambe, and Illiniza, each one taller than the greatest mountain in the Alps. "Nature," Ulloa and Juan wrote, "has here scattered her blessing with so liberal a hand."

Quito and its daily life were equally captivating. Stone bridges spanned the deep ravines that transected the city, adobe homes were built on steep streets, and soaring cathedrals seemed to grace every other block. Throughout the day, the peal of church bells could be heard, and inside the great chapels were "vast quantities of wrought plate, rich hangings (tapestries) and costly ornaments," Ulloa marveled. Markets in the city were filled with an abundance of meats—beef, veal, pork, rabbit, and fowl—and a dazzling array of colorful fruits. There were apricots, watermelons, strawberries, apples, oranges, pineapples, lemons, limes, guavas, and avocados to try, and all the members of the French expedition agreed that the most delicious New World fruit was the chirimoya, its pulp "white and fibrous, but infinitely delicate."

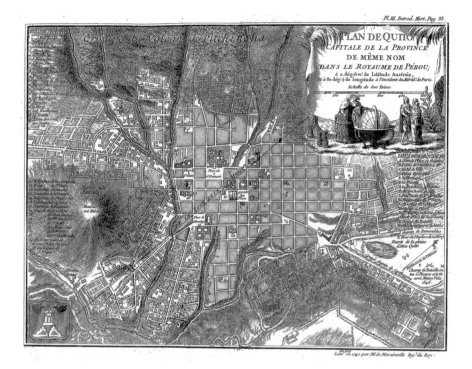

**Map of Quito in 1736.**

*From Charles-Marie de La Condamine,* Journal du voyage fait par
ordre du roi à l'équateur *(1751).*

The evening festivities were formal affairs, and the two
groups—guests and hosts—did their best to impress one another.
The French powdered their wigs and wore their finest silk coats,
while the Spanish men of Quito polished their swords, put on their
black capes, and in every way possible "affected great magnificence
in their dress," Ulloa wrote. The women of Quito were breathtak-
ing, too, and they did not seem to mind the attention from the visitors. "Their beauty," Ulloa confessed at the end of one particularly
festive evening, "is blended with a graceful carriage and an amiable
temper."

Every part of their dress is, as it were, covered with lace, and
those which they wear on days of ceremony are always of the
richest stuffs, with a profusion of ornaments. Their hair is gener-

97

*1. A Spanish Lady of Quito.*
*2. An Indian woman of Distinction.*
*3. An Indian Barber*
*4. A Mestizo of Quito.*
*5. An Indian Peasant.*
*6. An Indian Woman of the common sort.*

**The clothing of different castes in Quito.**
*From Jorge Juan and Antonio de Ulloa,* Relación histórica del viage
a la América Meridional *(1749), from the 1806 English*
*translation* A Voyage to South America.

ally made up in tresses, which they form into a kind of cross, on
the nape of the neck, tying a rich ribbon, called balaca, twice
round their heads, and with the ends form a kind of rose at their
temples. These roses are elegantly intermixed with diamonds
and flowers.

But perhaps none of the visitors were so smitten as the youngest
two members of the French expedition. As Couplet whispered to
Jean Godin on more than one occasion, "These women are
enchanting."

WHEN LA CONDAMINE ARRIVED, he did not join his colleagues at the royal palace. Instead, he slipped quietly into town,
doing his best to go unnoticed. He was very much the scruffy traveler, bemoaning the fact that he had nothing to wear. He had left
the one suitcase he had been carrying in the mountains, and Louis
Godin had left his other trunks in Guayaquil, which La
Condamine was certain his colleague had done just to spite him.
"*Seventy* mules used to carry cargo as well as persons, and it had not
been possible, in my absence, to find a place for a single one of my

trunks, nor even for my bed," he bitterly complained in his journal. La Condamine had no clothes other than the soiled hunting outfit he had been wearing since Manta, attire that left him "incapable of appearing in public in any decent fashion." He had a letter recommending him to the Jesuits, and he holed up with them in their compound. He remained there, out of sight, for more than a week, working on his maps while a servant fetched the goods he had left behind.

Although La Condamine felt justified in secluding himself, his behavior constituted a major diplomatic gaffe, which Alsedo took as a personal insult. A guest of La Condamine's rank was expected to enter a city after giving advance notice so that a proper welcome could be provided. Godin and the others had understood this; they had paused a few leagues outside of Quito and sent a messenger ahead, asking the audiencia president for permission to proceed. But not only had La Condamine sneaked into town, unaccompanied by a Spaniard, he then did not even deign to introduce himself. Alsedo found this unimaginably rude, and it stirred up his underlying mistrust of these "foreigners."

Months earlier, Alsedo had heard whispers that the French were not complying with the terms of their passports. In Cartagena, they had drawn several thousand pesos from the royal Peruvian treasury, which Philip had authorized them to do. However, while Spain had not put any limit on the amount that it would advance the expedition, the French consul in Cadiz, in a last-minute mix-up, had said it would cover these draws only up to 4,000 pesos (about 20,000 French pounds). This was a ridiculously small sum given the expedition's expenses, and rumors had reached Alsedo that the French, while in Cartagena, had tried to sell contraband valued at 100,000 pesos. The Quito president had immediately written the viceroy of Peru in Lima for advice; the viceroy had cautioned him to carefully "watch that the said astronomers didn't use the royal permission for purposes that weren't proper." Alsedo had been on his guard even before the French had arrived, and now La Condamine had slighted him.

On June 14, La Condamine finally wrote to Alsedo, telling him that he was in town and would like to visit. But the letter did not contain the apology that Alsedo expected, and the audiencia president responded with an icy warning: La Condamine was to comport himself "within the boundaries" set by his passport, he was to refrain from investigating matters that had not been approved by the king, and he should have come to the audiencia palace earlier to explain himself. Why had he separated from his companions in Manta, and why was he now lodged apart from them? Did he realize this violated the terms of his passport? Alsedo also fired off a missive to the viceroy, assuring the Marqués de Villagarcía, "I will always be suspicious of the foreigners, and I have taken precautions that would be considered necessary to protect the security and interests of Spain."

This ill will did not portend well for the future success of the mission, and yet La Condamine, who seemed to have a particular fondness for diplomatic dustups, responded in a way that could only exacerbate matters. In a few days, he informed Alsedo, he was planning to travel to Nono with Ramon Maldonado, Pedro's brother, in order to view the June 21 solstice. This village, he noted rather snootily, "would be found near or next to the equator," where he was supposed to do his work, but if the president did "not like it that I take a walk there with Don Ramon, I will not go." La Condamine was holding up his passport to trump Alsedo—theirs was a sanctioned trip to the equator, after all—and, pleased that he could call on Philip's words in this way, he took his trip to Nono. It was, he wrote, "the first time that I had emerged from my retreat."

When he returned, Alsedo was—as La Condamine subtly put it in his journal—"indisposed" toward him. His Jesuit hosts warned him not to take this dispute any further, particularly since the expedition had other problems to solve. First among them was money. Godin had expected that there would be new letters of credit waiting for them in Quito, but not a single letter from Maurepas or any one else in France had reached the city, even though more than a year had passed since they had departed from La Rochelle. Godin had immediately asked Alsedo for an advance, but the audiencia president had refused—4,000 pesos was all that France had guaranteed. Something needed to be done, and with the rector of the Jesuits, Father Hormaegui, acting as a go-between, La Condamine arranged to see the president.

There was every reason to believe this meeting would go badly. Honor was of such overwhelming importance in colonial Peru that men waged duels over squabbles much more trivial than this one. La Condamine was famously stubborn, unlikely to back down just because it might make things proceed more smoothly. Yet once he arrived at the audiencia palace and bent forward ever so slightly in greeting—about as much deference as La Condamine could muster—the bad feelings began to dissipate. La Condamine explained that it was because of his lack of decent clothes that he had not come to pay his respects right away: How could he call on an honorable representative of the king of Spain in such a state? He had needed to wait until a servant had fetched his suitcase and Bouguer, coming in from Guayaquil, had arrived with his trunk. "I completely satisfied the President on all counts," La Condamine happily concluded, and indeed, Alsedo was so charmed that he insisted that La Condamine, from that moment forward, become a frequent dinner guest. Alsedo even begged the Jesuits to keep their doors open until 8:30 P.M., past their usual hour of closing, so that he and La Condamine could enjoy an after-dinner brandy together. Theirs was a budding friendship, and La Condamine, at ease now in Quito, opened a shop of sorts in the Jesuit rectory, putting up for sale an array of his personal belongings in order to raise money for the expedition. This was just the type of contraband activity that Alsedo had been worried about, but times had changed, and he quickly became one of La Condamine's best customers.

The president was not alone in enjoying the new shopping opportunity—many of Quito's elite found their way to the rectory. Ramon Maldonado bought a number of books, including a history of the French Academy of Sciences, while his wife picked out some diamonds and emeralds. Pedro Maldonado acquired some elegantly embroidered cloth. Alsedo, for his part, purchased fine Holland shirts and cotton clothes. Others bought bedsheets, silk stockings, gloves, switchblades and other knives, needles, gunflints, jewelry, a "prize gun" of La Condamine's, a diamond-encrusted cross of Saint Lazarus, and various French novelties and trinkets. Tomás Guerrero, a member of the Quito town council, was a regular customer, as was José Benavides, a rich property owner. The flow of goods out of the Jesuit rectory was such that a resale market opened: Alsedo put an assistant, Manuel de Escabo, in charge of buying things and reselling them in Otavalo, while another prominent Spaniard, Antonio Suarez, simply resold the contraband in his shop in Quito.

All in all, La Condamine had turned a difficult situation to his advantage. He had had the good sense to sell his goods at a price that provided the elite in Quito with a fair deal and even offered them the possibility of turning a profit. After a bungled beginning, he had found a way to get along with Quito's high society, and the expedition was now able to go about its business unfettered by any overly scrupulous supervision, at least as long as Alsedo was president.

ALTHOUGH THE CASSINIS, in their earlier work, had always measured a degree of latitude along a north-south meridian, the French savants were considering measuring both a degree of latitude and one of longitude on this mission. Not only would the east-west measurement enable them to calculate the earth's circumference along its equatorial axis, but by comparing the two (a degree of latitude versus one of longitude), they might be able to answer the question of the earth's shape from their "operations alone without needing to refer to anyone else's," La Condamine noted. According to Newton's theory, the diameter of the earth along the equatorial plane was thirty-four miles longer than it was along an axis through the poles, and thus a degree of longitude at the equator should be ever-so-slightly longer than a degree of latitude. If, as the Cassinis believed, the earth was elongated at the poles, then the reverse would be true—a degree of latitude would be slightly longer than a degree of longitude. Taking both measurements was another way of resolving the question of the earth's shape, and it would complement their initial plan of comparing a degree of latitude at the equator to the one measured by the Cassinis in France or by Maupertuis in Lapland.

Godin, Bouguer, and La Condamine had a basic plan for determining a degree of longitude. After using triangulation to mark off a distance of seventy miles or so along the equator, they could synchronize pendulum clocks stationed at the two ends of this measured line. This synchronization could be done with a luminous signal, such as the flash from a cannon, or, if a mountain obstructed their sight, with a sonic signal, such as the sound of cannon fire. With their clocks in harmony, observers could train their sights on a particular star and mark the time—at each station—that it reached its halfway point in its east-west passage across the sky. The difference in time would tell them how far apart they were in degrees of longitude, and since they would also know the distance between the two stations in miles (or toises), they would have all the information they needed to calculate the circumference of the earth at the equator.

Although this was in theory a relatively straightforward process, Godin, Bouguer, and La Condamine were not of one mind about whether it could be done with sufficient accuracy to produce a useful result. The difference between a degree of longitude and one of latitude at the equator would be very small, less than half a mile. Rather than try to resolve that question now, Godin decided that they should set down a baseline that could be used for triangulation in either a north-south or an east-west direction. In August, Verguin and several of the others scouted around Quito for terrain that might be suitable for this task, and they settled on the plain of Cayambe, thirty-five miles north of the city.

The entire group traveled to Cayambe in early September, and while the academicians debated whether it would do—the land was awfully uneven and was divided by two rivers—Couplet fell gravely ill. He was bled and purged, as was the European custom, and was probably given a dose of local medicine for *mal del valle,* as fever was called in the Quito area. This Peruvian treatment, Ulloa and Juan noted, was rather painful, "as a pessary, composed of gunpowder, guinea pepper and a lemon peeled, is insinuated into the anus, and changed two or three times a day, till the patient is judged to be out of danger." Despite such ministrations (or perhaps because of them), Couplet died on September 17, only two days after the fever set in.

Although the scientists were saddened by this tragedy, they were not at all surprised by it. Everyone had experienced a bout of fever, which could turn deadly at a moment's notice. Indeed, no sooner had they buried Couplet than Juan fell ill. Someone was always sick, death was an ever-present possibility, and there was nothing for the others to do but go on with their work. Cayambe, they decided, would not serve their purposes well, so they moved their baseline operations to the plain of Yaruqui, twelve miles northeast of Quito. Although the terrain was not as hilly at Yaruqui as at Cayambe, they would need to cross a fifty-foot ravine, which presented a formidable challenge.

It was essential that they determine the length of the baseline to an excruciating degree of accuracy. This measurement would serve as the first side of the first triangle and thus would be "the base of the whole work," Ulloa observed. From the two ends of the baseline, they would then measure the angles to a third point, and this information would enable them to mathematically calculate the length of the other two sides of the triangle. This process could then be repeated over and over again, with a side of the most recently determined triangle serving as the first side of the next one, so that only the length of the initial baseline actually had to be measured. An imprecise measurement here would corrupt all that followed.

Their proposed baseline ran from Oyambaro to Caraburu, the land dropping 760 feet between these two villages. They marked the terminals of the baseline with large millstones, cleared the brush between these two points, and set up a straight path to follow by carefully aligning intermediate markers every 3,000 feet. As a way of checking their work, they broke into two groups to measure this distance in opposite directions. One group was led by Bouguer, La Condamine, and Ulloa, the other by Godin and Juan, who, after a week of rest, had regained his strength.

Each group employed three twenty-foot-long wooden rods to mark off the distance. They laid the rods, which were color coded to ensure they were always kept in the same order, end to end and moved one rod at a time. By utilizing three rods instead of two (as the Cassinis had done), La Condamine and the others reasoned that there would be less chance that moving a rod to the front would jiggle the others—two stationery rods would be more stable than one. The rods also had thin pieces of copper wire on their ends so that when placed together they would touch at a single contact point, making the measurement more precise. Every possible source of error was considered, the academicians even fretting that changes in temperature or humidity could cause the rods to expand or contract, throwing off their results. Each day they checked the wooden rods with Langlois's iron toise, which they kept in the shade lest it expand in the hot sun—they needed their ruler to maintain an exact length. Yet another problem was presented by the sloping land. To keep the rods perfectly horizontal, they placed them on sawhorses and used wedges to level them off. When necessary, they utilized a plumb line to move the rods up or down to a new tier, and in this manner they proceeded steplike across the hilly plain.* They used this same method to cross the ravine.

As they performed this delicate operation, they had to contend with weather of the most miserable sort. Although the valley south of Quito might have been a pastoral Eden, the environment north of the city was totally different. Few shrubs or plants grew in the sandy soil, Ulloa and Juan reported, and "violent tempests of thunder, lightning and rain" regularly swept down from the mountains.

---

* A plumb line points to the center of the earth, and thus the French academicians could move their sawhorses up or down along a vertical axis.

Such dreadful whirlwinds form here that the whole interval is filled with columns of sand, carried up by the rapidity and gyrations of violent eddy winds, which sometimes produce fatal consequences. One melancholy instance happened while we were there; an Indian, being caught in the center of one of these blasts, died on the spot. It is not, indeed, at all strange, that the quantity of sand in one of these columns should totally stop all respiration in any living creature who has the misfortune of being involved in it.

With the wind constantly blowing their rods askew, it took the French academicians twenty-six days of dawn-to-dusk labor to measure the baseline. Their results, however, were phenomenal. The two groups' conclusions varied by only *three inches* across a distance of nearly eight miles, and so they split the difference: Their baseline was 6272.656 toises long. They returned to Quito on December 5, confident that they had done this all-important first measurement well.

**A panoramic view of the plain of Yaruqui.**
*From Charles-Marie de La Condamine,* Journal du voyage fait par ordre du roi à l'équateur *(1751).*

. . .

THROUGHOUT THIS PERIOD, everyone in Quito was keeping up with the progress of the French expedition, even though they were not quite sure what the visitors were up to. Their presence even stirred a passing fancy for things French. Ever since Spain had come under the rule of a Bourbon king, the elite in Quito, influenced by a steady stream of Crown-appointed administrators who came to the town, had come to think of French customs as superior to their own, and now, with the French scientists nearby, the wealthy residents of Quito could more easily imagine being part of that elegant world. The women practiced their curtsies and memorized a few French phrases, and, according to one account of the times, no party was complete unless the host could provide a bottle of French wine.

Pedro Gramesón and his family became personally acquainted with the French mapmakers. The general spoke passable French, having learned it from his father, and his house, one Ecuadorian historian has noted, "was always open for all the French men." In fact, he could boast that his brother-in-law had played a small role in making the expedition happen. When the French had first proposed it to King Philip V, Spain's Council of the Indies, which oversaw all colonial matters, had sought advice from several notables in Peru, one of whom was José Augustín Pardo de Figueroa, the Marqués de Valleumbroso. Pardo had a keen interest in science, and he had given his whole-hearted approval. He particularly liked the idea that two Spaniards would be assigned to this expedition, although not because they would keep tabs on the French. Instead, he saw their presence as a way that Spain could participate in this endeavor and learn "the practice of astronomy and trigonometry." After the academicians had arrived, Pardo and La Condamine had quickly become friends, La Condamine writing in his diary of how impressed he was "by his [Pardo's] knowledge and how well read he was." There were other ties as well that brought the Gramesóns closer to the expedition. The Gramesóns and Jean Godin's family shared mutual close friends, the Pelletiers from Lignieres, a village near Saint Amand. Members of the Pelletier clan living in Cadiz, Spain, shared business interests with the Gramesóns there, while in France the Pelletiers and the Godins had known each other for at least three generations. The connection may have been a distant one, but it made Jean Godin feel welcome at the Gramesóns, and he became a regular guest.

Although Isabel was still in a convent school, she heard all about the French men from her father and through other gossip that filtered into the cloister. The school had not turned out to be such a dismal place. She and the other girls had learned to read and write, and they all enjoyed singing in the choir. Occasionally, the nuns even hosted small fiestas, having musicians and singers in to entertain. And every day, visitors were allowed into the convent parlor to call on the girls, enabling them to keep up with all that went on in Quito. Often they wondered whether it was true, as had been whispered, that the French men had shown the women of Quito a Parisian dance step or two. That was a deliciously scandalous thought, and it naturally caught Isabel's fancy. She had particular reason to be fascinated by this world—her grandfather, after all, was French, and her family personally knew the scientists—and this interest was starting to blossom into an unusual ambition for a Peruvian girl. She had yet to turn nine years old, but—as would later become evident—she had already begun to dream of one day seeing France for herself.

# CHAPTER SEVEN

# High-Altitude Science

**W**ITH THE BASELINE MEASURED, the French academicians thought that they could complete their mission within eighteen months. Bouguer was even more optimistic. He believed that they might finish by the end of 1737, and he wrote to his colleagues in Paris that he now had "hope of seeing France once more." But in January of 1737, the French academicians began to realize that they were being overly optimistic, their efforts certain to be delayed by a lack of money, the upside-down world of colonial politics, and their own internal squabbling.

Although it was now twenty months since they had left La Rochelle, they had yet to receive any letters from France. Nearly everyone had sold personal goods to keep the expedition going— even a telescope had been peddled—but in the absence of any new letter of credit, they were, as a group, once again nearly broke. The Peruvian viceroy, the Marqués de Villagarcía, had denied Louis Godin's request for an advance beyond the 4,000 pesos already given to the expedition. To further complicate matters, Alsedo was no longer the president of the Quito Audiencia. He had been replaced on December 28, 1736, by Joseph de Araujo y Río, a small-minded man who immediately began harassing the French academicians and the two Spanish officers accompanying them. Without any money or political support in Quito, La Condamine decided to travel to Lima, 1,200 miles distant, in order to make a personal appeal to the viceroy. If that failed, he hoped to cash a personal letter of credit that he had brought with him from a French businessman in Paris.

La Condamine left Quito on January 19, 1737, and on his way to Lima, he stopped in Loja to investigate the famous cinchona tree that grew nearby in the tropical rain forest, on the eastern slopes of the Andes. The bark of this tree was in great demand in Europe as a treatment for fever, particularly when the fever was accompanied by terrible sweats and chills (an illness soon to be named malaria.) It was sold there as "Jesuits' bark" or as "the countess's powder," the latter name arising from a story that Francisca Henriquez de Ribera, the Condesa de Chinchón, wife of a Peruvian viceroy, had been miraculously cured of a high fever by a preparation from this tree in 1638. Indians in the Loja area referred to it as *quina quina* (the bark of barks), and on February 3, La Condamine spent a night with a *cascarillero,* an Indian skilled in stripping the bark from the trees.

The opportunity to learn more about this tree could easily have justified an entire expedition. While a dose of the countess's powder often worked wonders, the preparations varied widely in their efficacy. The problem was that there were many species of cinchona, and not all had the same therapeutic value. The Indians of Peru used the same name, *quina quina,* to describe a balsam tree, and its bark, which regularly showed up in European apothecaries, was worthless. Old World merchants and pharmacists were eager to know how to separate the good from the bad, and La Condamine, after his three-day stay in Loja, wrote a scientific treatise, "Sur l'arbre du quinquina," on the tree, complete with a drawing of its leaves. He noted that the inner bark came in three colors,

La Condamine's sketch
of *Cinchona officinalis.*
*The Wellcome Trust*
*Medical Photographic*
*Library.*

white, yellow, and red, and the red one, which was more bitter than
the others, appeared to be the most potent against fevers. No one
had ever published a detailed botanical description of cinchona,
and when the treatise  was published by the French Academy of
Sciences in 1738, it caused a sensation.

La Condamine arrived in Lima on February 28, only to find that
it was an inopportune time to be seeking a loan. Funds were scarce
in the capital. Nearly all of the gold and silver from the mines had
recently been loaded on a frigate for shipment to Spain. Even if the
viceroy had been willing to lend the expedition money, there was
little in the royal coffers. Three weeks later, La Condamine
received more bad news: The new president of the Quito
Audiencia, Araujo, had filed criminal contraband charges against
him and sought his arrest. Authorities in Lima searched his belongings thoroughly, and while nothing illegal was found in his possession, his motives were now seen as suspect. All of Lima was

buzzing over this scandal when Juan unexpectedly showed up in the capital, with an even more salacious tale involving the new president.

The viceroy's appointment of Araujo had been unusual, for Araujo was a Creole, a native son of Lima. The relationship between Creoles and *chapetones,* as those born in Spain were called in Peru, was contentious throughout the viceroyalty, and particularly so in Quito, which was known for being thoroughly dominated by the chapetones. The Creoles disliked the chapetones for their superior airs, and they had been quick to make fun of Ulloa and Juan, too, referring to them as the *caballeros del punto fijo* (knights of the exact)—men who preferred the pencil to the sword, a put-down that nobody could miss. But the disdain was mutual. The chapetones complained that the Creoles were spoiled and lazy, living off the labor of slaves and Indians and devoting all their energies to frivolous affairs. They have "no employment or calling to occupy their thoughts, nor any idea of intellectual entertainment," Ulloa and Juan observed. Instead, they said, the Creoles spent most of their time drinking, gambling, and going to "balls and entertainments." Alsedo, during his term as president, had exacerbated the bad feelings between the two groups by excluding Creoles from the local cabildo, and when Araujo had replaced him, the Creoles had danced with joy, eager to see the tables turned.

Araujo did not disappoint them. Even though he himself had arrived with a mule train of goods to sell in Quito, which was forbidden, he immediately launched an investigation into La Condamine's contraband activities, confident that it would embarrass Alsedo.* He also found a way to needle Ulloa and Juan, repeatedly addressing them with *usted,* the common form for "you," instead of the more formal *usía.* Given the diplomatic protocol of

---

* When Araujo's investigation revealed that Alsedo had been one of La Condamine's customers, Alsedo responded by accusing Araujo of selling contraband, a much worse offense. This set off a court battle between the two that dragged on for years. In many ways, the case typified the legal wrangling that strangled colonial Peru in the eighteenth century.

the day, this was the rankest kind of insult. Ulloa and Juan were members of the Guardias Marinas, in Peru as representatives of the king, and, just as Araujo had hoped, they were outraged. A Creole was acting as *their* superior, and doing so in public for all of Quito to hear? When Araujo ignored several admonishments to stop, Ulloa reached his breaking point. He charged into the president's house one morning, brushed aside servants who tried to stop him, and confronted Araujo in his bedroom. *Usted?* He told off the president with a few choice words of his own, then turned on his heel and left, returning home—as a biographer later wrote—a much "happier man."

Naturally, Araujo escalated the battle. He sent out armed officers to arrest Ulloa and Juan. The two Spaniards, however, refused to be taken into custody and instead drew their swords, badly wounding one of Araujo's men before fleeing to the Jesuit church where La Condamine had holed up the previous summer. Enraged, Araujo ordered his men to surround the church. He swore he would starve them out, by God, and he promised bystanders that if the two cowards dared to show their faces, he would have them killed. All of Quito found this a spectacle not to be missed, but the show ended a few nights later when Juan slipped out under the cover of darkness and hurried to Lima to seek relief from the viceroy, whom he had befriended on his trip across the Atlantic.

Once La Condamine and Juan were together, they were able to get the expedition back on track. The viceroy wrote them letters of support and assured them that they could safely return to Quito— Araujo would be counseled to that end. La Condamine, meanwhile, used his personal letter of credit to obtain a loan of 12,000 pesos from a British merchant, Thomas Blechynden, who, by a stroke of good fortune for the French, had come to Lima to collect on a debt owed his trading company. La Condamine also obtained a letter from the viceroyalty authorizing the expedition to draw 4,000 pesos from the royal treasury in Quito, and on June 20, he and Juan returned there, ready to get on with the work of triangulation.

. . .

WHILE THESE FEUDS were playing out, the other members of the expedition had been surveying possible triangulation routes. Louis Godin, who wanted to measure a degree of longitude, had headed west from Quito, while Bouguer scouted out the region to the north, and Verguin and Jean Godin reconnoitered the terrain to the south. Once La Condamine returned, they all agreed that they would head south to measure three degrees of latitude first and worry about measuring one of longitude later.

The triangulation would enable them to measure a distance of 200 miles or so along a north-south line. They would run their triangles—a long-distance tape measure, so to speak—down the Andean valley that had been the old Inca highway. The valley was twenty-five to thirty-five miles broad and lined on both sides by mountains that rose to over 12,000 feet, including a number of individual volcanoes that soared above 16,000 feet. By setting up their triangulation points on the top of peaks or on the sides of the higher volcanoes, they figured that they would have clear lines of sight from one point to the next, making it easy to measure the interior angles of each triangle. Partly because of the tensions between the academicians, they decided to break into two groups and divide the work. La Condamine, Bouguer, and Ulloa would form one party, Louis Godin and Juan the other. The assistants would help both groups.

On August 14, La Condamine's group set out for the first triangulation point, the summit of snow-covered Mount Pichincha. From there, they expected to be able to clearly see the two ends of their baseline in Yaruqui.* However, Pichincha is roughly 15,500 feet high, nearly equal to the tallest peak in the Alps, Mont Blanc, which at that time had never been climbed. During their ascent, first by horseback and then on foot, several members of the group

* Their initial triangle would be formed by Pichincha and the two ends of their baseline. Once they determined the interior angles of this triangle, they could—since they already knew the length of the baseline—calculate the lengths of the triangle's other two sides.

suffered fits of vomiting, and all were "considerably incommoded by the rarefaction of the air," Bouguer reported. Ulloa fared the worst, fainting and falling face first into the snow. "I remained a long time without sense or motion, and, as I was told, with all the appearance of death in my face." After Ulloa spent a night in a cave, several Indians helped him reach the summit, where the others were huddled up inside a small hut.

The top of the peak was too small to accommodate the large tents they had had made in Saint Domingue. Instead, their "lodging," as La Condamine referred to the hut in his journal, was about six feet high, made from reeds lashed to posts that served as a frame. Five or six people crowded into it at a time, Verguin and Jean Godin joining La Condamine, Bouguer, and Ulloa in this humble abode. Their Negro slaves were close by in a "little tent," the two groups camped out on a summit that dropped off steeply on all sides.*

Along with a quadrant for measuring angles, they had brought a thermometer, a barometer, and a pendulum clock to the summit, and during the first few days, they exulted at the opportunity to do science at such an altitude. They charted temperatures that plunged below freezing each morning, hung the pendulum clock from the posts to measure the earth's gravitational pull at this great height, and marveled at how low the mercury in their barometer dipped. "No one before us, that I know of, had seen the mercury go below sixteen inches," La Condamine wrote in his journal. "That is twelve inches lower than at sea level, indicating that the air we were breathing was diluted by almost half of what it is in France, when the barometer goes up to 29 inches." He calculated that the peak was a "large league" in height (roughly three miles) and that it would take 29,160 steps to climb it from sea level.

* The peak they were on is known today as Rucu Pichincha (15,413 feet). The volcano's rim, Guagua Pichincha (15,728 feet), is a mile away. Neither Rucu Pichincha nor Guagua Pichincha is regularly snow-covered today, evidence of the changing climate in Ecuador. Pichincha remains an active volcano; it erupted in 1999, sending ash down on Quito.

At times, they put aside their scientific duties to play around like little kids, "rolling large fragments of rock down the precipice" to amuse themselves, Ulloa wrote. They were living on top of the world, so high that often they could look down on storms roiling the valley below:

> When the fog cleared up, the clouds, by their gravity, moved nearer to the surface of the earth, and on all sides surrounded the mountain to a vast distance, representing the sea, with our rock like an island in the center of it. When this happened, we heard the horrid noises of the tempests, which then discharged themselves on Quito and the neighboring country. We saw the lightnings issue from the clouds, and heard the thunder roll far beneath us, and whilst the lower parts were involved in tempests of thunder and rain, we enjoyed a delightful serenity, the wind was abated, the sky clear, and the enlivening rays of the sun moderated the severity of the cold.

But for the most part they suffered, and horribly so. They were pounded regularly by snow and hail, the wind so violent that they feared being blown from the summit should they dare step outside the hut. They spent whole days inside, each trying to warm his hands over a "chafing dish of coals." They ate a "little rice boiled with some flesh or fowl," Ulloa noted, and had to boil snow for water. Even a swig of brandy in the evenings did not do anything to chase away the cold, and they soon gave up even this comfort.

The nights were long on the mountain. Each afternoon, at five or so, an Indian servant would fasten the door shut with a leather thong and then hurriedly descend to a cave lower down, where the Indians kept a perpetual fire. The academicians and their assistants would now be shut in for the next sixteen or seventeen hours, their imaginations haunted by the noise of howling winds, the "terrible rolling of thunder," and crashing rocks. Most mornings, the hut was covered with a "thick blanket of snow," La Condamine wrote, with such a wall of ice forming against the door that they could not push it open. The Indians usually arrived at nine or ten to dig them out, but one morning—their fourth or fifth on the mountain—no one came. They hollered for help, but the winds were so fierce that their Negro slaves either did not hear them or were in such pain, with swollen feet and hands, "that they would rather have suffered themselves to have been killed than move," Ulloa wrote. At last, a lone Indian arrived at noon to free them. All of the other Indians had fled, unwilling to endure such hardship any longer, even though they were being paid several times the going rate for their labor.

Despite this harsh environment, the French academicians hoped to measure angles to distant points with an amazing accuracy. Their quadrant, two feet in diameter, was built with reinforced iron to make it steadier, and Langlois had calibrated the instrument so that a degree could be divided into minutes (1/60 of a degree) and seconds (1/3,600 of a degree). The French academicians hoped to make measurements accurate to ten seconds, readings that they could verify by determining if the three angles added up to 180 degrees, plus or minus thirty seconds. Without this precision in the angular measurements, their subsequent calculations of the lengths of the sides of the triangle would not be sufficiently exact. But Mother Nature was not cooperating. There were few moments when it was calm enough to set up the quadrant, and during those brief interludes, Bouguer reported, "we were continually in the clouds, which absolutely veiled from our sight every thing but the point of the rock upon which we were stationed." Only once or twice were they able to glimpse through their binoculars the markers they had erected at the ends of the Yaruqui baseline. They spent one week on the summit, then a second and a third, and all the while their health deteriorated. "Our feet were swelled and so tender," Ulloa wrote, "that walking was attended with extreme pain. Our hands were covered with chilblains; our lips swelled and chapped, so that every motion, in speaking or the like, drew blood. Consequently we were obliged to a strict taciturnity and but little disposed to laugh, an extension of the lips producing fissures, very painful for two or three days together." Their slaves were in equally bad shape, and several "vomited blood."

Finally, on September 6, after twenty-three days on "this rock," they came down from Pichincha, defeated. They set up a camp lower on the mountain, humbled by this encounter with the great Andes. "The mountains in America are in comparison to those found in Europe what church steeples are to ordinary houses," La Condamine sighed. It took them three months to complete their angular measurements from lower down on the mountain, and this, as they all knew, was simply the first of several dozen field stations they would have to inhabit. The year 1737 had nearly come to an end. By this time, Bouguer had hoped they would be ready to return to civilized France, and yet their "severe life," as Ulloa dubbed it, had only just begun.

WITH THE FIRST SET of triangles completed, Jean Godin's role became more defined. After Couplet's death, he had become the youngest member of the expedition, expected to run errands for the three academicians and otherwise be at their beck and call. Most of the other assistants had specific tasks to do or were not even expected to stay with the academicians. Jussieu was off collecting plants, Senièrgues was tending to patients in Quito, and Hugo's primary role was caring for the instruments, repairing them or even constructing new ones as the need arose. Morainville at times traveled with Jussieu, drawing the plants he collected. That left only Verguin and Jean Godin to regularly assist the three academicians, and Godin was being sent to and fro with such frequency that, as he would later write, he was becoming a "veteran" at moving around the Peruvian landscape. Now that they had come down from Pichincha, Jean was assigned the duty of signal carrier. His job was to head out in advance of the others to set up markers at the triangulation points they had mapped out earlier. One or the other of the two parties, La Condamine's or Louis Godin's, would then catch up, setting up a new observation post where Jean had placed the marker. He might stay a short while with them, running errands as they did their critical observations, and then he would scurry on ahead, traveling alone or perhaps with a single servant. He crisscrossed the Andean valley numerous times as he performed this task, bouncing back and forth between the two cordilleras. As he did so, he suffered all the hardships and difficulties that the academicians recorded in their daily journals, although he was often without the solace of companionship. A French historian later wrote what it was like for Jean:

> He was always in movement along a meridian line of around 300 kilometers, climbing massive mountains crossed by torrents, walking along the sharp edge of precipices, or through ravines along the banks of the rivers. In these areas in a primitive state, where every step represented a victory of valor and of physical strength, he acquired strength of will and familiarized himself with the country and with the Indians.

This was the sort of life that fostered independence and self-reliance, and a touch of bitterness, too. La Condamine, Bouguer, and his cousin Louis may also have been suffering hardships, but they were almost certain to be hailed for their achievements upon their return to France. But how would he leave his mark? He had left Saint Amand thinking that perhaps he would study the language of the indigenous people in Peru, which had been Quechua throughout the Andes since the time of the Incas. And now, out and about as he was, running errands and carrying signals to distant posts, he often spoke with the local Indians. He began to pick up the Quechua vocabulary, and his ambitions turned more concrete: He would one day produce a grammar of the Incan language, which he would present to the French Academy of Sciences or even to the king of France.

And so his life went: Young Jean spent many of his days and nights in isolated camps, and there, alone and confronting the most frigid conditions, his tent battered by snow and hail, he would scribble the new words of Quechua he had learned into his note-book, struggling to understand how the Indians put these words together into sentences to describe the rugged land they inhabited.

As THE EXPEDITION headed south from Quito, starting in early 1738, the two groups—La Condamine's and Louis Godin's—worked increasingly apart. The tensions between the three acade-micians remained, and rather than simply dividing the labor of triangulation, each group began producing its own measurement of a meridian line stretching south across the Andes. But this separa-tion, Bouguer reasoned in a letter to the academy in Paris, was not such a bad thing, for the duplication would make for the "strongest and most convincing proof possible." The two groups were still col-laborating in some ways. In the region around Quito, they had plot-ted off different triangles, but south of the city they "shared" some triangles, each checking the other's work.

The problems they encountered were numerous, and one that slowed both groups was that they could not keep intact the wooden pyramids they were using as markers. Each pyramid was covered with a light-colored cloth to make it more visible, and to work, the academicians would set up a quadrant atop this pavilion, sighting through the instrument's telescope similar markers off in the dis-tance. But when the pyramids were not being "carried away by tempests," Bouguer reported, they were being taken by Indians, who had other uses for the timber and ropes. Jean Godin was not always able to watch over the pyramids until the others arrived, and even when the main party arrived at a camp, the local Indians were apt to creep in at night and grab what they could. After La Condamine and Bouguer rebuilt one of their stations seven times, they grew so frustrated that they decided to start using the smaller tents as markers. "Mr. Godin des Odonais preceded us," La Condamine wrote, "and had these [tents] placed on the two moun-tain ranges, at designated points, according to the agreed location of the triangles, leaving an Indian to guard them." While this pro-

**A field camp in the Andes.**
*From Charles-Marie de La Condamine,* Mesure des trois premiers
degrés du méridien dans l'hémisphere austral *(1751).*

cedure worked better than erecting the pyramids, the tents also disappeared more than once, stirring the academicians to lash out in their journals against the Indians, whom they disparaged, in the manner of the times, as slovenly "beasts."

With every camp they set up, they had new mishaps and close calls to write about. As they worked on the slopes of towering Mount Cotopaxi, Juan fell into a twenty-five-foot-deep ravine with his mule, luckily escaping with only a few cuts and bruises. Bouguer regularly complained about the nasty conditions, and La Condamine, while riding between two camps, was caught in a fierce storm and had to spend two days in a snow-covered tent without food or water. At last, he used the lens of his glasses to focus the sun's rays on a pot of snow, which provided a few drops of water that saved him "from this sad situation."

Despite these hardships, the team members explored their world in every way imaginable. They did not limit themselves to their triangulation work, difficult as it may have been. Through their experiments with a pendulum clock, they discovered—just as Newton had predicted—that the earth's gravitational pull weakened with altitude. They needed to make the seconds pendulum about one-twenty-fourth of an inch shorter at an altitude of 10,000 feet than it was at sea level, which led La Condamine and Bouguer to calculate that a body that weighed 1,000 pounds at the seashore would weigh one pound less atop Pichincha. They also dragged a barometer to the top of Mount Corazon, a volcano 200 feet higher than Pichincha. Atop the summit, their "clothes, eyebrows and beards covered in icicles," they figured that no humans had ever "climbed a greater height." They "were at 2,470 toises [15,794 feet] above sea level," La Condamine wrote, "and we could guarantee the accuracy of this measurement to four or five toises." * Their experiments with the barometer were paying off, as Bouguer had come up with a "very simple rule" for using barometric pressure to calculate altitude. Air pressures at higher elevations, he had concluded, "alter in a geometrical progression, while the heights of places are in arithmetical progression." His method for determining the height of a mountain involved taking a reading at its base and at its summit, and then applying the logarithmic rule he had devised.

The French scientists were men of the Enlightenment at play. They investigated the climate of the Andes, the expansion of metals in response to variation in temperature, the speed of sound at high altitudes, the rocks and plants, and Inca ruins. Ulloa, meanwhile, was fascinated by some of the clever methods the Indians had devised for navigating this landscape. The road south of Quito regularly crossed ravines several hundred feet deep, and at several of these the Indians had built a "cable car" of sorts, known as a *tarabita*. Men and animals alike were winched across the ravine, riding in a leather sling attached to the cable, which was a rope made from twisted strands of leather. One such tarabita they came upon was strung at a height of more than 150 feet, the river below charging through a boulder-strewn gully.

As might be expected, all of this activity stirred a great deal of gossip among the locals. The behavior of these visitors was so

---

* While the French academicians were not the first to climb Pichincha, theirs was indeed the first recorded ascent of Corazon.

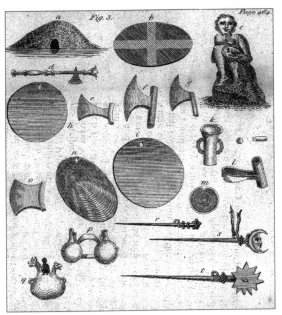

**Inca artifacts.**
*From Jorge Juan and
Antonio de Ulloa*, Relación
histórica del viage a la
América Meridional *(1749),
from the 1806 English
translation* A Voyage to
South America.

**Bridges in
eighteenth-century Peru.**
*From Jorge Juan and
Antonio de Ulloa*, Relación
histórica del viage a la
América Meridional *(1749),
from the 1806 English
translation* A Voyage to
South America.

*strange.* They climbed to absurd heights on the mountains, peered into odd-looking instruments, and furiously scribbled away in their notebooks. Their three-week stay atop Pichincha had earned them the reputation of being "extraordinary men," La Condamine noted, and there were whispers among some of the Indians that these strangers were superior beings, shamans of a sort. At a camp near Latacunga, a group of four men even got down on their knees to pray to them. Could they use their powers to help them locate a lost mule? When Ulloa told them they had no such knowledge, the Indians refused to believe him. "They retired with all the marks of extreme sorrow that we would not condescend to inform them where they might find the ass, and with a firm persuasion that our refusal proceeded from ill nature, and not from ignorance." Others, Ulloa added, were convinced that they were prospectors looking for gold. Wasn't Mount Pichincha rich in minerals? Hadn't Atahualpa buried his treasure there? And wasn't that the reason that everyone came to this land, to get rich?

> Even those of the best parts and education among them were utterly at a loss what to think. … Some considered us little better than lunatics, others more sagaciously imputed the whole to covetousness, and [said] that we were certainly endeavoring to discover some rich minerals by particular methods of our own invention; others again suspected that we dealt in magic, but all were involved in a labyrinth of confusion with regard to the nature of our design. And the more they reflected on it, the greater was their perplexity, being unable to discover any thing proportionate to the pains and hardship we underwent.

Indeed, as the months passed, the physical hardships began to wear the men down. They moved steadily from one camp to another, their daily lives, Ulloa noted, marked by "continual solitude and coarse provisions." Their only respite from this difficult life came when they were passing between camps, when they might have time to spend a day in a little town, everyone so starved for the comforts of civilization that "the little cabins of the Indians were to us like spacious palaces, and the conversation of a priest, and two or three of his companions, charmed us like the banquet of Xenophon." Loneliness was now creeping into their writings, and by mid-October it was clear they needed a respite. Ulloa fell gravely ill and had to be taken to the nearby city of Riobamba. Louis Godin suffered a similar bout of sickness and returned to Quito to recuperate. The expedition was once again short of funds, supplies were low, and Riobamba, a city of 16,000, offered them a civilized place to rest. They had also recently received a cache of letters from France that had delivered an emotional blow and left them wondering how to proceed.

THE DIFFICULTY IN CORRESPONDING with colleagues in France had led La Condamine, at one point, to complain that he had nearly given up on ever hearing from Paris. The first letter the expedition received arrived in late 1737, shortly after they had come down from Pichincha. In it, Maurepas—the minister who had promoted their expedition to the king—had sought to resolve the ongoing dispute between Godin and Bouguer over the merits of measuring a degree of longitude. Each of the academicians had written Paris to argue his case, and the academy, Maurepas wrote, had agreed with Bouguer's opinion that it would be a "completely imprudent enterprise." While Godin had not immediately given up on the idea, his own subsequent experiments on the speed of sound, which he had completed in July 1738, supported the academy's decision. Godin had determined that sound at this altitude traveled between 175 and 178 toises a second, but that imprecision—of three toises per second—was too great to allow them to use a sound, such as the noise of a cannon being fired, to synchronize watches at two spots along a line measured at the equator. The margin of error would be greater than any difference in distance between degrees of longitude and latitude at the equator, Bouguer noted, and thus "one might even come to believe that the earth is flattened or oblong when in fact it may have a completely different shape."

So that issue had been resolved, but now, as a result of letters they had just received, they had to question the merits of proceeding even with their latitude measurements. Maupertuis, they had learned, had already returned with his results from Lapland.

The Maupertuis expedition had not lacked its own controversies. Maupertuis was a committed Newtonian, as were the other leaders of the expedition, such as Alexis Clairaut. As a result, many in the academy were ready to dismiss their results even before they left, certain that Maupertuis and Clairaut were too biased to do the work fairly. "Do the observers have some predilection for one or the other of these ideas?" asked Johann Bernoulli, the Belgian mathematician who was a supporter of the Cassinis. "Because if they believe that the Earth is flattened at the poles, they will surely find it so flattened. ... [T]herefore I shall await steadfastly the results of the American observations." Despite such skepticism, Maupertuis and six others had gone to Lapland in April 1736 and returned seventeen months later with an answer. They had determined that a degree of latitude in Lapland was 57,437 toises, which was 477 toises longer than a Parisian arc, as measured by the Cassinis in 1718. Thus, Maupertuis told the academy, "it is evident that the earth is considerably flattened at the poles." Newtonians naturally pounced on this news, Voltaire gleefully praising Maupertuis as the "flattener of the earth and the Cassinis."

But as Bernoulli had predicted, the Lapland results did not end the dispute. Many of the old guard in the academy were outraged, Jacques Cassini complaining that Maupertuis was trying to destroy in one year the work his family had taken fifty years to create. He and others criticized Maupertuis's work as sloppy and snidely suggested that the expedition members had all taken mistresses in Lapland, evidence that they were moral degenerates. Maupertuis was so disheartened that he hurried away to Germany, where he became president of the Berlin Academy of Sciences. "The arguments increased," he wrote bitterly, "and from these disputes there soon arose injustices and enmity."

Even though sour grapes may have affected Cassini's criticisms, from a scientific point of view, he did have a point. The Lapland expedition had measured only one degree, and upon close inspection, its results did not match up with Newton's mathematical equations. "This flatness [of the earth] appears even more considerable than Sir Isaac Newton thought it," Maupertuis admitted. "I am likewise of the opinion that gravity increases more towards the pole and diminishes more towards the equator than Sir Isaac supposed." Something was not quite right with their measurement. The controversy was still alive. A famous Scottish mathematician, James Stirling, declared that he would "choose to stay [neutral] till the French arrive from the South, which I hear will be very soon." Similarly, Clairaut, in the letter he wrote to La Condamine, noted that the dispute remained so violent that the Peruvian findings were vital to confirming their work in Lapland.

Clairaut had meant to encourage La Condamine with such words, but they had the exact opposite effect. *Vital to confirming the Lapland work*—this was just what the Peruvian team had always feared. They had been away from France three and one-half years, they were still less than halfway done, and they were now in the position of being viewed by history as having come in second, with all the scientific glory going to Maupertuis. Their own experiments with the pendulum had already led them to suspect that Newton was right, that the earth was flattened at the poles and that Cartesian physics would have to be scrapped. Should they continue their triangulation work another year—or longer—simply to bring this debate to a tidier conclusion?

RIOBAMBA, where they had stopped for rest in October 1738, turned out to be just the place for them to mull over this question and to rethink their expedition. Although smaller than Quito, this city, tucked in the shadow of Mount Chimborazo, was one of the most sophisticated cities in all of Peru, perhaps second only to Lima in this regard. Artisans of all kinds—jewelry makers, painters, sculptors, musicians, and carpenters—lived in Riobamba, and a number of Peru's most prominent families had come here to live, drawn by the pleasant climate and the city's reputation as a place of culture. This was the birthplace of the Maldonados, and both Pedro and Ramon Maldonado had become so close to the expedition that they had loaned La Condamine and Louis Godin several thousand pesos. The "agreeable reception provided us [in Riobamba]," La Condamine wrote, "helped us forget the hard times we had spent on their mountains." The arts, he added, "which were barely cultivated in the province of Quito, seemed to flourish here." There were Jesuits in Riobamba who spoke French, the town council welcomed them with great warmth, and all of the best families competed to entertain the French savants in their homes. The teenage children of the family of Don Joseph Davalos even put on a play and concert for the visitors, and La Condamine was clearly smitten by their eldest daughter: "She possessed every talent. She played the harp, the harpsichord, the guitar, the violin, the flute. … [She had] so many resources to please the world." La Condamine, so often bashful around women because of his smallpox scars, was close to falling in love, but alas, as he later wrote, "her sole ambition was to become a nun."

With the comforts of civilization rejuvenating their spirits, the members of the expedition were able to see with a new clarity what they were accomplishing. They were not measuring one degree of latitude but three, and it was hard to imagine that the Lapland group, up and back so quickly, had conducted its triangulation with the same obsessive attention to detail that characterized their work. They also knew that they were accomplishing much more than simply measuring the arc at the equator. The very enterprise was forcing them to deepen their understanding of the physical properties of the world. They had needed to investigate the atmosphere's refractory properties, Bouguer concluding that "contrary to all received opinion [it] diminished in proportion as we were above the level of the sea." They had developed a better understanding of how barometric pressure varied with altitude. They had studied the expansion and contraction of metals in response to temperature change in order to understand how their toise might shrink in the cold. They had needed to perform all these investigations because, in one manner or another, these factors would have to be accounted for in their final calculations of the distance of a degree of latitude at the equator. On this expedition, they were advancing the *art* of doing science, and learning about nature as they did so.

They were aware too that measuring the arc was not the expedition's only purpose. They were also unveiling a continent. They were investigating its flora and fauna, with Jussieu gathering bags full of seeds and plants to bring back to France. They were making observations on the social mores and customs of colonial Spain. They were newly curious about earthquakes and volcanoes, and a volcano to the southeast of Riobamba, Mount Sangay, was threatening to erupt even as they convalesced in the city. A few months earlier, La Condamine and Bouguer had climbed to a height never before reached by Europeans, and perhaps by no one on earth. Their stay in Riobamba was giving them an opportunity to nurse their tired spirits and heal their bodies, and soon they could appreciate that they had been set loose in a savant's playground. Even Bouguer, so often grumpy about the rigors of this trip, was ready to change his tune. "Nature," he wrote, "has here continually in her hands the materials and implements for extraordinary operations."

IN MID-JANUARY 1739, they returned to the countryside. Their destination was Cuenca, 100 miles distant, and to get there, they had to map their way through a mountain range that intersected the valley and crossed between the two cordilleras, like a rung on a ladder. In this region, known as the Azuays, they no longer enjoyed the clear lines of sight that had made it possible to bounce their way south from Quito, with signal points set up on mountains on each side of the plain. Instead, they had to triangulate their way through terrain filled with "sandy moors, marshes and lakes," and they had to do so during the rainy season.

As had been the case in the past, Jean Godin and Verguin went ahead to mark the triangulation points, and the others followed close behind. Everyone was battered as they struggled through this wilderness. La Condamine was robbed at one camp, thrown by his horse and injured at another, and rendered tentless by fierce winds at a third. "I spent eight days wandering around the moors and marshes, without finding any shelter other than caverns in the rock," he wrote. Bouguer suffered a grave fall in these mountains, and he complained that at night his "sleep was continually interrupted by the roarings of the [Sangay] volcano," a "noise that was so frightful."

There were a few moments when the weather cleared and they enjoyed amazing vistas. To the north, the great Andean valley stretched out, with Mount Corazon visible 125 miles away. It was "the most beautiful horizon that one can imagine seeing," La Condamine enthused. And on March 24, they were treated to the spectacle of an eruption on Sangay. "One whole side of the mountain seemed to be on fire, as was the mouth of the volcano itself," La Condamine wrote. "A river of flaming sulfur and brimstone forged through the snow."

But such moments were rare. Their work was hampered at every step by fog, rain, and sleet. In the final days of April, they were blasted by hail and snow. The raging winds destroyed three of their tents, their Indian servants deserted them once again, and they were forced to huddle together in a breach in the rocks. Twenty miles away, in the town of Cañar, a priest led a prayer vigil for them, the people of that town fearful that they "had all perished" in the horrible storm. All seemed hopelessly grim, until, a few days later, a messenger arrived at their newly established camp with a letter that offered some comic relief. Their colleagues in France, it seemed, were worried that with the expedition taking place so close to the equator, they might be "suffering too much from the heat."

**A volcano erupts.**
*From Jorge Juan and Antonio de Ulloa,* Relación histórica del viage a la
América Meridional *(1749), from the 1806 English translation*
A Voyage to South America.

By mid-May, they had finally punched their way through the
Azuays. The worst was now behind them, and with the terrain
becoming gentler, they were able to rapidly make their way down
to Cuenca. They arrived there in early June, and over the course of
the next month, both groups, La Condamine's and Godin's,
mapped the last of their triangles. La Condamine and Bouguer
determined that they had measured off a meridian that was 176,950
toises long (214 miles). Godin and Juan had measured one that was
slightly longer.

The final step in the triangulation process involved proofing
their work. To do so, each group used a toise and wooden rods to
measure the last side of their last triangle. This was known as a second baseline, and the logic of the proof was simple. Since this line
was part of a known triangle, its length could be mathematically
deduced. Physically measuring this distance would verify the calcu-

**Bouguer's map of the triangulation area in Peru.**
*By permission of the Houghton Library, Harvard University.*

lated result. If the two were not equal, it would mean that unacceptable error had crept into their triangulation work, and much of it would have to be redone.

Each group had its own second baseline to measure. Although they had shared triangles part of the way, they had mapped out separate finishing triangles in the Cuenca region. Neither of the sites they had picked for this work was ideal. Godin and Juan had selected a plain that was bisected by a broad river; La Condamine, Bouguer, and Ulloa had chosen a spot a little further south, known as the plain of Tarqui, where they had to measure across a shallow pond one-half mile across. There they worked for days on end in the waist-deep water, tying the floating rods to stakes and then moving them forward in the same manner as on land.

As the men placed their final rods, they grew noticeably anxious. Two years of effort would be wasted if their results did not match up. They would have to retrace their steps and recheck all of their measured angles to find the source of the error. But both groups were able to breathe a sigh of relief: Their results were stunningly good. Godin and Juan determined that their baseline, as physically measured, was 6,196.3 toises long, which was only three-tenths of a toise—about two feet—less than its length as mathematically calculated. La Condamine and Bouguer achieved similar results. Their numbers for their second baseline—as measured and as mathematically calculated—differed by only two-tenths of a toise. The two groups had marked off meridian lines stretching more than 200 miles, through mountainous terrain and in miserable weather, and their proofs were accurate to within a couple of *feet*. At last, La Condamine wrote with understandable pride, "our geometric measurements were completely finished."

All they needed to do now was measure the height of a star from both ends of their measured meridians, and their work in Peru would be done. This would give them the difference in latitude of their meridians' endpoints, and with this information in hand, they could precisely calculate the length of a degree of latitude at the equator. Although they would need to build observatories, this would take six months at most. Their results put them in a festive mood, and so they retired to Cuenca, where they hoped to enjoy themselves for a few days before their final push. They would—or so they thought—be on their way home soon.

# CHAPTER EIGHT

# Death in the Afternoon

C UENCA WAS NEARLY THE SAME SIZE as Riobamba and had an equally pleasant climate, which made it seem an ideal place to rest. Both groups—La Condamine's and Louis Godin's— had in fact been coming and going from Cuenca ever since June, for they had used a bell tower in a church in the city's *plaza mayor* as a triangulation point. Yet when they returned on August 23, they found the city all stirred up, like a bee's nest that had been disturbed. Tensions were so high that Senièrgues, who had been living in Cuenca since March, did not dare go out in public without a loaded pistol.

Since the expedition had left Quito, Senièrgues had rarely been with the others. As they moved south through the mountains, he had regularly gone ahead to the nearest city in order to hang out his shingle as a traveling doctor. In one town, he had removed cataracts from a rich merchant, who had rewarded him with a princely sum. Senièrgues, La Condamine wrote, perhaps with a touch of envy, was making a "fortune" in the New World. Initially, Senièrgues had enjoyed similar success in Cuenca, but then he foolishly became involved in a lover's quarrel.

One of Senièrgues's patients, Francisco Quesada, had a beautiful daughter, Manuela, who had recently been jilted by her fiancé, Diego de Leon. Leon, a guitar-playing Lothario, had dumped Manuela for the daughter of Cuenca's mayor, Sebastián Serrano. In order to get free of his marriage contract with Manuela, he had promised to pay her family a sum of money. But then he reneged, and the Quesadas asked Senièrgues if he would help collect the debt. This was clearly a delicate situation, and to complicate matters, as Senièrgues was making his initial overtures to Leon, he moved into the Quesadas' house, prompting a great deal of gossip in town about what the doctor's real motives might be.

Senièrgues's initial discussions with Leon went poorly. Even though Leon had jilted Manuela, he still felt jealous on hearing rumors linking Senièrgues and his former girlfriend. Negotiations broke down completely after one of Leon's slaves came to the Quesadas' house and "loudly insulted" Senièrgues. As La Condamine later recounted, his friend immediately went looking for Leon: "Senièrgues stopped Leon at a street corner and picked a fight with him. Leon, for an answer, pulled out a loaded pistol, which did not prevent Senièrgues from advancing with his saber in his hand toward Leon, with such a rush that he took a false step and fell. Those that accompanied Leon intervened and separated the two."

This scene was soon being reenacted in every bar in Cuenca. The local men—would-be comics all—took turns mimicking the clumsiness of the great doctor, falling over their feet in an exaggerated way while shouting out a few words of badly pronounced French. And there things might have ended, except that a few of Leon's friends continued to boil over with anger, a sentiment that gradually spread. No one could understand what the French were doing in their town in the first place, and now they were wooing their women and threatening people with their swords. Could this be allowed to stand? A local priest, Juan Jiménez Crespo, asked a Cuenca judge to start a criminal investigation of Senièrgues. His crime, Crespo declared, was that he had stayed overnight in the house of an unmarried woman. The priest also denounced the French from his pulpit, further whipping up ill feelings toward the doctor, and such was the foul mood of Cuenca when La Condamine and the others arrived on August 23, hoping for a little peace and quiet.

EVER SINCE ARRIVING IN MANTA, the expedition members had been running into this darker side of Peru, where violence was constantly in the air. In Quito, the French had enjoyed the parties thrown for them and had been impressed by the fine clothes and refined manners of the Quito elite. But only a few blocks away from the elegant *plaza mayor,* they had discovered, "troublesome activities" began. There they found mestizos and others stumbling about drunk, thieves so bold that they would "snatch a person's hat off" and run, and, most disturbing of all, Indians being dragged about by their hair as they were taken to work in the *obrajes,* or textile mills. Ulloa and Juan were carefully compiling notes on this aspect of Peru as part of their planned report to the king of Spain, and Cuenca, they wrote, was a particularly hard place: The men "have a strange aversion to all kinds of work. [Many] are also rude, vindictive, and, in short, wicked in every sense."

At the root of this "evil," as Ulloa and Juan dubbed it, was an economic system built on the forced labor of Indians. In the colony's early years, the exploitation of the Indians had been accomplished through the encomienda laws, which placed entire native villages under a Spaniard's control. However, this gave the spoils of Indian labor to a few, and the Crown quickly realized that the resulting concentration of wealth would nurture an aristocracy so powerful that it could challenge the authority of a distant monarchy. Spain passed legislation making it difficult for encomenderos to pass their encomiendas on to their descendants, and by the end of the sixteenth century, it had put in place a new system of compulsory labor.

Indians in mita service mining silver.
*By Theodore de Bry. Private collection/Bridgeman Art Library.*

The labor law, which was known as the *mita,* required a percentage of the population in every Indian village to work for several
months each year in mines, textile mills, and haciendas owned by
the colonists. The responsibility for doling out this labor to the
colonists was left up to the corregidors, who were agents of the
Crown. The Indians were paid fixed wages for their work, which
made the mita, in the eyes of the Spanish monarchy, fair and just.
But as Ulloa and Juan documented, the reality in eighteenth-century
Peru was quite different:

Work in the *obrajes* begins before dawn when each Indian enters
his assigned room. Here he receives his work for the day. Then
the workshop overseer locks the doors, leaving the Indians
imprisoned in the room. At noon he reopens the doors to allow

the laborers' wives to deliver a scant meal for their sustenance. After this short interval, the Indians are again locked up. In the evening when it is too dark to work any longer, the overseer collects the piecework he distributed in the morning. Those who have been unable to finish are punished so brutally that it is incredible. Because they seemingly do not know how to count any lower, these merciless men whip the poor Indians by the hundreds of lashes. To complete the punishment, they leave the offenders shut up in the room where they work or place them in stocks in one of the rooms set aside as a prison.

The physical abuse of Indians conscripted into mita service was never-ending. Those who kicked too much while being dragged off to work were tied by their hair to a horse's tail and brought in that manner to the shop. Ever since the 1500s, authorities had required Indians to keep their hair long so that they could be shunted about in this way. The whip used to punish the Indian laborers, Ulloa and Juan added, was "about a yard long, a finger's width or a bit less, made of strands of cowhide twisted together like a bass guitar string, and hardened." When a whipping was ordered, the Indians were

commanded to stretch out on the ground face down and remove their light trousers. They are then forced to count the lashes given them until the number set by the sentence has been inflicted. After getting up, they have been taught to kneel down in front of the person who administered the punishment and kiss his hand, saying, "May God be pleased, and may He give you thanks for having punished my sin."

At times, in order to inflict more pain, the overseers would light two bundles of maguey stems on fire and then beat the bundles together "so that the sparks fall on the victims' open flesh as they are being whipped."

Indians assigned to work on rural haciendas fared only slightly better. They would be assigned the task of caring for a flock of sheep or a herd of cattle, and although they might not be subjected to the same steady physical abuse that obraje workers were, they were certain to lead hopelessly impoverished lives. In theory, Spain had outlawed the enslavement of Indians, but the way the system worked ensured their bondage. A shepherd caring for a flock of 1,000 sheep was paid fourteen to eighteen pesos a year. Out of this, Ulloa and Juan found, the Indian was expected to pay a tribute—an annual tax that all Indians between the ages of eighteen and fifty-five were expected to pay—of eight pesos. Each month, the Indian laborer was also forced to buy a 100-weight bag of corn at inflated prices, which cost him a total of nine pesos annually. If a sheep died or wandered off, the shepherd had to pay for it. In this manner, an Indian drafted into the mita ended up perpetually in debt and thus "remains a slave all his life," Ulloa wrote.

This exploitation of Indian labor colored every aspect of Peruvian culture. Since those at the top of the rigid caste system looked down upon manual labor, so did those lower on the totem pole, and every group sought to dominate the one below it. The Creoles and Spaniards looked down on everyone who was not white, mulattos and mestizos fancied themselves better than Negroes, and everyone lorded it over the Indians. Even slaves could be seen dragging Indians about by their hair, and at one home Ulloa and Juan visited, slaves went out into the street and corralled Indians to do *their* work.

The clergy in Peru—save for the Jesuits, Ulloa and Juan reported—were equally abusive and corrupt. They were supposed to save the Indians' souls, but their attention more often than not was focused on a decidedly worldly concern: making money. Clergy would bid for the right to tend to a parish and then apply "all their efforts to enriching themselves." Priests would not say mass until they had received gifts, and Indians who did not bring a gift or lacked goods to give were whipped. One priest reported that while traveling through his parish over the course of the year, he collected

An Indian porter
carrying a Spaniard.
*Museo de America,
Madrid, Spain.*

more than 200 sheep, 6,000 chickens, 4,000 guinea pigs, and 50,000 eggs, all of which were profitably resold.

All of this produced a society in which violence was ever-present. The French had seen it often. While in Quito, La Condamine wrote, "[T]here were times when there would not be a week that passed, and sometimes not a single day, without some murder taking place." Bouguer's slave had been killed, and while the expedition was working around Riobamba, even the mayor of that graceful city was "stabbed by a mulatto in broad daylight in the center of town." Creoles and Spaniards carried swords and pistols, and nearly everyone else went about armed with a knife. At the top of Peruvian society, people worried about whether they were being addressed with the proper grammatical form, and young girls were taught to be pure and virginal. But beneath that patina of civilization was a very rough society. The French had reason to worry, and now this: Senièrgues was enmeshed in a quarrel, and a five-day festival of bullfighting was set to begin.

SPAIN'S LOVE FOR BULLFIGHTING dated back to the Middle Ages, the ritual having become popular during the Reconquest. In its earliest incarnation, several nobles mounted on horseback and armed with long lances would fight a bull that had already been repeatedly stabbed by commoners on foot. Later, the bullfight evolved into a more dramatic form in which a lone toreador faced the animal head on, killing it with a single thrust of his sword. The spectacle evoked both a sense of violence and sexual prowess, and when a bullfight was held to celebrate a noble's wedding, it was viewed as a fertility ritual, the bull's sexual potency transferred in the killing to the groom. In the early eighteenth century, France and other European countries under the influence of the Enlightenment began to scorn the bullfight as a barbaric relic of the past, but in Spain, where medieval values still held sway, it became more deeply ingrained than ever. "Bullfights," remarked the Spanish writer Fray Luis de León, "are in the blood of the Spanish people."

During a festival, passions tended to rise with each passing day. The bullfights in Cuenca were being staged in a makeshift arena erected in San Sebastián Plaza on a bluff high above the Rio Tomebamba, and each afternoon, long before the gates opened, men and women would gather, eagerly awaiting the spectacle that was about to unfold. On the morning of the fifth day, August 28, Crespo denounced the French once again in his sermon, and by that afternoon, there was a palpable tension in the air, as though everyone knew that something was going to happen.

All of the members of the expedition went to the corrida that day. La Condamine, Bouguer, Morainville, and one or two others had been invited to sit with Gregorio Vicuna, the priest of San Sebastián Church, which graced the square where the bullfight was being staged. A former corregidor of Cuenca joined them in Vicuna's box. While they were waiting for the festivities to begin, they engaged in small talk about Crespo and his anti-French tirades, La Condamine dismissing the sentiment as coming from a few rabble-rousers led by a priest who "did not have any virtue beyond a grand indifference to the beautiful sex." As usual, La Condamine was in some ways enjoying their ongoing feud with the locals—everyone in the box understood his subtle dig at Crespo's manhood—but even he did a double take when Senièrgues entered the stadium with Manuela hanging on his arm. "This was the first time that he had showed up in public with her," La Condamine later wrote, "and it was, if you wish, imprudent." But Senièrgues played the moment for all it was worth, slowly strolling to his box, where he took out a handkerchief and made an exaggerated show of dusting off Manuela's seat.

A murmur of disbelief rose from the crowd. The director of the bullfight, Nicolás de Neyra, rode up to where Senièrgues was seated and angrily told him that his behavior—indeed, his very presence—was disturbing the festival. And, Neyra asked, did Senièrgues understand that neither he, nor anyone else in Cuenca, was afraid of him? More insults were exchanged, and then the French doctor, unable to "contain himself" any longer, threatened to climb down into the ring and give Neyra a thorough beating.

At that, Neyra turned and rode off. The crowd now rained jeers down upon his head for this seeming retreat. The turmoil was mounting, and once outside the ring, Neyra told those gathered for the opening parade that he was calling off the bullfight because Senièrgues had threatened to kill him. "There was," La Condamine confessed, "nothing that could infuriate the common man more." As the news that the bullfight had been canceled swept through the crowd, a chant of "Death to the Frenchmen" leapt from their throats, and suddenly Neyra was leading a mob of 200 men, armed "with lances, swords, slings, and guns," back into the ring. Even the mayor, Serrano, joined Neyra and, stopping before Senièrgues, demanded that he surrender. Others were threatening to clamber into the stands to get at the French doctor, who responded with a blast of Gallic pride: Who, he asked, were Serrano and Neyra to give *him* such an order? And then he jumped into the ring, holding a pistol in one hand and a sword in the other, all the while promising to "give them a spectacle more interesting than that of the bulls."

At first, nobody dared to approach Senièrgues. But then, as La Condamine later wrote, the mob surged forward:

> Seeing himself surrounded, Senièrgues tried to retire from the scene, always facing his attackers, using his sword and stopping their blows, without receiving a single injury. In that manner, he arrived at the corner of the plaza, next to the fence that served as a barrier to the bulls, persecuted at every step by a hailstorm of stones, from which he tried to protect himself with his arms. The continuous throws of the stones knocked the weapons from his hands, and seeing himself disarmed, he could not think about anything other than fleeing. He retreated through the door that shut the fence, leaving his head and half his body exposed, and while he was like that, the mayor shouted to his followers: Kill him! Too quickly and too well was he obeyed: Senièrgues fell punctured with wounds, and if one is to believe the public testimony, it was Neyra who delivered the mortal thrust.

La Condamine, Bouguer, and the others had all sought to rush to Senièrgues's aid the moment he had jumped into the ring, but Vicuna had held them back, certain that they too would be killed. With blood having been spilled, chaos was erupting everywhere. Senièrgues stumbled to the patio of a house in the corner of the plaza, the crowd continuing to kick and beat him. The deputy of the town drew his pistol to shoot him in the head, but at the last moment, the owner of the house cried out in protest, taking "up in his arms the wounded man and helping to lay him in a bed." Meanwhile, those in the stands turned their rage on the other members of the French expedition, including Ulloa and Juan, chasing

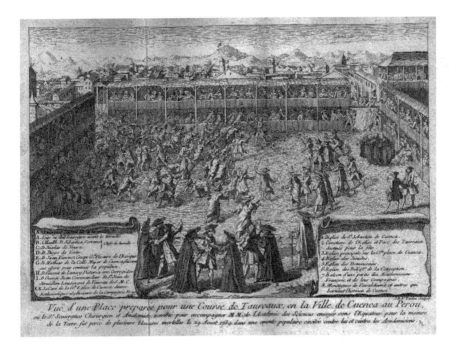

**The murder scene in Cuenca.**

*From Charles-Marie de La Condamine,* Journal du voyage fait par
ordre du roi à l'équateur *(1751).*

them into the streets of Cuenca. As they fled, the mob hurled stones
at them, and Bouguer was at some point stabbed in the back. "We
ran in fear of our life," La Condamine later recalled, and even as
they were scrambling into the sanctuary of a Jesuit's house, a knife
was hurled at Bouguer's head that barely missed its mark. The
priest and his servants quickly barred the door, the mob banging on
it and trying to force it open, until at last their fury was spent and
they retreated.

For the next four days, Senièrgues lay dying. He was brought to
the home where the others had found refuge and where Jussieu
tended to his gaping wounds and to Bouguer's back. "Senièrgues
alone has paid for all of us," Jussieu wrote in an August 31 letter to
his brother. The locals, he concluded, had become enraged by all
things French. Bouguer had not been badly injured, but Senièrgues
died the next day. The news of his murder spread throughout the

colony and even to Europe, although there the details of what happened became somewhat garbled in the retelling. "It seems," wrote the Scottish mathematician Colin Maclaurin, in a letter to a colleague, "that they were shewing some French gallantry to the natives' wives, who have murdered their servants, destroyed their Instruments, & burnt their papers."

LA CONDAMINE AND THE OTHERS had planned to return to the surrounding area to do their astronomical observations. But in the wake of the riot, this seemed the height of folly. On the day that Senièrgues had been stabbed, the mob had eventually descended on the ranking official in town, an assistant to the corregidor, and forced him to promise that the Frenchmen would be made to leave the city. Serrano, meanwhile, had decided that *he* would direct the investigation of the killing, and as a first step, he told Neyra—the very person who had stabbed Senièrgues—to gather information about the doctor's criminal activities. Even the arrival of the corregidor of the Cuenca district, who had hurried to town to restore order, did not make the French feel safe. At their urging, he did initiate criminal proceedings against Neyra, Serrano, and Leon, who had been a leader of the mob as it surged through the streets. But he feared that if he arrested them, the town would revolt. Many in Cuenca were toasting Leon for having vanquished his rival, and Neyra, La Condamine wrote bitterly, had been publicly praised "for having done the killing." All that the corregidor dared to do was send a secret indictment to judges in the Quito Audiencia, which allowed the three ringleaders of the riot to remain at liberty.

Even so, after a few weeks, La Condamine and the others resumed their scientific work, and they did so in and around Cuenca. They were not going to let death threats keep them from completing their measurements.

At first glance, this last step in their mission—apart from the danger that the people of Cuenca presented—seemed simple.

Determining latitude by measuring the altitude of the sun or another star was an age-old science. However, as had been the case with their triangulation work, the French savants were intent on making measurements that were accurate down to one second of a degree. That precision had never before been achieved.

The instrument they would use for this purpose was the zenith sector. Rather than measuring a star's altitude above the horizon, a zenith sector determined the complement of this angle: It measured the difference between the star's position and a point directly overhead. The sector's long stationery arm would be aligned along the vertical axis,* while its telescope would be pointed at the star as it crossed the local meridian (the imaginary line of longitude drawn through the observatory and the earth's two poles). The telescope was attached by a swivel to the sector's vertical arm, and thus pointing it at the star created an angle that could be measured, which was known as a star's zenith distance. By taking zenith-distance readings of the same star from different points on a north-south line, astronomers could determine the difference in latitude of those two points.

The academicians had brought a sector with a twelve-foot radius from France, the instrument having been skillfully constructed by Graham in England. However, Louis Godin, anticipating this moment in their work, had asked Hugo to construct a twenty-foot sector, which, since it had a larger radius, could theoretically provide more accurate measurements. La Condamine and Bouguer took the twelve-foot sector to the plains of Tarqui, where they built an observatory during the month of September, while Godin set up his twenty-foot sector in Cuenca, using the bell tower of the church in the *plaza mayor* as a makeshift observatory. Because the two groups had measured separate meridian lines, they needed to continue working apart. Each would determine the latitudes of the endpoints of its own meridian.

* A plumb line is used to determine the point directly overhead. Gravity will cause a plumb line to point toward the earth's center, and the extension of that line in the opposite direction identifies the point directly overhead.

The use of a zenith sector required spending long hours in an awkward position. A pendulum clock can be seen on the observatory wall.
*From Charles-Marie de La Condamine,* Mesure des trois premiers degrés du méridien dans l'hémisphere austral *(1751).*

In early October, both groups began making measurements, training their sights on a star in the Orion constellation. However, bad weather slowed their progress. Clouds obscured the night sky for weeks on end, and with Senièrgues's murder so fresh in their minds, the constant rains cast a pall over the whole enterprise. It was a "series of sad and difficult observations" they were trying to make, La Condamine wrote in his journal, and they were having to conduct them in a "lonely place." By December, they were still not finished, and it seemed certain that 1739 would close with their spirits flagging. But their gloom was lifted by an unlikely group: Indians and mestizos holding a festival at Tarqui. The brightly costumed Indians, mounted on horseback, performed choreographed dances, and during an intermission, a group of mestizos put on a pantomime that, for the moment anyway, washed away their grief:

> They had the talent of mimicking anything they saw and even things they did not understand. I had seen them observing us sev-

eral times while we took the measurements of the sun to adjust our pendulums. This must have been for them an impenetrable mystery to see a man on his knees at the base of a quadrant, head facing upwards in an uncomfortable position, holding a lens in one hand and with the other turning a screw on the foot of the instrument, and alternately carrying the lens to his eye and to the divisions to examine the plumb line and from time to time running to check the minutes and seconds on the pendulum and jotting some numbers down on a piece of paper and once again resuming the first position. None of our movements had escaped the observations of our spectators and when we least expected it they produced on stage large quadrants made of painted paper and cardboard which were rather good copies and we watched as each of us was mimicked mercilessly. This was done in such an amusing manner that I must admit to not having seen anything quite as pleasant during the years of our trip.

In early January, both groups completed their celestial observations in Cuenca. All they had to do now was perform similar observations in the plains north of Quito, and they would be done. After two long years in the mountains, they looked forward to the relative comforts of that city, where, they knew, friends like Pedro Gramesón would welcome them once again. Jean Godin in particular thought happily about returning to the Gramesóns. Indeed, he went to their home the minute he reached Quito, and he heard from the general this news: Isabel had turned twelve years old, the age when girls in Peru began to wed.

# CHAPTER NINE

# Marriage in Quito

THE LIFE COURSE THAT WAS PLOTTED for upper-class girls in Peru sent them down one of two paths. After six or seven years of convent school, they were expected to "take a state." Either a girl would prepare to marry a man, or, by becoming a nun, "marry God." This moment of decision usually came at around age twelve, the age when Catholic doctrine deemed girls to be physically capable of intercourse. However, families who did not want to wait that long to arrange a favorable union for their daughters could obtain a dispensation from the church. Child brides nine and ten years old were not uncommon in colonial Peru.

Although Creoles and Spaniards wrangled endlessly in the political arena and often confessed their loathing for one another, the parents of a Creole daughter typically put aside such feelings when it came to marriage. A Spaniard was viewed as a superior choice. Everyone understood that Creole men did not have the same access to political power that Spaniards did, and Creole men, by and large, had a reputation for being lazy, spoiled, and vain. "Creole women,"

Ulloa wrote, "recognize the disaster of marrying those of their own faction." A Spanish groom would also be certain to have *limpieza sangre* (clean blood), and thus a white Creole family could be assured that the offspring of such a union would enjoy the many privileges that came with being white in colonial Peru. Those of pure Spanish blood were exempt from many colonial taxes and had a privileged claim on civil and ecclesiastical positions.

Most elite families would pick older men for their young daughters to marry. Six to twelve years of age difference was the norm. At times, however, a father would contract with a forty-year-old man to wed his twelve-year-old daughter, even though this was an age difference that the girls found loathsome. They would sing:

*Don't marry an old man*
*For his money,*
*Money, money disappears*
*But the old man remains.*

However, Peruvian girls did want to marry, and at an early age. A girl who passed through puberty and turned twenty years old without marrying risked being thought of as an old maid, and rumors would likely fly that she was no longer a virgin, which would make it impossible for her to ever find a husband. And while elite families looked upon an arranged marriage as a business transaction, the girls naturally had their romantic fantasies. Courtly love was part of the same knightly tradition that prompted their seclusion.

The Amadís novels that were so popular in sixteenth-century Spain were, first and foremost, *romances*. Although the beautiful maiden may have been locked away in her castle, kept from the world by bars on her windows, such sequestration was necessary precisely because she pined so for her knight, and did so in a feverishly physical way. These books, lamented one sixteenth-century bishop, "stir up immoral and lascivious desire." Yet another priest lamented that "often a mother leaves her daughter shut up in the house thinking that she is left in seclusion, but the daughter is really reading books like these and hence it would be far better for the mother to take the daughter along with her." Indeed, Spanish girls devoured the books. Saint Teresa de Jesus of Ávila confessed in her autobiography that as a child she had been "so utterly absorbed in reading them that if I did not have a new book to read, I did not feel that I could be happy."

In Peru, this vision of romance found a real-world outlet in the amorous liaisons between men of Spanish blood and lower-caste women. As seventeenth-century visitors noted in their travelogues, Spanish men in Peru thought of mulattos and mestizos as their "women of love." The woman who was the object of such affection was a recognized type in Peruvian society, known as a *tapada*. She was, American historian Luis Martín has noted, the "sex symbol of colonial Peru."

> She was always dressed in the latest fashions, and her clothing was made of the most expensive, imported materials. She favored lace from the Low Countries, exquisite silks from China, and exotic perfumes and jewelry from the Orient. The length of her gown was shortened several inches to reveal the lace trim of her undergarments, and to draw attention to her small feet covered with embroidered velvet slippers.

While upper-class girls in the convent schools were taught to assume a different role, to be honorable and chaste in their thoughts, they still were greatly influenced by this culture. Rare was the Peruvian girl, one historian wrote, who did not fancy sneaking away at night for "an amatory conversation through the Venetian blinds of the window of the ground floor." The girls' seclusion, which allowed their imaginations to run rampant, only reinforced this feeling. Their "frantic desire to marry," a Peruvian scholar noted, was "aggravated still more by the ban on speaking to men, except cousins." Moreover, even in the convents, there was an ever-present undercurrent of sexuality. All of the girls would giggle in private over the nicknames that locals gave to the pastries and candies that the nuns produced and sold—the sweets were known as "little kisses," "raise-the-old-man," "maiden's tongue," and "love's caresses."

As Isabel reached this moment in her life, she was by all accounts quite fetching. Petite and with delicate features, she had the slender fingers and tiny feet that men in colonial Peru so fancied. While she had the usual dark hair of the Spanish, her skin was milk-white, and in this regard, she looked very much a daughter of Guayaquil, for the women of that port city were known to be "very fair" in complexion. Those who knew her spoke of her "good soul" and of how "very pretty" she was, and of her obvious intelligence. She could speak both French and Quechua, having learned this latter language as a child, when she had had an Indian wet nurse. Even La Condamine, usually so discrete in his comments, pronounced her "delicious" upon meeting her, and remarked that she had a "provocative" mouth. He was, in the manner of the times, simply stating what everyone saw: Isabel Gramesón, who was both pretty and from a prosperous family, was going to be quite the catch.

THE FRENCH ACADEMICIANS finished their astronomical observations around Quito in April 1740, prompting La Condamine to triumphantly declare their work complete. "After four years of a traveling life, two of which had been spent on mountains, we were ready to calculate the degree of the meridian which was the purpose of so many operations." Yet even at this apparent moment of success, they were gnawed by doubt. Their measurements of stars in the Orion constellation had consistently varied "8 to 10 seconds" from one night to the next. Although this was a small discrepancy, it still prevented them from feeling secure about the precision of their work. They had not quite reached the ambitious goal that they had set for themselves, and as they mulled over this problem, they concluded that the fault must lie with their zenith sectors. If the long telescope flexed by so much as one-sixth of an inch between viewings, a star's apparent position would shift by twenty seconds. Everyone glumly realized what they must do: Hugo would have to make the instruments more stable or build new sectors altogether, and then they would have to repeat their celestial observations.

While waiting for Hugo to do his work, the others busied themselves in various ways. La Condamine, for his part, returned to Cuenca, intent on bringing Senièrgues's killers to justice. He wrote to the viceroys in both Lima and Santa Fe de Bogotá,* collected statements from witnesses to the murder, and even mounted a legal case against the priest whose sermons had helped spark the riot. "I love my country," La Condamine wrote in his journal. "I believe that I have an obligation to defend the honor and interests of my sovereign, of my nation, and of my academy." That case seemed to stoke his appetite for other legal battles as well. La Condamine sued three individuals who had not returned goods he had loaned them, and then he got into an argument with Ulloa and Juan that also headed to court.

The dispute with Ulloa and Juan was over how the French planned to commemorate the expedition's work. Even before they departed from France, they had decided to build monuments at the ends of their first baseline. This had been thought out in such detail that the academy had written the inscription that was to be used. La Condamine had taken charge of this task, and he had decided to build pyramids, rather grand in size—twelve feet by twelve feet at the base and fifteen feet tall—to mark their Yaruqui baseline. There was a scientific rationale for putting up markers, as it would enable other geodesists to check their work. But the pyramids would also serve to glorify those who performed the deed, and therein was the problem: La Condamine, as he fiddled with the

---

* Santa Fe de Bogotá was the capital of the Viceroyalty of New Granada, which Spain had created in 1717, carving it out from the northern part of the Viceroyalty of Peru. The Quito Audiencia was shifted out of Peru and into Granada in 1739.

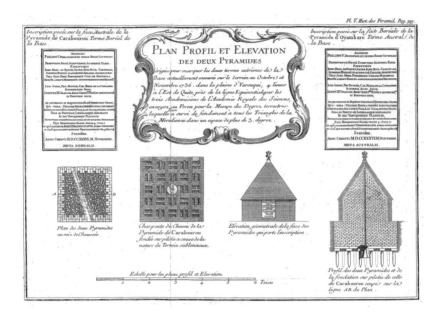

La Condamine's blueprint for pyramids marking the Yaruqui baseline.
*From Charles-Marie de La Condamine,* Journal du voyage fait par
ordre du roi à l'équateur *(1751).*

wording of the inscription prepared by the academy, sought to
describe the two Spanish naval officers as "assistants."

From La Condamine's point of view, this was exceedingly generous. None of the French helpers—Verguin, Morainville, or Jean
Godin—was going to see his name on the marble tablet. But Ulloa
and Juan had grown up in a society where swords could be drawn
over the use of *usted,* and they perceived the wording as an unfor-
givable slight. They informed La Condamine that the inscription
should describe them as Spanish academicians—they wanted equal
status. Replied La Condamine: "Only the French members of the
Academy were charged with this mission [and] we have always
remained the masters of our work." To describe Ulloa and Juan as
academicians, he wrote, would be to award them "qualities which
they did not possess." One bemused observer of this squabble—
Isabel's uncle, the Marqués de Valleumbroso—deemed it worthy of
"a new comedy by Molière." But this was colonial Spain, and the

argument blew up into a legal contest that clogged the Quito court with hundreds of documents, with the Creoles in the city cheering on La Condamine, for they rather enjoyed seeing two Spaniards humiliated.

The expedition, however, was clearly sputtering as the academicians tried to bring it to a close. The zenith sectors were in the repair shop. Louis Godin's relationship with La Condamine and Bouguer remained so strained that more often than not they communicated with each other by letter. Senièrgues and Couplet were dead, and yet another member, Jussieu, was in bed with a raging fever, so sick that he had "put his affairs and his conscience in order." As a group, the expedition was falling apart, and then, late in 1740, the Peruvian viceroy called Ulloa and Juan to Lima. A British armada was sailing around Cape Horn with plans to attack Peruvian ports, and he wanted the two Spaniards to help prepare the colony's defense. The expedition, at least for the moment, had come to a halt.*

EVEN MORE THAN THE OTHER ASSISTANTS, Jean Godin was left at loose ends by this scattering of the expedition members. The others still had tasks to do. Hugo was working on the instruments, Morainville was building the pyramids, and Verguin was assisting La Condamine with his drawing of maps. But Jean's job

---

* The War of Jenkins's Ear had its roots in the 1713 Treaty of Utrecht, when Britain obtained the right to have one British merchant ship a year trade with Spain's New World colonies. That very limited right blossomed into a much larger English smuggling enterprise, which the Spanish Guardias Marinas was constantly trying to rein in. In 1731, Spain detained a British ship, captained by Robert Jenkins, that was allegedly loaded with contraband. Jenkins insulted the Spanish commander, who responded—or so the story went—by cutting off Jenkins's ear with a sword, spitting into the severed organ, and vowing that he would like to do the same to England's King George II. In 1738, Jenkins recounted his tale to the House of Commons, even presenting to them his carefully pickled ear, and the furor was such that England declared war on Spain.

had been to act as a signal carrier during the triangulation work, and now there was little for him to do. Nor was there money left for the expedition as a whole. His cousin Louis was descending ever deeper into debt, while La Condamine was relying on his personal funds to pay for his expenses and for the construction of the pyramids. In order to earn some money, Jean decided to travel to Cartagena, planning to trade in textiles. Before he left, however, La Condamine gave him a trunk filled with "natural curiosities" to take to the port, where he could arrange for its shipment to France. This request picked up Jean's spirits, for it made him feel connected, in some small way, to the others.

He departed from Quito on October 3, 1740. It was 900 miles to Cartagena, along a tortuous route that could take three months to travel. The first 500 miles involved a trek by mule across the dry plains north of the city and then along the spine of the Andes. The most treacherous segment in the mountains was Guanacas Pass, "the most famous in all South America" for its perils, Bouguer later wrote. The peaks in this region near Popayán were covered with snow, and so many mules had perished while crossing the pass that their bones covered the trail, making it impossible "to set a foot down without treading on them." This route, Bouguer concluded, was "never hazarded without the utmost dread."

Jean Godin found it slow going; at times he was able to cover only three or four miles a day. It took him until the middle of November to make his way through the mountains and to reach the Magdalena River, where he was able to trade his mule for a canoe. This was a much more comfortable form of transport. Near Bogotá, he even took a short detour to Tequendama Falls, a waterfall "200 toises" in height that, at the time, was thought to be the tallest in the world.

When Jean arrived in Cartagena, the city was busily preparing for an attack by the British. Jean found some textiles to buy, and handed off La Condamine's trunk to the captain of a French frigate. It contained a number of archaeological items certain to intrigue the Europeans: fossil axes, rock samples, petrified wood,

Tequendama Falls.
*From John
Pinkerton, ed.,* A
General Collection of
the Best and Most
Interesting Voyages
and Travels in All
Parts of the World,
*vol. 14 (London,
1813).*

the skin of a small crocodile, a stuffed coral snake, several Incan artifacts, and antique clay vases that were shaped with such skill that the water whistled when poured. Unfortunately, the ship did not sail right away and was still docked in Cartagena on March 15, 1741, when the British launched their assault. They set fire to ships in the bay, including the frigate loaded with La Condamine's trunk of curiosities, and all of the items were lost.

Godin's journey to and from Cartagena took more than six months, and as had so often been the case during his time in South America, he had traveled alone. He had grown quite accustomed to this difficult life. His trek to Cartagena, he wrote, reminded him of the years he had spent "reconnoitering the ground for the meridian of Quito, fixing signals on the loftiest mountains." But back in Quito, he was once more at loose ends. As La Condamine said, "His duties regarding the objective of our mission had ceased." He was adrift in a Spanish colony far from his home, and it was then, over the next several months, that he became engaged to thirteen-year-old Isabel Gramesón.

There is no record of their courtship, either in Jean's writings or La Condamine's. The match, however, could only have been made with Pedro Gramesón's approval, and in that regard, it was surprising. While he may have welcomed the French visitors into his home and delighted in their tales, he almost certainly would not have considered Jean Godin a good husband for his daughter. It was true that the two families shared common friends, the Pelletiers from Lignieres—alliances often lay behind arranged marriages. And Jean, during his years of service to the expedition, had proven himself to be a person of industry. But he was not Spanish and was planning to return to France, and it would hardly make sense for Pedro Gramesón to invest Isabel's dowry in such a suitor.

His daughter, however, was strong-willed, and this was a union that would fulfill many of her wishes. She had often stated her desire to go to France. As Jean later wrote, she was "exceedingly solicitous" of traveling there. Hers was a childhood dream woven from many strands: Her grandfather on her father's side was French, her father had entertained these famous visitors in his home, and all of Quito had gossiped about the wonders of Paris when the expedition had first come to the city. Women there, or so she had been told, presided over salons, attended the theater in fancy gowns, and danced the minuet at elegant balls. Marrying Jean promised to make all of that a reality, and at last Isabel's father consented: He would provide the couple with a dowry that consisted of jewelry, textiles, 7,783 pesos in silver, and two slaves.

Jean and Isabel were married by Father Domingo Terol on December 29, 1741, in the Dominican College of San Fernando in Quito. La Condamine, Verguin, and Jussieu—who had recovered from his fever—all attended, as did many of the elite in Quito and other rich Creoles from miles around. The large crowd was a reflection of the Gramesóns' prominence, particularly on Isabel's mother's side. It is likely that Louis Godin, Bouguer, and Morainville also attended, bringing together all the French members of the expedition one final time.

The marriage ceremony was followed by a grand feast and dance. The guests sipped on liquors chilled by ice chipped from Mount Pichincha, drank grape brandy, and ate to their hearts' content. Great plates of fish, fowl, and meats were served, and the dining tables were loaded with bowls of succulent fruits—chirimoyas, avocados, guavas, pomegranates, and strawberries. After the food was put away, everyone danced the fandango, the rhythm tapped out with a tambourine and castanets. More than one guest had brought a guitar, and according to one account, the Gramesóns had shipped in a clavichord from Guayaquil for the occasion. Isabel's parents had spared no expense, and everyone could see how happy Isabel and Jean looked. Theirs, it seemed, was a marriage certain to bring good fortune to both.

After the wedding, Isabel went into seclusion for a month. In a society in which the cult of the Virgin Mary held sway, it was considered improper for a woman to be seen during the time of her "deflowering." Once the thirty days had gone by, she and Jean began a round of visits to family and friends, a ritual signaling that she had passed into adulthood. Although it was expected that Isabel, in the future, would rarely venture out alone—social protocol required that she have a maid or her husband with her—she no longer needed to be to be hidden. She was fourteen years old and he was twenty-eight, a match that seemed right and proper to all, and even as they made their social rounds, she was already pregnant with their first child.

During this period, La Condamine, Bouguer, and Louis Godin repeated their celestial observations, but without success. Hugo's repairs to the zenith sectors did not make any difference. A star's zenith position would vary from five to twenty seconds from night to night. They now had to confront a painful possibility: Perhaps they were trying to do the impossible. Perhaps they could not measure a degree of latitude with sufficient precision to definitively answer the question of the earth's shape. They were sure that Maupertuis's measurements in Lapland were not as accurate as theirs already were, and yet they knew that if they went ahead and used these imprecise celestial observations to calculate the length of a degree of latitude at the equator, some doubt would remain.

There were any number of factors that might be causing the variation. Perhaps, they speculated, atmospheric refraction was not constant. Perhaps its strength varied from night to night. Or perhaps the adobe walls of their observatories contracted or expanded ever so slightly in response to changes in temperature and humidity, which in turn caused a slight movement in the wire strung up to align the zenith sector along the meridian plane. Or could the star's position actually be changing? Maybe, in their effort to make measurements more precise than anyone had ever made before, they had discovered something new about the universe: A star's movement through the heavens might not be quite as fixed as previously believed. Perhaps a star could *wobble*. They mulled over all these possibilities and then, in late 1741, Bouguer wrote La Condamine with "devastating" news. He had concluded that the problems with their two zenith sectors had never been resolved. Hugo would have to make additional improvements to one of the sectors and build a second one anew. Sighed La Condamine: "At a time when I was flattering myself that all of the obstacles that had been holding us back for so long were going to be removed and that I could finally set off en route back to France, I found myself forced to begin the work again. Although it was painful, it was clear to me that our work was not nearly done."

As frustrating as this all was, the problems with the zenith sectors enabled La Condamine and Bouguer to pursue other investigations, which turned out to be very fruitful. La Condamine took advantage of the hiatus to travel with Pedro Maldonado along his newly opened road to Esmeraldas. In 1736, La Condamine had stumbled through the rain forest along this route, but now the journey could be fairly easily made. This was progress, and once La Condamine was back in Esmeraldas, he happily renewed his study of a thick, white liquid called caoutchouc, which Indians took from the hevea tree. On his first visit to Esmeraldas, he had noticed that local Indians poured caoutchouc between shaped plantain leaves, let it harden, and then used it "for the same purpose we use waxcloth." La Condamine fashioned a waterproof pouch for his scientific instruments from this amazing material, sent back samples of it to France, and, in collaboration with Maldonado, wrote a monograph on its properties, helping to introduce rubber to Europe. La Condamine also came upon an Indian tribe that used a curious white metal to make jewelry, and when metallurgists in France received a sample of it from him, they immediately saw that this "platinum" was going to be very useful. La Condamine was in his element again, mining the New World for plants and minerals— *quinquina,* rubber, platinum—that would, in the years ahead, lead to important advances in medicine and industry.

He and the others chalked up numerous achievements during this time. After his trip to Esmeraldas, La Condamine collaborated with Verguin and Maldonado to produce a map of the Quito Audiencia that was far more accurate than any that had been drawn before. With Bouguer, he continued conducting experiments on the speed of sound and on the expansion and contraction of materials in response to temperature changes. The two observed solar and lunar eclipses, calculated the "obliquity of the ecliptic"— the tilt of the earth toward the sun—and investigated the strength of the magnetic attraction to both poles. "It matters not on what place of the earth we stand," Bouguer concluded, "we shall always feel the action of one pole as powerfully as the other." Perhaps most important of all, La Condamine came up with the idea of using the "length of a seconds pendulum at the equator, at the altitude of

Quito" as a "natural measurement." This would be a ruler defined by the gravitational pull of the earth rather than something arbitrary like a king's foot, and it could provide a standardized measurement for all nations. "One wishes that it would be universal," La Condamine wrote, giving voice to a sentiment that, fifty years later, would inspire France to invent the meter.*

As a final adventure, La Condamine and Bouguer climbed the Pichincha volcano in June 1742. The crater was about a mile away from the summit where they had camped in 1736. They struggled once again with the elements, and at one point, La Condamine, while hiking apart from Bouguer, became lost. The night closed in on him, he was soaking wet and his feet were stuck in the "melting snow," and once more he showed how resourceful he could be:

> I tried in vain to keep moving my feet so as to provide them some heat and by around four in the morning I could no longer feel them at all and feared they had frozen. I remain convinced that I would not have escaped this danger, which was difficult to foresee when setting off for a volcano, if I had not come upon a successful solution involving the bathing of my feet in a natural bath, the nature of which I shall leave to the reader's imagination.

After returning from that climb, La Condamine and Bouguer were ready to say their last good-byes to Quito. Hugo had reengineered their sectors for one final round of celestial observations. Bouguer would go north to their observatory at Cotchesqui (near Yaruqui), while La Condamine would head south to Tarqui. They planned to make simultaneous observations of the same star and exchange results by messenger. After they were done, Bouguer intended to head to France via Cartagena, while La Condamine was planning to go down the Amazon. Only a few had ever traveled from the Andes to the Atlantic coast via this great river, and

---

* The meter is also a "natural measurement," for it was defined as one-ten-millionth of the distance from the equator to the North Pole.

certainly no scientist ever had. Pedro Maldonado was contemplating joining him, although his friends and family were begging him not to go, warning him that it was much too dangerous.

By this time, both of La Condamine's legal imbroglios had concluded, although not quite to his satisfaction. A year earlier, he had won a victory in his pursuit of Senièrgues's killers, the Quito prosecutor in the case deciding that he would seek the death penalty for Leon, Neyra, and Serrano. However, that decision had not been at all popular in Cuenca, and when authorities had tried to arrest the killers, only Leon could be found and put in jail. The Quito court subsequently pronounced the three guilty but commuted their death sentences to eight years of exile, a decision that everyone in Cuenca could accept because, as La Condamine bitterly wrote, "no one obeyed it."

The war of the pyramids, as locals called La Condamine's dispute with Ulloa and Juan, had come to a similar confused end. After his initial argument with the two Spaniards in 1740, La Condamine had erected the monuments without listing their names, since they had insisted on being described as academicians. He also carved a fleur-de-lis, the French coat of arms, on the two pyramids, which of course brought him more trouble. In late 1741, Ulloa and Juan had made a brief visit to Quito, and when they discovered that the pyramids had been built in this manner, they filed suit, arguing that the inscription and presence of the fleur-de-lis "insulted the nation of Spain and his Catholic Majesty personally." The first judge to review the case ordered the pyramids destroyed. A second judge set that order aside and ruled that the inscription had to be changed— the names of the two Spaniards had to be added and they were to be described as participants, not assistants. In addition, the judge ordered La Condamine to carve the escutcheon of the Spanish monarchy *above* the French coat of arms. But that was not the end of the matter. On July 10, 1742, the Quito Audiencia issued a third decision: The escutcheon and the names of Ulloa and Juan were to be inscribed, but La Condamine would be allowed to call them assistants. This lengthy court battle led Isabel's uncle to quip that "justice in Quito is constant and perpetual because the trials never end," and indeed, the Quito Audiencia also sent the matter to the Council of the Indies in Madrid for further review.*

In late August, La Condamine wrapped up a few last matters in Quito. He had a bronze ruler made that was the length of a seconds pendulum at the equator, which he placed into a marble tablet and gave to the Jesuits. This commemorative, humble in kind, was eagerly welcomed. He also sold his quadrant, and in order to do the same with his tent, he set it up in Quito's *plaza mayor,* a spectacle, he reported, that "attracted the attention of the ladies of the city, which I had foreseen and whom I was pleased to honor." Even at this moment of good-bye, the rich women of Quito still viewed the French expedition through romantic eyes.

La Condamine and Bouguer spent the next six months in their respective observatories, and this time they found that their zenith measurements were consistent from one day to the next. Their instruments were working well, and when they exchanged letters in early 1743, it was evident that at last they had a cohesive result. The two ends of their meridian were three degrees, seven minutes, and one second apart in latitude. Since their meridian was 176,940 toises long, this meant that the distance of one degree of arc was 56,749 toises (68.728 miles). There could be no doubt now about the earth's shape. Maupertuis had found that an arc of meridian in Lapland was 57,497 toises. A degree of arc clearly lengthened as one went north from the equator, proving, La Condamine wrote, "that the earth is a spheroid flattened toward the poles." Newton— and not the Cassinis—had been right.

Louis Godin, Ulloa, and Juan finished their celestial observations a year later. The War of Jenkins's Ear fizzled to an end, allowing the two naval officers to return to Quito and resume working

---

* In 1747, the Spanish Crown ordered the pyramids destroyed. As a result, the exact location of the baseline was lost. In honor of the 100-year anniversary of the La Condamine expedition, Ecuador rebuilt the pyramids in 1836, but it lacked the information to erect them on the proper spot.

*Introduct. histor. vis-à-vis la page*

**OBSERVATIONIBUS**
LUDOVICI GODIN, PETRI BOUGUER, CAROLI-MARIÆ DE LA CONDAMINE,
È REGIÀ PARISIENSI SCIENTIARUM ACADEMIÂ,
INVENTA SUNT QUITI:

LATITUDO HUJUSCE TEMPLI, AUSTRALIS GRAD. 0, MIN. 13, SEC. 18: LONGITUDO OCCIDENTALIS AB OBSERVATORIO REGIO, GRAD. 81, MIN. 22.
DECLINATIO ACUS MAGNETICÆ, À BOREA AD ORIENTEM, EXEUNTE ANNO 1736, GRAD. 8, MIN. 45: ANNO 1742, GR. 8, MIN. 21.
INCLINATIO EJUSDEM INFRÀ HORIZONTEM, PARTE BOREALI, CONCHÆ, ANNO 1739, GRAD. 12: QUITI 1741, GRAD. 15.
ALTITUDINES SUPRÀ LIBELLAM MARIS GEOMETRICÈ COLLECTÆ, IN HEXAPEDIS PARISIENSIBUS,
SPECTABILIORUM NIVE PERENNI HUJUS PROVINCIÆ MONTIUM, QUORUM PLERIQUE FLAMMAS EVOMUERUNT,
COTA-CACHE 2567, CAYAMBUR 3028, ANTI-SANA 3116, COTO-PAXI 2952, TONGURAGUA 2623, SANGAY ETIAMNUNC ARDENTIS 2676, CHIMBORASO 3220, ILINISA 2717:
SOLI QUITENSIS IN FORO MAJORI 1462, CRUCIS IN PROXIMO PICHINCHA MONTIS VERTICE CONSPICUÆ 2492:
ACUTIORIS AC LAPIDEI CACUMINIS NIVE PLERUMQUE OPERTI 2492: UT ET NIVIS INFIMÆ PERMANENTIS IN MONTIBUS NIVOSIS.
MEDIA ELEVATIO MERCURII IN BAROMETRO SUSPENSI, IN ZONÀ TORRIDÀ, EAQUE PARUM VARIABILIS,
IN ÔRÀ MARITIMÀ POLLICUM 28, LINEARUM 0: QUITI POLL. 20, LIN. 2½: IN PICHINCHA, AD CRUCEM, POLL. 17, LIN. 7: AD NIVEM POLL. 16, LIN. 0.
SPIRITÙS VINI, QUI IN THERMOMETRO REAUMURIANO, À PARTIBUS 1000, INCIPIENTE GELU, AD 1080 PARTES IN AQUÀ FERVENTE INTUMESCIT
DILATATIO: QUITI, À PARTIBUS 1008, AD PARTES 1028: JUXTÀ MARE, À 1017 AD 1029: IN FASTIGIO PICHINCHA, À 995 AD 1012.
SONI VELOCITAS, UNIUS MINUTI SECUNDI INTERVALLO, HEXAPEDARUM 175.
*PENDULI SIMPLICIS ÆQUINOCTIALIS, UNIUS MINUTI SECUNDI TEMPORIS MEDII, IN ALTITUDINE SOLI QUITENSIS, ARCHETYPUS*

( MENSURÆ NATURALIS EXEMPLAR, UTINAM ET UNIVERSALIS! )
ÆQUALIS HEXAPEDÆ, SEU *PEDIBUS* 3, *POLLICIBUS* 0, *LINEIS* 6: MAJOR IN PROXIMO MARIS LITTORE LIN: MINOR IN APICE PICHINCHA LIN.
REFRACTIO ASTRONOMICA HORIZONTALIS SUB ÆQUATORE MEDIA, JUXTÀ MARE 27 MIN: AD NIVEM IN CHIMBORASO 19′ 51″: EX QUÀ ET ALIIS OBSERVATIS, QUITI 22′ 30″.
LIMBORUM INFERIORUM SOLIS, IN TROPICIS DEC. 1736 ET JUNII 1737, DISTANTIA INSTRUMENTO DODECAPEDALI MENSURATA GRAD. 47, MIN. 28, SEC. 56:
EX QUÀ, POSITIS DIAMETRIS SOLIS, MIN. 32, SEC. 37 ET 31′ 37″: REFRACTIONE IN 66 GRAD. ALTITUDINIS 0′ 15″: PARALLAXI VERÒ 4′ 40″.
ERUITUR OBLIQUITAS ECLIPTICÆ, CIRCA EQUINOCTIUM MARTII 1737, GRAD. 23, MIN. 28, SEC. 38.
STELLÆ TRIUM IN BALTHEO ORIONIS MEDIÆ (BAYERO 1) DECLINATIO AUSTRALIS, JULIO 1737, GRAD. 1, MIN. 23, SEC. 41.
EX ARCU GRADUUM PLUSQUÀM TRIUM REIPSÀ DIMENSO, *GRADUS MERIDIANI SEU LATITUDINIS PRIMUS, AD LIBELLAM MARIS REDACTUS, HEXAP. 56768*
QUORUM MEMORIAM,
AD PHYSICES, ASTRONOMIÆ, GEOGRAPHIÆ, NAUTICÆ INCREMENTA,
HOC MARMORE PARIETI TEMPLI COLLEGII MAXIMI QUITENSIS SOC. JESU AFFIXO, HUJUS ET POSTERI ÆVI UTILITATI V. D. C.
IPSISSIMI OBSERVATORES ANNO CHRISTI M. DCCXLII.

*La mesure ci-dessus qui, pour représenter le Quart du Pendule équinoctial, devoit avoir près de 9 pouces 1 ligne ⅓, est trop longue d'environ ¼ de ligne de trop.*

La Condamine's inscription on a marble tablet advocating the use of the seconds pendulum as a universal measurement.

*From Charles-Marie de La Condamine,* Journal du voyage fait par ordre du roi à l'équateur *(1751).*

with Godin, and the trio concluded that a degree of arc at the equator was 56,768 toises. This was only nineteen toises different from the number obtained by La Condamine and Bouguer; the similarity of the results was evidence that both groups had done their work well. Indeed, more than 200 years later, geodesists would find that their measurements were amazingly accurate, much superior to the ones Maupertuis had made in Lapland.

So much had happened that would have caused lesser men to give up. As Ulloa wrote, theirs had been a mission marked by a "series of labors and hardships, by which the health and vigor of all were in some measure impaired." But they never had, and the fact that they had kept on until they achieved these results spoke volumes about their character. La Condamine and the others may have been deeply flawed human beings—often vain, fractious, and petty—but they had proven themselves to be men of resolve and courage, Enlightenment scientists through and through.

# CHAPTER TEN

# Down the Amazon

J EAN GODIN SAW LA CONDAMINE for the last time in
August 1742, just before La Condamine left for Tarqui. They
embraced, and Jean asked La Condamine to advise the mission stations strung along the Amazon that he, Isabel, and their first child
would soon be following in La Condamine's footsteps. "I reckoned
on taking the same road along the river of Amazons, as much
owing to the wish I had of knowing this way, as to insure for my
wife the most commodious mode of travelling, by saving her a long
journey overland [to Cartagena], through a mountainous country,
in which the only conveyance is by mules."

The expectation of returning home must have helped Jean cope
with his sense of loss at watching La Condamine go. He had always
looked up to La Condamine, who, even more than his cousin
Louis, had appreciated what he had done for the expedition, publicly praising him for the "zeal" he had shown as a signal carrier.
Jean and the other assistants—Verguin, Morainville, Hugo, and
Jussieu—were also having to face the fact that the expedition had

ended, Bouguer and La Condamine were on their way back to France, and yet there was no money for their own return. They had, in some ways, been abandoned by the country they had served for so long.

Although Jean and Isabel had intended to go to France in 1743, the date came and went. They settled for a time in Quito, where Isabel gave birth to their first child, a girl. This was a moment of great joy for the Gramesón family—their first grandchild had arrived—but it turned to sorrow when the baby succumbed at four months to one of the many infectious diseases that so often killed children in colonial South America. Jean, meanwhile, struggled with his business ventures. He dabbled in the textile business and lost money in an ill-fated term as a tax collector. He had obtained the right to collect a 2 percent duty on goods, known as an *alcabala*. The Crown often auctioned this position to the highest bidder, who would then try to make a profit by collecting more than he had paid. This was a risky bet even in the best of times, and Jean had the distinct disadvantage of being French, which only encouraged merchants to ignore him. In early 1744, a devastating epidemic broke out in the Quito area, killing 8,000 in the audiencia, and with Isabel pregnant again, the entire Gramesón clan moved 110 miles south to Riobamba, where they hoped the air was healthier.*

The Riobamba valley, which had so enchanted the expedition members, had been inhabited for several thousand years. When the Incas began their conquest of the Andes, a group known as the Puruhás lived here, many gathered in settlements along a long, beautiful lake, which the Spanish later named Laguna del Colta. The surrounding fields were fertile, and the Puruhás harvested reeds from the shores of the lake to weave mats and baskets. It took the Incas three tries to conquer the proud Puruhás, but once they did, they built a town called Liripamba on the flat plains north of the lake. The buildings in the Inca town were constructed with

---

* This is the distance from Quito to Old Riobamba, or the village of Cajabamba today. Modern Riobamba is about ten miles closer to Quito.

mortarless stonework and included a temple of the sun and other religious buildings.

Diego de Almagro, Pizarro's original partner in the conquest of South America, founded Riobamba atop the ruins of Liripamba on August 15, 1534. He constructed it according to the usual Spanish plan, with a *plaza mayor* and with streets laid out along a rectangular grid. The valley here is slightly higher than at Quito, around 9,000 feet, and the air is further cooled by the nearby presence of Mount Chimborazo, the tallest volcano in the Quito Audiencia at 20,700 feet. Although nights can be chilly, daytime temperatures are warm and springlike, and as early as 1545, a traveler who stopped here, Pedro Cieza de León, waxed eloquent over the town. He was in the midst of a seventeen-year trek by horseback through the viceroyalty, and he found no place he liked as much: "Riobamba is situated in the province of the Puruhás in beautiful fair fields, whose climate, vegetation, flowers and other features resemble those of Spain."

With its rich soil and pleasant weather, Riobamba attracted a number of eminent families, whose names told of nobility and purity of blood. Also living there were many men who could boast of high military rank—sergeants, captains, and generals of the cavalry or infantry. These families, Ulloa noted in his journal, had "been very careful not to diminish either the luster of their families, or their wealth, by promiscuous alliances, marrying only into one another." The Maldonados were one such clan in Riobamba, and several others could trace their roots back to the conquistadors. These wealthy families built several churches that were equal in grandeur to any in Quito, and the one that graced the *plaza mayor,* they liked to boast, had a "steeple that was the tallest in the viceroyalty."

In 1699, the city was nearly destroyed by an earthquake, which killed more than 8,000 people in Riobamba and other Andean towns along the fault line. But the survivors rebuilt their beloved town, erecting homes of light stone and adobe that were, for the most part, only one-story tall, lest another earthquake strike. In the ensuing decades, Riobamba reached the peak of its flowering, and people in other parts of the viceroyalty spoke of its "splendor." More than 16,000 people lived in the city, and the surrounding fields were so fertile, sown with clover and various cereals, that—as Ulloa wrote—it created a "landscape elegantly adorned with such an enchanting variety of colours as painting cannot express." This agricultural bounty was complemented by profits from the textile business. Huge flocks of sheep grazed in the rolling hills above the valley, providing the raw wool for more than twenty textile mills in the district. The town's location, with Quito to the north, Cuenca to the south, and Guayaquil to the west, also made it a vital transportation hub. All of this economic activity in turn attracted a number of jewelry makers, painters, carpenters, and sculptors, their work gracing the sumptuous parlors and dressing rooms in the homes of the elite.

Most wealthy families in Riobamba owned both a country hacienda and a city house, and that was true of the Gramesóns as well. They acquired a large hacienda called Subtipud in Guamote, a village about fifteen miles south of Laguna del Colta, where they produced potatoes and barley. Isabel also purchased several vegetable gardens in Chambo, which was ten or so miles to the east of Riobamba, and some other small properties in that area. Nearer to Riobamba, she bought several alfalfa fields from Franciscan nuns. The fact that she owned these properties in her own name reflected yet another contradiction of colonial Peru: Although elite women were not supposed to work and were expected to stay sheltered in their homes, they nevertheless did enjoy certain legal rights that provided them with a measure of independence. Such laws were the work of humanists in Spain who, since the sixteenth century, had sought to make Spanish society more equitable and just. Even the marriage dowry theoretically remained the property of the woman; the husband was supposed to safeguard these assets during their lives together, and then it would be returned to her upon his death.

In Riobamba, Jean and Isabel lived on the east side of town, just up from the main square. As their home was on the side of a hill,

Mount Chimborazo. Eighteenth-century drawing
by Alexander von Humboldt.
*By permission of the British Library.*

fifty feet or so above the valley floor, they had a particularly good
view of Mount Chimborazo when they stepped out their front
door, and if they climbed up the hill a few blocks more, to the top of
the ridge, they could see a number of volcanoes in the snow-capped
eastern cordillera. To the north was graceful Tungurahua and closer by was rugged Altar, and these volcanoes, forever rumbling and
threatening to erupt, were like living entities to the people of
Riobamba. One tale handed down from the local Indians told of
the three volcanoes being involved in a messy "affair." Massive
Chimborazo was married to slender Tungurahua, but Tungurahua
had betrayed Chimborazo in the past, having had a passionate
romance with fierce-looking Altar. How could Chimborazo not
notice such goings on? One day Chimborazo had looked out over
the entire valley and had blown his top in fury, putting an end to
the adulterous liaison. And now when Tungurahua spit smoke and

fire, locals mused that she must be remembering her old lover and was displaying her anger with Chimborazo for having denied her such pleasure.

The constant rumblings of the earth influenced the religious habits of the people of Riobamba as well. They constructed a large statue of the Virgin Mary atop a nearby mountain, and from this lofty perch she looked over the town and protected them from nature's wrath. On holy days, the priests would lead a procession to the foot of the statue, the people of Riobamba hopeful that their veneration of the Virgin would keep them safe.

While social life in the town centered on the church, as it did in all Peruvian cities, the people enjoyed their games too. Dice and cards were common pastimes, bullfights were held in the *plaza mayor* at regular intervals, and the city was known throughout the audiencia for its cockfights. The young boys in town also crowded neighborhood plazas to play *un juego con una pelota* (a game with a ball), which led church fathers at times to complain about their rowdiness. An attorney for the San Augustín Church wrote to the cabildo,

> There are a great number of young people of bad habits that have established a ball game that has demoralized the spirituality of my convent. They block the street where they gather, and so many are they that they impede the path to the church and that doesn't allow us to celebrate mass.... Furthermore, the ball strikes the convent and causes cracks in the walls, all to the disadvantage of said convent.

The Gramesóns prospered in this lively town. General Pedro Gramesón enjoyed a society where so many had titles—at mass, the pews would be crowded with men wearing medals and other insignia that told of their importance. Isabel's older brother Juan became a priest in the San Augustín order, while her younger brother, Antonio, helped manage Subtipud. Antonio married and some years later became the father of two boys. Isabel's younger sister, Josefa, also wed, and she became the mother of several children. The one person who struggled in Riobamba was Jean Godin. He helped out with the Gramesón properties and continued to trade in textiles, but his business ventures in Riobamba were as unsuccessful as they had been in Quito. Every year he filed a list of his debtors with the town council, and every year it got longer. He simply was not good at getting people to pay him what they owed.

While he and Isabel never stopped talking about France, the years began to slip by. He continued to work on his grammar of the Incan language, always thinking of the moment he would present it as a gift to the king. Since Isabel spoke Quechua, she was able to help him in this endeavor. But they had set down roots in Riobamba—Isabel's family was here and she was a property owner as well—and any possibility of going to France was delayed time and again by her repeated pregnancies. They had a second child and then a third, although each time the joy of birth was followed by grief. Neither child lived more than a few days, and with each death Isabel fell into a period of melancholy. Even Jean began to wonder if he would ever see Saint Amand again. His plans for traveling down the Amazon grew ever dimmer, until, in late 1748, he received a letter, written *eight years earlier,* from his siblings. His father had died, and his family wanted him home at once.

ALTHOUGH PORTUGUESE SLAVE TRADERS had been regularly making their way up the lower part of the Amazon since the early 1600s, by the late eighteenth century, only a few people had ever traveled from the Andes down the river to the Atlantic coast. Indeed, when La Condamine set out, only three or four parties had ever made the 3,000-mile trek, there was no good map of the river, and fantastic tales of Amazón women and El Dorado still swirled about.

The mouth of the Amazon, which is a delta more than 200 miles wide, was discovered by Vicente Yáñez Pinzón, a Spaniard, in 1500. He named it La Mar Dulce, the Sweet Sea. According to the

1494 Treaty of Tordesillas, in which Spain and Portugal divided up the undiscovered world, this part of the New World belonged to Spain. But the coast here was not inviting. To the north were dense forests and swamps, and traveling southeast was difficult because of trade winds and shallow reefs. The Spanish attempted to establish a colony in the mouth of La Mar Dulce in 1531 but quickly gave up, and efforts to explore the Amazon from this direction lay dormant for the next seventy years.

From high up in the Andes, however, the conquistadors could look out at the vast jungle below and dream of riches hidden there. After Pizarro's conquest of the Incas, everyone was certain that there were other wealthy kingdoms to conquer, and rumors were rampant about El Dorado, where gold was said to be so plentiful that the king covered himself in gold dust and washed it off each evening. There were also stories of a magical land in the jungle where cinnamon trees grew. The bark of this tree could provide a fragrant spice highly valued in Europe.

Lured on by such accounts, Pizarro's brother, Gonzalo, headed out from Quito in February 1541 at the head of a large army—220 Spaniards in clanking armor and 4,000 Indians—that brought with it 2,000 hogs, 2,000 hunting dogs, and vast flocks of llamas. This expedition was larger than the one Francisco had mounted to conquer the Incas, but it quickly bogged down in the dense rain forest at the base of the Andes, where Pizarro and his men were plagued by incessant rains and hordes of insects. Although this area was sparsely populated, whenever Pizarro did encounter Indians, he tortured them to reveal the location of El Dorado, and if they professed not to know, he had them burned alive or fed to the dogs. Finally, a local chief, having learned of such interrogation methods, told Pizarro what he wanted to hear—there was a fabulous kingdom ruled by a powerful overlord further to the east. Pizarro and his men wandered deeper into the wilderness until, at last, they came upon a navigable river, the Coca, a tributary of the Napo. Here they stopped long enough to build a small boat to carry their supplies and munitions. The horses and men, however, proceeded on foot along the banks of the river, hacking their way through thick brush, and at the end of ten months, Pizarro and his band of men were still only 300 miles from Quito. They were also struggling to stay alive. They had eaten most of their animals, nearly all of the 4,000 Indians had died, and they had not discovered a speck of gold.

On Christmas Day 1541, Francisco de Orellana, who was the second in command, proposed that he take the boat and sixty men and head downstream in search of food. Pizarro agreed, a decision he came to rue, for he never saw Orellana again. At first, Orellana found nothing. There were no settlements along the river, and his troops were reduced to eating their leather belts and the soles of their shoes, which they cooked with herbs. "They were like madmen, without sense," wrote Friar Gaspar de Carvajal, who accompanied Orellana. But shortly after New Year's Day, they came upon an Indian village, and after Orellana made peace with its chief, the villagers provided them with "meat, partridges, turkeys, and many kinds of fish." They had found the food they had been seeking, but they had proceeded so far down the swift-moving river—as much as seventy-five miles each day—that they realized it would be impossible to return to Pizarro. After waiting three weeks to see if he would come to them, during which time they built a second boat, they decided that they had no choice but to go on without the others. Their only plan was to follow the unknown waterway to its end.

As they proceeded down the Napo, they entered a world that was more and more heavily populated, and shortly after they reached the Amazon, in mid-February, they came upon the kingdom of Aparia the Great, who brought them cats and monkeys to eat. Now they began encountering one "nation" after another— first the Machiparos, who were rumored to number 50,000, and then the even larger kingdom of the Omaguas, which stretched for several hundred miles. "We continued to pass numerous and very large villages," Carvajal wrote, "and the farther we went the more thickly populated and better did we find the land." The Indian tribes, he reported, kept turtles in pens and often supplied Orellana and his men with eggs, partridges, parrots, fish, and a variety of fruit to eat, including pineapples, pears, plums, and custard apples.

By this point, the Amazon was so wide that they could not easily see from one side to the other. There was an endless horizon of green trees along the riverbank, the water moved languidly along, and lush clouds piled up overhead. In early June, they came upon a great river that flowed into the Amazon from the north, which they named the Río Negro after its inky black color. So powerful was this river that its black water did not completely mix with the Amazon's brownish current for twenty leagues, Carvajal reported. Here they began to be attacked with some regularity by Indians, who paddled out in canoes to fight, at times firing so many arrows that the Spaniards' boats looked like porcupines. Even so, Orellana reached the Atlantic in August 1542 with forty-nine of his men still alive. Only eleven had died on the long journey, and eight of the deaths had been due to "natural causes." While he had not found El Dorado, he had discovered a populated world, where food was abundant and the natives were variously welcoming and hostile. Carvajal also told of a tribe of women warriors on the banks of the river, below the Río Negro, and of an encounter with four giant white men. As a result of his account, La Mar Dulce came to be known as the River of the Amazons.

Gonzalo Pizarro and his men had not fared as well. Left behind in the forest, they were reduced to eating lizards and drinking the blood of their horses, which they cooked with herbs in their helmets. A band of eighty half-naked, emaciated, and slightly crazed men arrived back in Quito in August 1542, Pizarro seething with bitterness toward Orellana, whom he accused of treason. In the fate of the two groups, though, one could see a picture of two wildernesses. Along the foot of the Andes was a dense and forbidding jungle. But after passing through it, one came to the navigable waters of the Amazon, along which game and food could be found. Travel along this waterway, except for attacks from natives, was fairly easy.

Although Spaniards in Peru continued to dream of El Dorado, only a few dared to venture into the jungle after Pizarro's failed adventure. The next expedition of any note was sent in 1560 by the viceroy of Peru, who did so partly as a way of getting rid of trouble-makers in the colony. Three hundred men led by Pedro de Ursúa departed from Lima, heading into the jungle via the Huallaga River and with orders to find El Dorado and conquer the Omaguas. Ursúa brought along his mistress, which stirred up jeal-ousy among his men, and on New Year's Day 1561, Lope de Aguirre—one of history's great psychopaths—led a mutiny, killing Ursúa and hatching a plot to return to Peru to conquer it. The route Aguirre took across the Amazon basin to reach the Atlantic is uncertain even today. Either he followed the Amazon to its end, or he turned up the Río Negro, crossed over into the Orinoco River, and followed that waterway north to the Caribbean. What is known is that on July 20, 1561, he seized the island of Margarita, slaughtering anyone who dared to stand in his way. He then launched an invasion of the mainland, where he was defeated by royalist troops and beheaded.

Aguirre's was the last transcontinental journey through the Amazon basin for nearly eighty years. Heading east from the Andes, through the dense rain forest of the mountains, was so diffi-cult that it seemed to bring ruin to those who tried. However, at the end of the sixteenth century, the Dutch, English, and French all established colonies at the mouth of the Amazon, kicking off European exploration of the Amazon from the eastern end. The Portuguese arrived in 1616, setting up a military fort named Belém do Pará. Although this was supposed to be Spanish land, at that time Spain and Portugal were united under one king, and so Spain, struggling to manage its colonies in Peru and Mexico, was only too happy to see the Portuguese take on the settlers from other coun-tries. Over the next ten years, the Portuguese drove the French, Dutch, and English out of the Amazon, and they moved north to the swampy coasts of Guiana.

South of the Amazon, Portuguese settlers along the coast had already carved out huge sugar plantations, and they now looked to the river as a source of slave labor. The Indians, in their words, were "red gold." Although enslavement of the indigenous people was theoretically illegal, both Spanish and Portuguese law provided the settlers with loopholes to exploit. Settlers were allowed to make slaves out of "prisoners taken in just wars," and a just war was in the eye of the beholder. They were also allowed to enslave Indians captured by other tribes. The rational for that provision was that the "freed" Indians became their indentured servants who had to work the plantations in order to "repay" the ransom. Once the Portuguese gained control of the river's mouth, the slave trade exploded and the mass migration of Indians along the Amazon began. Some tribes, such as the Omaguas, moved further upriver to escape, and others fled into the interior.

As the slave traders conducted their hunting expeditions, they expanded Portugal's control over the Amazon. Although Portugal and Spain may have shared a king, the two countries remained separate, and the Amazon—in the 1630s—was clearly up for grabs. Portugal was laying claim to the vast interior of the continent, which was why, in February 1637, Portuguese military commanders in Pará, on the southern shore of the delta, reacted with alarm when two Spanish Franciscan monks and five Spanish soldiers arrived in their port after having canoed *down* the river. Were the Spanish going to push forward territorial claims from the west?

The Franciscans had not made their voyage with any such intention. They had left Quito several years earlier in order to establish a mission on the Napo River, but hostile Indians had driven them off, and they had subsequently traveled several thousand miles to Pará. Even so, their visit stirred the Portuguese to mount a huge expedition, under the command of Captain Pedro Teixeira, to march up the river and formally stake Portugal's claim to it. He led a force of seventy soldiers traveling in a fleet of forty-seven canoes, with 1,200 Indians and Negroes manning the oars, and even after he had reached the end of the navigable part of the Napo River, he and his soldiers continued on, arriving in Quito in October 1638. Their trip had taken a year, and now it was Spain's turn to be alarmed. The authorities in Quito ordered the Portuguese crew back to Pará but placed several Spaniards on board, including a Jesuit priest, Cristóbal de Acuña, who was told to produce a report on the river. It was the first time that Spain had sought to survey this vast region.

The party left Quito on February 16, 1639, and reached Pará ten months later. Along the way, Teixeira staked out an arbitrary boundary line between the two countries, using a carved log to mark the spot. He also drew up a formal "Act of Possession" to back Portugal's legal claim to the lion's share of the Amazon. Meanwhile, Acuña published an account of their voyage in which he sang of the river's riches and recommended that Spain should occupy all of it. The Amazon, he marveled, had more people than the "Ganges, Tigris, or Nile." Many of the natives were friendly, and he hailed the Omaguas as the "most intelligent, the best governed on the river." There were healing drugs to be found in the forest, huge trees that could be harvested for shipbuilding, and fertile riverbanks that could be used to grow manioc, sweet potatoes, pineapples, guavas, and coconuts. The river was swimming with fish, the woods were full of game—including tapirs, deer, peccaries, monkeys, and armadillos—and the lagoons were populated by numerous birds. His was a wilderness that was more bountiful paradise than fearsome jungle. "Settlements are so close together that one is scarcely lost sight of before another comes into view," he wrote. "It may be imagined how numerous are the Indians who support themselves from so plentiful a country." Yet lower on the Amazon, closer to the mouth, he found a river undergoing a transformation, its banks emptied by the slave trade, "with no one [left] to cultivate the land."

Acuña's book was titled *New Discovery of the Great River of the Amazons,* and in many ways he provided a straightforward account of what he saw. However, he also gave credence to what he had heard along the way about strange people living inland from the Amazon. He wrote of lands inhabited by giants and dwarfs, and of a race of people whose feet grew backward so that those hunting them would be led astray by their tracks. He confirmed that a tribe of warrior women inhabited this jungle, up north toward Guiana. These tales kept alive the picture of the Amazon as a wilderness that was both bountiful and magical, a world where explorers could indeed find great treasures.

Portugal now had little motivation to rein in its slave trade, which exploded in earnest. Entire tribes were "descended" down the river by slave traders, and the enslaved Indians died in great numbers from disease, despair, and malnutrition. "They killed them as one kills mosquitoes," protested a Jesuit priest, João Daniel. One after another the Indian tribes disappeared, falling like dominoes as one went upriver. One slave trader complained, in 1693, that it was necessary to travel two months from Pará to find any natives to capture.

Daniel and other Jesuits sought to protect Indians from the slave trade by building missions where they could come and live, and presumably find a safe refuge. However, the Portuguese stations were something of a double-edged sword, for the priests would convert the Indians to Christianity and often force them to adopt Christian ways, thereby destroying their culture and tribal identity. Meanwhile, Spain turned to the Jesuits and their missionary work with a political goal in mind: By encouraging the black-robed priests to build missions along the upper Amazon, Spain could hope to take possession of this region and thus prevent the Portuguese from grabbing an ever greater share of the Amazon. The boundary between the two countries would effectively be established by the mission stations rather than by any formal treaty between the two countries.

Spanish Jesuits erected their first such mission at Borja in 1658, at the foot of the Andes, where the Marañón River* pours through a nasty strait called the Pongo de Manseriche. A little while later, they established a second settlement further downstream at

---

* The Marañón is the name used for the upper Amazon.

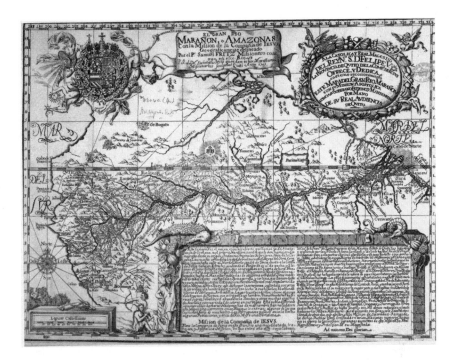

**Samuel Fritz's Map of the Amazon, 1707.**
*By permission of the British Library.*

Lagunas, where the Huallaga flows into the Amazon. In 1681, representatives of the Omaguas traveled upriver to Lagunas to request that a missionary be sent to them—they needed protection from the Portuguese slave traders—and the priest who arrived five years later was a memorable, ruddy-faced German, Samuel Fritz. For the next thirty-seven years, he worked along the banks of the Amazon, tending to a "parish" that extended for more than 1,000 miles. During this time, he produced the first somewhat reliable map of the river.

Fritz's mapmaking journey arose from what is possibly the longest trip ever made in search of medical help. In 1689, he was struck by malaria and for days lay dying in a flooded Yurimagua village. Everyone had fled to higher ground except for a lone boy, who tried to comfort him. Fritz was so weak that lizards and rats ran across his body, and at night his sleep was disturbed by the malevolent grunting of crocodiles outside his hut. At last, he gathered enough strength to get into a canoe and head downriver for help. Once in motion, he stayed in motion, and he traveled more than 2,000 miles to Pará, where the Portuguese promptly arrested him, reasoning that he was a spy. After eighteen months in prison, he was freed by an order from Portugal's King Pedro II. On his return upriver, with the aid of a few crude instruments, he was able to roughly chart the Amazon. He traveled all the way to Lima, and it was this map, along with Cristóbal de Acuña's book, that inspired La Condamine to take this route home.

FROM THE BEGINNING of the French expedition, there had been some talk that the group, as a whole, would return via the Amazon. But as the mission went on and on and the group came to be rent by dissension, that idea faded away. However, La Condamine never lost interest in the route, and as early as 1738, he had initiated the process of obtaining a passport from the Portuguese. "As for the discomforts," he wrote in his journal in 1741, "I knew these would be great, and everything which I had heard only served to increase the wish I had to experience it for myself."

At the last minute, La Condamine also coaxed Pedro Maldonado to join him. Maldonado, who had finished his Esmeraldas road by 1742, had initially begged off, his family urging him not to go on such a dangerous venture. By the time Maldonado made up his mind to ignore his family's advice, it was too late for him to leave with La Condamine, so they decided to take different routes to the river and meet up in Lagunas. Maldonado, leaving from the Riobamba area, would skirt around the base of Mount Tungurahua and head east on foot down a steep gorge that spilled out of the Andes; then he would follow the Bobonaza and Pastaza Rivers to the Amazon. La Condamine, who would be departing from Tarqui after finishing his celestial observations, decided to head south to Jaen, where, after a short journey overland, he could pick up the

La Condamine's Voyage Down the Amazon, 1743

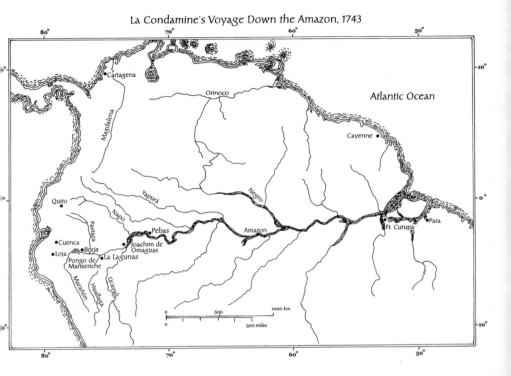

Marañón. This would allow him to draw a map of the entire navigable part of the Amazon and would also enable him to see whether "the famous strait known under the name of Pongo de Manseriche was as terrible up close at it had been described to me from afar." In Quito, he noted, they spoke of this passage "only in hushed tones of admiration and fear."

La Condamine's journey got off to a rough start in Tarqui. He went to Cuenca to hire mules and porters, but the people there were still furious over his efforts to prosecute Senièrgues's killers, and most refused to help. When he left on May 11, 1743, for his long journey down the Amazon, La Condamine was accompanied only by a Negro servant, and he was hauling along a sixteen-foot telescope as well as his precious scientific papers. These got soaked when his mule stumbled and fell into a river, and when he arrived in the town of Zaruma, only a short distance south of Tarqui, he was told it was fortunate he had taken an uncommon route, for several friends of Neyra and Leon had been laying "in wait on the high road," eager to play him a "bad game."

In Loja, La Condamine stopped long enough to collect nine saplings of the cinchona tree, along with some seeds. He placed the plants in an earthen box, hoping to bring them back alive to Paris. By late June he had arrived in Jaen, and there he paused long enough to summarize all his observations and arc measurements. He gave this report to a local official in case he "should die en route."

As he expected, his descent into the jungle proved memorable. He had to cross numerous boiling streams and rivers, either by inching his way along the swaying bridges he had always found so nerve-racking or by floating across "on rafts constructed on the spot." His papers and other goods were stuffed into baskets covered with ox hides, and in the incessant rain, they began to rot and "exhale an intolerably offensive smell." When he reached the small hamlet of Chuchunga, he hired local Indians to build a balsa raft, and there, at an altitude he calculated to be about 1,500 feet above sea level, he entered the flow of waters out of the Andes that would eventually take him to the Atlantic. The Chuchunga River flowed into the uppermost reaches of the Marañón, where, over the course of the next four days, he encountered one obstacle after another on his way to the Borja mission. At one point, he was caught in a whirlpool for more than an hour, "incessantly whirled about" until four Indians on the riverbank threw him a liana rope and pulled him free. On another occasion, he had tethered his raft to tree branches in order to sleep on it for the night and awoke to discover that the river was dropping so fast that he needed to hurriedly untie his craft, lest it end up "suspended in the air," dangling by the rope. The river, he determined, fell *twenty-five feet* over the course of the night, a dramatic illustration of how its flow was affected by rain—or the relative absence of it—along the eastern slopes of the Andes. La Condamine also had to pass through a stretch of riverbank that was home to the Jibaros, a fierce tribe who had fled to this remote region in order to escape from the Spanish, who were forcing them to work in gold mines in the Andes. "Ever since," La Condamine wrote, "secluded in inaccessible woods, they preserve themselves independent, and impede the navigation of the river."* Finally, on July 12, he arrived at the infamous Pongo de Manseriche, where the Marañón narrowed from 1,500 feet to 100 feet, the water surging between two huge walls of rock. La Condamine held his breath as his raft gathered speed:

> The waters seem to hurl themselves and as they dash against the rocks, deafen the ear with a tremendous noise. ... I was flung two or three times violently against the rocks in the course of the different windings. It would have been terrifying if I had not been warned. A canoe would be dashed into a thousand pieces, but since the beams of the raft are neither nailed nor dovetailed together, the flexibility of the lianas, by which they are fastened, have the effect of a spring, and deadens the shock so, that when the strait is passed in a raft, these percussions occur unheeded.

The six-mile straight was nature's portal into the Amazon. After the Pongo, La Condamine and his raft popped out onto a lazy river, and just as he had once marveled at his first glimpse of Quito, he was now transfixed by the jungle:

> I found myself in a new world, separated from all human intercourse, on a fresh-water sea, surrounded by a maze of lakes, rivers, and canals, penetrating in every direction the gloom of an immense forest. ... New plants, new animals, and new races of men were exhibited to my view. Accustomed during seven years to mountains lost in clouds, I was wrapped in admiration at the wide circle embraced by the eye, restricted here by no other boundary than the horizon.

---

* The Jibaros later became known for their custom of shrinking the heads of those they killed.

La Condamine rafts
through the Pongo de
Manseriche.
*Bibliotheque de l'Institut
de France, Paris.
Lauros-Giraudon-
Bridgeman Art Library.*

La Condamine reached Lagunas a week later, where Maldonado, who had experienced "many dangers and great fatigue" on his trek down the Bobonaza, had been waiting for six weeks. There they picked up new transportation, two dugout canoes "42 feet and 44 feet long," each fashioned from a single tree trunk. Indians paddled from the front of the canoes while La Condamine and Maldonado sat in the rear, each beneath a canopy of palm fronds, and in this relative comfort, they headed out on their 2,400-mile journey, taking notes of the flora, fauna, and human inhabitants, and mapping the Amazon's course.

La Condamine had brought along the telescope in order to observe Jupiter's moons, as this would enable him to establish his longitude, and once he had that bearing, he and Maldonado used a compass, watch, and portable gnomon—an instrument for determining latitude from the sun's position—to plot the river's course, carefully penciling in on their charts its many bends and turns, its islands, and the tributaries that flowed into it. They also measured the river's breadth and how fast it flowed, and they tried to determine its depth at various places, although on several occasions, even after letting out a line 600 feet long, they could not find its bottom. "Every instant of my time was employed," La Condamine joyfully reported. Along the way, he described the many animals he found, including turtles, crocodiles, tigers, monkeys, sea cows, and electric eels. This last creature, he noted, delivered a shock so powerful that it could "lay one prostrate." They observed blood-sucking bats, toucans, porcupines, sloths, and boars; measured snakeskins longer than fifteen feet; and cataloged exotic insects. He preserved in wine a particularly nasty worm called "suglacuru," which "grows in the flesh of men and animals to the size of a bean, and occasions intolerable anguish." La Condamine investigated too the blow-gun and poison arrows that natives used to hunt game, and he figured out why the jungle toxin—which centuries later would gain a valuable place in medicine as the muscle-paralyzing agent curare—did not make the meat inedible:

> By a strong puff of the breath, they dart these arrows to the distance of thirty or forty paces, and scarcely ever miss their aim. This simple instrument serves as an admirable substitute among all these savages for firearms. The points of these diminutive arrows, as well as those they shoot from their bows, are steeped in a poison of such activity, that it kills any animal from which the instrument dipped in it may chance to draw blood. We scarcely ever, in going down the river, ate of game killed by other means than these arrows, the tips of which we often discovered in eating, between our teeth. There is no danger from such occurrences, for the venom of this poison is only mortal when absorbed by the blood, in which case it is no less fatal to man than to animals. The antidote is salt, but of safer dependence, sugar.

For the first time ever, the Amazon was being seen through the eyes of an Enlightenment scientist. The chroniclers who had come before him, Carvajal and Acuña, were men of the cloth, and while they had sought to be faithful recorders, they belonged to an earlier age, when the world was seen through the prism of religious teachings and medieval mythologies. La Condamine poked into the tales of El Dorado and Amazon women with reason as his guide. The story of a kingdom with "roofs and walls of gold plates," he said, was one that "nothing but a thirst for gold could render credible," and yet he did find a kernel of truth in it. In the past, a fierce tribe called the Manaos had obtained gold from an isolated people living along the Yapurá River, a tributary of the Amazon just above the Río Negro, and they had pounded this gold into plates and other trinkets, which they traded with other nations along the Amazon. Moreover, about 100 miles up the Yapurá River was a small lake, and from these few facts, he concluded, there arose a fantastic tale of a golden city of Manoa on Lake Parima. The Europeans arrived in the Amazon wanting to believe in this story, and Native Americans—by pointing to an El Dorado some distance away— lent credence to it in order to "rid themselves of unwelcome guests." He came to a similar conclusion about the story of the Amazons. Throughout his trip, he queried natives about this legend, and everyone replied in a similar fashion: There had once been a tribe of women who lived without husbands and who wore green stones, and everyone said they had moved away from the river to a place of low-lying mountains near the sea. This described the hills of Guiana. Thus, La Condamine reasoned, there probably had once been a group of women along the Amazon living without men, but all the other fantastic details—of women who cut off one of their breasts to shoot arrows better or killed their sons at birth— were "probably exaggerations or inventions of Europeans informed of the practices attributed to the Amazons of Asia, and which a fondness for the wonderful may have caused the natives of America, upon learning these tales from them, to interweave in their narratives."

La Condamine's investigation of these two tales was evidence, yet again, of his insatiable curiosity. He had been gone from France for more than eight years, but rather than hurrying down the river, he stopped time and again in order to learn about this world. He investigated the course of the Río Negro, and he continued his studies of rubber, observing with delight how the Omaguas used it to fashion a hollow ball, into which they would stick a cane and in this manner manufacture a syringe. He wrote of the resins and oils that flowed from different trees in the jungle, queried a Carmelite priest about how he inoculated natives against smallpox, and gathered samples of the toxic barbasco root that Amazon Indians threw into marshes and small lakes to stun the fish: "While thus torpified," he wrote, "the fish float on the water and are taken with the hand; by means of these plants, the Americans catch as many fish as they please." Scientists later followed up on La Condamine's report to develop an insecticide from this natural toxin, a chemical known today as rotenone.

Maldonado and La Condamine reached Pará on September 19, 1743. The town boasted such amenities that they fancied themselves "at once transported to Europe." Indeed, having reentered the civilized world, they could now see that their journey had unfolded in three stages: The first and most difficult segment was the descent down the slopes of the Andes to the Amazon, which required travel by foot, mule, balsa rafts, and small canoes. The second was the voyage in dugout canoes from Lagunas through the rest of Spanish territory, to slightly below the Napo River. The third, after crossing the border into Portuguese land, was the trip in a much larger canoe, with fourteen rowers, during which their Portuguese hosts provided them with "courtesies which made us for the time forget we were in the center of America." Their journey had become progressively easier as they had gone along, and in each of these three segments, they had encountered natives in different stages of change, away from what they had been before the Europeans arrived.

As La Condamine had made his way to Borja, he had scurried through lands newly inhabited by the Jibaros, who had fled from their original homes, higher up in the cloud forests, in order to escape from the Spanish. Maldonado also had encountered many "dangers" as he made his way down the Bobonaza. This strip of jungle on the eastern edge of the Andes had been very sparsely populated when the Spanish conquistadors arrived, but now it was becoming a last refuge for native groups, with some coming down from the Andes to flee the Spanish and others moving upriver to escape the Portuguese. Partly as a result, this was the one part of the wilderness where travelers still had to fear encountering hostile Indians, including a few, La Condamine wrote, who were "man-eaters."

However, once La Condamine and Maldonado reached the upper Amazon, this worry disappeared. "On the banks of the Marañón there is now no warlike tribe hostile to Europeans, all having either submitted or withdrawn into the interior," La Condamine reported. Yet along this stretch of the Spanish Amazon, many natives still retained their traditional dress and customs. Around Pebas, the last Spanish mission before the border with Portugal, La Condamine and Maldonado met Indians who put bones through their nostrils and lips, wore feathers through their cheeks, and used narrow cylinders of wood to prolong their ear lobes. "The chief decoration is a large nosegay or tuft of herbs and flowers, which is drawn through this hole, forming most uncommon pendants," La Condamine wrote. The Omaguas were now living along this part of the river as well. Whereas they had once ruled over a 600-mile stretch of river below the Napo, they were now gathered above it, around the mission station of Saint Joachim de Omaguas. But they too had kept many of their old ways. "Of all the savages who live on the borders of the Amazon River," La Condamine wrote, "they are the most civilized despite their strange use of flattening their forehead, the artificial length of the ears, and their exceptional liking of witchcraft." The Omaguas used two boards to flatten the foreheads of their newborns, he noted, in order "to make them more perfectly resemble the full moon."

A much different scene unfolded once La Condamine and Maldonado entered Portuguese territory. Below the Napo, the

La Condamine's map of the Amazon.

*From Charles-Marie de La Condamine,* Relation abrégée d'un voyage
fait dans l'intérieur de l'Amérique Méridionale *(1778).*

banks of the Amazon were silent, even empty. They traveled for
several days and nights "without coming across any signs of life."
This was a stretch of river where Acuña, a century earlier, had
come upon one village after another, the natives farming and raising turtles in pens. That world was gone. There were five lonely
Carmelite missions spaced out along the Amazon between the
Napo and the Río Negro, a distance of more than 1,000 miles, and
the handful of Indians living in these stations had been thoroughly
transformed: The "native women [were] all clad in Britany linen,"
and the Indians used "coffers with locks and keys, iron utensils,
needles, knives, scissors, combs and a variety of little European articles." When La Condamine and Maldonado reached the Río
Negro, they found that slave traders, known as "redemption
troops," were scouring that river clean as well, every year advancing "farther into the country." The Jesuit João Daniel estimated
that the population along the Amazon and its main tributaries had
declined to a thousandth of what it had been 200 years earlier. In
his journey down the Amazon, La Condamine had revealed the
wonders of a great wilderness and at the same time—somewhat
unwittingly—borne witness to the tragic tale of a civilization lost.

· · ·

LA CONDAMINE AND MALDONADO parted ways in Pará. Maldonado, mindful that the Portuguese had imprisoned Father Fritz as a spy, told the authorities in Pará that he was French, traveling on La Condamine's passport, and on December 3, he sailed for Portugal. La Condamine traveled by sea canoe to Cayenne, and along the way, the trunk containing his cinchona saplings was swept overboard. In Cayenne, he repeated Richer's 1672 experiments with the seconds pendulum, and then—fearful that if he traveled on a French boat, he might lose his cherished papers to English pirates—he traveled to Dutch Guiana in order to find passage to Europe on a ship sailing under the flag of the Netherlands. He departed on September 3, 1744, and while his trip across the Atlantic was not uneventful—pirates attacked the Dutch ship twice—he successfully arrived back in Paris on February 23, 1745, a full decade after he had left.

Initially, La Condamine did not receive the welcome he hoped for. Debate over the earth's shape was fizzling to an end by this time. Not only had Maupertuis returned with his results many years earlier, but the academy had also recently remeasured a degree of arc in France, which had shown that the Cassinis' earlier work had been in error. Voltaire even made fun of La Condamine with a witty put-down: "In dull, distant places, you suffered to prove what Newton knew without having to move."

Even so, the academy members understood the larger accomplishments of the mission. As La Condamine told his peers shortly after he returned, knowing that the earth bulged at the equator "furnishes a new argument and demonstration of the rotation of the earth on its axis, a rotation that holds for the entire celestial system." Their work at the equator, he added, "has put us on the path of even more important discoveries, such as the nature of the universal laws of gravity, the force that animates all heavenly bodies and which governs all the universe."

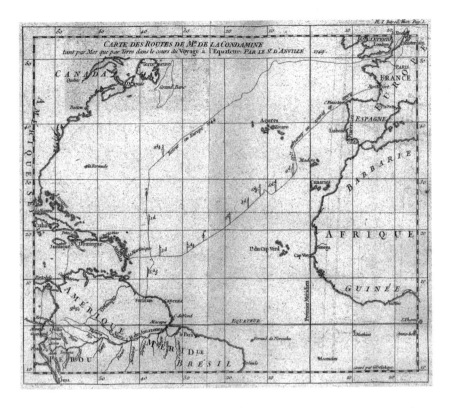

**La Condamine's map of his 10-year journey.**
*From Charles-Marie de La Condamine,* Relation abrégée d'un voyage
fait dans l'intérieur de l'Amérique Méridionale *(1778).*

Furthermore, this advance in physics was just the beginning of
what had been achieved by the Peruvian mission. La Condamine's
study of the cinchona tree promised to help Europe improve its use
of quinine as an antidote for malaria and other fevers. He had sent
back samples of a useful new metal, platinum, and his writings on
rubber were stirring imaginative thoughts on how to use it for
manufacturing purposes. Europe now had a detailed map of the
entire northern part of South America and a naturalist's view of the
Andes and the Amazon. Together these amounted to a grand
achievement: The mission had been a transforming moment in the
*development* of science, and it was Voltaire who understood this

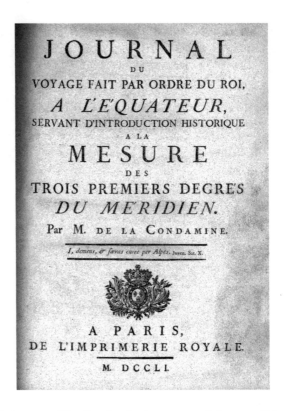

**Title page of La Condamine's account of the expedition.**
*From Charles-Marie de La Condamine,* Journal du voyage fait par
ordre du roi à l'équateur *(1751).*

best. "By all appearances our wise men only added a few numbers
to the science of the sky," he wrote, "but the scope of their work
was really much broader." The mission to Peru, he said, was a
"model for all scientific expeditions" to follow.

La Condamine's skills as a writer also brought him a great deal
of public adulation. He wrote a colorful account of his travels, complete with a blow-by-blow description of the war of the pyramids
and Senièrgues's murder. As his fame grew, science academies in
London, Berlin, Saint Petersburg, and Bologna all made him an
honorary member. The one sour note in this chorus of acclaim was
sounded, oddly enough, by Bouguer. Long jealous of La

Condamine's popularity, he published an account of their arc measurements in which he disparaged La Condamine's talents as a scientist, suggesting that he had brought little more than energy to the
project. "Bouguer could not disguise his feelings of superiority as a
mathematician over La Condamine," observed one of their peers,
Jacques Delille. He "felt that he should be the primary object of
public affection." Bouguer's unflattering words set off a pointless
quarrel that lasted for years, a dispute all the more difficult to com-
prehend, Delille wrote, because it was "between two men who for
several years had slept in the same room, in the same tent, and often
in the open air huddled under the same coat, and who in all this
time publicly acknowledged a great respect for one another."

Ulloa and Juan made an equally big splash in Europe upon their
return. They had sailed from Callao, near Lima, on October 22,
1744, but on different boats and each with a copy of their papers, a
precaution in case one of them did not return safely home. The two
left from Callao on French frigates, and while Juan made it back
with little difficulty, Ulloa's ship was attacked by an English vessel,
and he was taken to England as a prisoner. However, once the academicians of London understood who was in their prison at
Portsmouth, Ulloa was released and named a fellow of the Royal
Society of London, its members praising him as a "true caballero"
and "man of merit." This was a rare honor for a foreigner, and even
more so for one who had arrived in England in shackles. In 1748,
he and Juan became famous throughout Europe when they published a popular five-volume account of their travels, *Relación
histórica del viage a la América Meridional.* Their book pulled back
the curtain on South America and was translated into German,
French, English, and Dutch, the Jesuit scholar Andres Burriel
praising it as "one of the best and most useful books that have been
published in our tongue."

Naturally, bits and pieces of this news filtered back to the others
still in Peru. Maldonado was made a corresponding member of the
Royal Society of London and of the French Academy of Sciences

for having traveled the Amazon with La Condamine, and his election made all of Riobamba proud.* But hearing this was bittersweet for Jean Godin and the others, a reminder that they had been forgotten. Of all the assistants, only one, Verguin, had managed to make it back to Europe by the end of 1748. Hugo had married a Quito woman and settled there, writing plaintively to La Condamine that he had "no other wish but to find a way to return to France, to finish his days in his own country." He subsequently disappeared; by 1748, nobody knew where he was. Morainville, meanwhile, had become the third member of the expedition to die. He had fallen from a scaffold while helping to build a church in Riobamba, a job he had taken to earn money to return home. As for Jussieu and Louis Godin, both had been told by the Quito Audiencia at the end of the expedition that they would not be allowed to leave. Jussieu's medical skills were needed because a smallpox epidemic had erupted, and the audiencia was so insistent on this point that it promised to imprison anyone who tried to help him go. Louis Godin had been barred from departing because of his debts, and at the request of the Peruvian viceroy, he had taken a position as professor of mathematics at the University of San Marcos in Lima.

Their delayed departures had in turn led to greater heartache. The French Academy prohibited any member from taking an academic post in a foreign country, and Louis Godin's letter explaining why he had done so never made it to Paris, for the ship carrying his letter was raided by pirates. The French Academy learned about his professorship through a third party and expelled him, thinking that he had voluntarily chosen to leave the service of France. Jussieu, meanwhile, had become broken in body and spirit. When he was finally allowed to leave Quito, he traveled to Lima to see Godin and then headed further south on a plant-hunting expedition, dedicated to his botany, but enveloped in a sadness

---

* Maldonado never returned to Riobamba. He died in Europe on November 17, 1748, from a fever, at age forty.

so profound, he wrote, that his "heart [was] covering itself with a black veil."

As for Jean, he was hatching a half-crazed plan to bring Isabel, who was pregnant for a fourth time, to France.

His FATHER'S DEATH was not the only reason that Jean and Isabel had decided that it was time to leave Riobamba. Events were brewing that suggested the good times for the colonial elite in the village might be coming to an end. Growing social unrest was making all the landowners nervous. The War of Jenkins's Ear had forced Spain to greatly increase its military spending, and in order to raise that money, the Crown had hiked the duties and taxes that already so oppressed the Indian population. Bitter natives complained that colonial authorities wanted to tax the air they breathed. Some Indians had even taken up arms against their Spanish masters—there had been five revolts in the Andes since 1740. Equally troubling, the local economy was beginning to falter. Jean's difficulty in collecting debts owed him was simply part of a larger malaise. After Britain sacked Porto Bello in 1740, Spain had shut down its fleet system for carrying goods to Peru and had begun allowing individual ships—including some non-Spanish vessels—to sail to any number of colonial ports. Many trading boats had started sailing around Cape Horn to Lima, loaded with cheap textiles from the mills of Europe, and this competition was driving more than a few obraje owners into bankruptcy.

With such uncertainty in the air, both Jean and Isabel believed that the time was right for moving to Europe. For him it was a chance to return home, and for her—at age twenty-one—it was a dream revived. But there was no easy way to travel to France. One possibility was to head to Lima and find passage on a trading vessel that was planning to sail to Europe via Cape Horn, but that would require both a lengthy journey by land and a very long sea voyage. Heading north from Riobamba to Cartagena offered a slightly better option, yet it would still require several months of travel by mule along the rocky paths of the Andes and over a pass littered with the bones of dead mules, one that, as Bouguer had said, was "never hazarded without the utmost dread." The third route was the one "opened up" by La Condamine, and next to the other two alternatives, it offered an intriguing possibility. While the first part of the trip would admittedly be arduous—and almost everyone in the Andes spoke of it with fear—once the Amazon was reached, traveling by canoe from one mission station to the next might be fairly pleasant.

Or at least that was the thought, and so Jean concocted a plan: He would travel down the length of the Amazon to see if it would provide a suitable way home, come back up the river to pick up his wife and child, and then—if his scouting voyage had gone well— the three of them could follow this route to France. This meant he would have to travel the length of the river three times, an itinerary that covered more than 10,000 miles and could be expected to take at least two years. Even if all went as hoped, the plan had its evident shortcomings. Yet Jean, looking back on his past adventures, was certain that La Condamine would understand:

> Anyone but you, Sir, might be surprised at my undertaking thus lightly a voyage of fifteen hundred leagues,* for the mere purpose of preparing accommodations for a second; but you will know that travels in that part of the world are undertaken with much less concern than in Europe; and those I had made during twelve years for reconnoitering the ground for the meridian of Quito, for fixing signals on the loftiest mountains, in going to and returning from Cartagena, had made me perfectly a veteran.

He left on March 10, 1749, and although he said his good-byes to Isabel with some sadness and reluctance—she was now in her fourth month of pregnancy and was beginning to show—he felt a

---

* Fifteen hundred leagues is roughly equal to 4,500 miles; Jean apparently understood the journey to be even longer than it actually is.

great deal of excitement, too. He was embarking on an adventure that had brought fame and honor to those who had gone before—Acuña, Father Fritz, La Condamine, and even Maldonado. He intended to make his own observations of the Amazon along the way and gather plants and seeds for the king's garden. He had also purchased a grammar of the Incan language printed in Lima,* and once he made it to the Atlantic coast, he planned on sending it to the king as a gift. Although the grammar was not his own work, it would make the king's ministers aware of his interest in Quechua and of the fact that he hoped one day to complete his own study. Jean was nearly thirty-six years old now, and he saw this voyage as a chance to make a name for himself.

His trip downriver went well. He followed Maldonado's footsteps down the Bobonaza and Pastaza Rivers, and while this part proved difficult, just as it had for Maldonado, once he reached the mission stations on the upper Amazon, the priests treated him warmly. Even though six years had gone by, La Condamine's visit was still fresh in their minds. Further downriver, the Portuguese Carmelites provided him with the same welcome. "With no other recommendation to the notice of the Portuguese than arose from the remembrance of the intimation afforded by you in 1743," he wrote La Condamine, "that one of the companions of your travels would follow the same way, I was received in all the Portuguese settlements, by the missionaries and commandants of the forts, with the utmost courtesy." He reached Pará in September, his seven-month trip down the Amazon having unfolded "without incident," and the governor of the port, Francis Mendoza Gorjaô, treated him like a visiting dignitary. "He received me with open arms, and insisted on my making his house and table my own during a week that I stopped with him." Traveling on his own, Jean was at last stepping out into the limelight, or so it must have seemed. While still in Pará, he happily wrote La Condamine of his plan to return upriver to fetch his family as soon as he obtained the

---

* The printing press did not arrive in the Quito Audiencia until 1754.

necessary passport from Portugal. For this, he had written Antoine-Louis Rouillé, minister of the French navy, asking that he petition the Portuguese on his behalf. Jean was clearly in high spirits, confident that he could obtain the needed papers in fairly short order.

Even so, a letter still needed to travel across the Atlantic and back, and Jean decided to wait for Rouillé's reply in French Guiana. From Pará, he traveled back upriver to Fort Curupa, located at the head of the Amazon delta. From there he could take the northern arm of the river to the Atlantic (Pará is not on the main course of the river), minimizing the distance he would have to travel in the open sea. In Curupa, thanks to an order from Pará's governor, he found waiting for him "a large pirogue [canoe] of fourteen oars, commanded by a sergeant of the garrison." He was getting the royal treatment from the Portuguese, taxied about much in the manner that La Condamine and Maldonado had been. Once the canoe reached the ocean, it hugged the shoreline the rest of the way to French Guiana. He arrived in Cayenne on April 20, 1750, where he was greeted by a surprised—and somewhat baffled—governor, Gilbert Guillouet d'Orvilliers.

D'Orvilliers knew all about the La Condamine expedition, and years earlier he had spent many an evening dining with La Condamine during his stay in Cayenne. But he could not quite understand Jean's thinking. As he wrote in a June 7 letter to Rouillé, "Monsieur Godin" had come all this way simply to *familiarize* himself with the Amazon and now intended "by following the same route, to go and get a woman he had married in Riobamba, in Peru." Rouillé could read between the lines here—in d'Orvilliers's opinion, this devotion to a *Peruvian* woman seemed rather extreme—and what made Jean's intentions even more mysterious was that he was quite broke. "It doesn't appear that his time in Peru has made him rich," d'Orvilliers informed the French minister: "He arrived here with nothing at all."

Indeed, at that moment, at least a few doubts about the wisdom of his plan must have been creeping into Jean's mind. His trip downriver had taken nearly a year, he was 3,000 miles away from his wife, and he had no money. Moreover, he was a French citizen in need of a passport that would allow him to travel through Portuguese territory a second time, and across a Spanish-Portuguese border that was officially closed. It could take a year to send a letter back and forth to France, and letters were often lost in route. All of those obstacles were now in his way, and given the realities of eighteenth-century colonial politics, he could be certain that others would crop up.

# CHAPTER ELEVEN

# A Continent Apart

THE CIVILITIES THAT JEAN GODIN had known in Quito and Riobamba were largely absent from French Guiana in 1750. This was a stretch of the South American coastline where few wanted to live. More than 200 inches of rain fall annually, and during the colonial period, before drainage ditches were dug, much of the coastal strip was underwater in the rainy season and during high tides. The swamps gave rise to clouds of insects, and they were populated by crocodiles and deadly snakes. Bushmasters, fer-de-lance, rattlesnakes, coral snakes, and the mighty anacondas all found this a delightful habitat, making the Guiana forest much more dangerous than the Amazon basin. The coastal lowlands give way to grasslands and a dense rain forest, with the distant mountains rising to 2,600 feet. Monkeys, giant anteaters, sloths, and an array of cats—jaguars, pumas, and ocelots—lived in these woods. Not surprisingly, Guiana became known as the "wild coast" of South America.

The English were the first to attempt to colonize the land, settling along the Oyapock River in 1604. They were defeated by disease, starvation, and the fierce Carib Indians, who later became feared for their cannibalism. The French established a permanent settlement on Cayenne in 1635, but for the next sixty-five years few settlers bothered to come—this was no promised land. In 1700, the d'Orvilliers family assumed governorship of the colony, and under its leadership, France began to make a more concerted effort to populate the area. Slaves were brought from West Africa, and colonists began to carve out plantations where they grew cotton, coffee, spices, and sugarcane. But such efforts proceeded at a very slow pace, and in 1750, Cayenne and the handful of other settlements in the colony remained isolated outposts, with few cultural amenities. The heat, humidity, and poisonous snakes made it seem like a purgatory, and indeed, in the nineteenth century, France established a penal colony in Guiana for its worst criminals.

When La Condamine had arrived in Cayenne, he had fallen into a deep languor, the only time during his ten-year journey that his energy slackened. But Jean was revitalized. After fifteen years, he was glad to be back in French territory, in a colony governed by *his* king. In the first weeks and months after his arrival, he set enthusiastically to work, organizing his papers and writing up a report titled *Mémoire sur la navigation de l'Amazone,* which he sent to Rouillé. Having spent so many years in the shadows of others, he did so with a touch of overeagerness, trying to make a name for himself, and he ended up offering rather cheeky political advice to the minister. France, he wrote, should grab the northern banks of the Amazon. It could then share the river with the Portuguese, using it as a trade highway to the riches of Peru:

> France's interest in navigation along the Amazon lies in its immense commercial potential, touching upon all the provinces of the realms of Peru, with Spain hardly being able to do anything about it, given the infinite number of rivers, all navigable, flowing into the Amazon. I see also other interests for France in

## Colonial South America in 1750

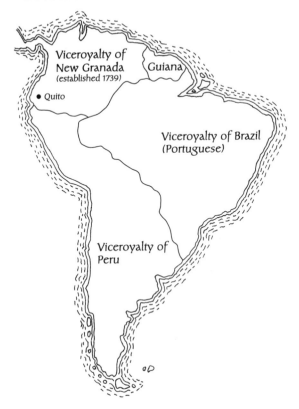

having the northern banks of the Amazon. For example, there are cacao, cloves, sarsaparilla, balm of copahu, vanilla, and precious woods for building. The Portuguese have built a substantial commerce out of all this, all maintained by the government at Pará.... Your Majesty could establish in this colony a shipbuilding works, the wood there is perfect. Your Majesty would get great use from this because the wood costs nothing.

Although Jean did not explicitly state that French Guiana should expand its boundaries into the neighboring Portuguese territories, that was the obvious implication of his report. "If France had a foothold in the Amazon," he concluded, "this colony would become the most flourishing in the world." This was a rather bold thing for someone in his position to say—after all, he had left France as a lowly assistant on the Peruvian mission—and a bit foolish, too. If his report were to fall into the hands of the Portuguese, it could cause a diplomatic furor, and even if Rouillé received it safely, he might be angered at the risk that Jean had taken. But Jean was apparently blind to these subtleties, and he eagerly sent off his report to Rouillé in June 1750, placing it in the hands of the captain of the king's vessel *L'Aventure*. He also sent along a collection of seeds he had gathered on his journey down the Amazon, as well as the grammar of the Incan language. He addressed this packet of New World treasures to Georges Leclerc de Buffon, who was the keeper of the Jardin du Roi in Paris and a member of the French Academy of Sciences. All in all, a productive first six weeks in French Guiana, or so Jean felt, and he was confident that he would soon hear news that his passport to Peru was ready.

Invigorated, he plunged ahead into a new scientific investigation. La Condamine, of course, was his model, and much as La Condamine had done with his studies of cinchona and rubber trees, Jean now took a careful inventory of the forests of Cayenne. He tested the various woods for their buoyancy and their resistance to insects and to find out how well they held nails, and he described how the various trees could be used to create a prosperous shipbuilding enterprise. The black cedar, he determined, was excellent for planking, while copahu was ideal for masts "owing to it being light and pliable." He noted which trees produced oils of potential value, and lauded in particular the merits of the cumaru tree, which "produces a fruit and a nut and almond, the odor of which is very agreeable and which produces an oil that is very good for treating dysentery." He finished this scientific treatise, *Mémoire sur differents bois dans l'ile de Cayenne*, on September 24, 1750, and in November, when another ship sailed to France, he mailed it to the academy, together with bottles of the tree oils. He also shipped a large trunk of wood samples "appropriate for construction purposes" to Rouillé and asked once again for a passport.

All that Jean had to do now was be patient. The king's vessel was expected to return in early 1751, and he passed the months trying to make himself useful to Governor d'Orvilliers, the other colonists, and the local Indians. He taught them about the various woods he had studied and how they could be put to use, and he was, by all accounts, a welcome addition to the colony. "He was well regarded by the Jesuits, and had the ear of other colonists and the Indians," wrote a nineteenth-century French historian, Henri Froidevaux. The governor of French Guiana, Froidevaux added, treated Jean "with consideration."

When the king's ship reappeared in the port on March 26, 1751, Jean was there to greet it. There would be letters from La Condamine, Buffon, and Rouillé, he was certain, and perhaps advice on how he should proceed. He had made it clear that he was placing himself at the service of both the Crown and the French Academy of Sciences. What would La Condamine, to whom he had written several times, think of his work? And would Buffon, having received his gift of a grammar, want to know more about his own studies of Quechua? Maldonado had been made a "corresponding" member of the French Academy of Sciences; perhaps such an honor would now be his. Best of all, his passport would be on the ship, and he would soon be on his way back to Isabel, and, God willing, their healthy child. At last the gangplank dropped, and the captain of *L'Aventure* strode toward the dock. But when their eyes met, the captain shrugged and held out his empty hands.

Crushed, Jean wrote anew to Rouillé, this time with a touch of panic:

> My Lord,
> I had the honor of writing to Your Grace in the month of June 1750 on the occasion of the vessel *L'Aventure* sailing to the port of Rochelle. I took the liberty of including my report on the potential utility that navigation of the Amazon would bring to this colony. I touched also on other advantageous points for our country. Last November, I had the honor of submitting to Your Grace a small trunk containing 14 or 15 types of wood that I deem

appropriate for building. I asked Your Grace to please examine them. I conclude that these little parcels never made it into your hands, since I have not had the pleasure to receive word from the vessel of the King, which was at anchor here in this port on March 26, to know if Your Grace received them and found them useful, which was the sole reason for giving my opinion.

Once more, Jean asked Rouillé for a passport. For the first time, he also requested money:

I beg you and implore of your justice to take into consideration the request that I take the liberty of making—that I be paid for having spent the best part of my life in service during our mission in Peru. This will help me survive for the remainder of my days by reimbursing the costs of my travel, if it is judged appropriate. I have the honor to extend my deep respect, Sir, Your Grace.
Your very humble and obedient servant,
Godin
Cayenne, April 8, 1751

Although Jean had no way of knowing it, this time the creaky wheels of the French bureaucracy began to turn. When Rouillé first received Jean's April 1751 letter, he had handled it in the same way he had the earlier ones: He had put it in a pile of papers that he planned to get to at some future date, scribbling on the top, "We have not yet responded to him." And there Jean's plea may have languished, had it not been for La Condamine, who was proving himself to be a true and loyal friend. La Condamine lobbied Rouillé on Jean's behalf, and he also personally called on Portugal's ambassador to France, Commander La Cerda, who provided him with a letter of recommendation for Jean to take to the governor in Pará. In addition, the ambassador promised La Condamine that Lisbon would send a passport for Jean directly to Pará.

Jean received La Condamine's letter in early 1752, and in it, La Condamine also provided him with news from Riobamba, which somehow had reached him in France. Isabel had given birth to a girl in August 1749, and both mother and daughter were said to be in good health. Other encouraging letters had arrived on the boat as well. The father general of the Jesuits in Rome, Ignatius Visconti, had written him a letter of recommendation that he could give to Jesuits living along the Amazon, Father Visconti requesting that the priests "facilitate, on my account, the travels of Mr. Godin, both for himself and for any others who accompany him." Best of all, Rouillé had written to say that all was now in place for him to return:

I write, Sir, to Monsieurs d'Orvilliers and [deputy-governor] Lemoyne to ask that they facilitate, in so far as possible, the voyage that you must undertake to Quito, passing through the Portuguese and Spanish colonies that are established along the Amazon River. I pointed out to them that the King finds it well that d'Orvilliers gives you the letters of recommendation for the governors of these colonies. I hope that this will turn out satisfactorily for you.

Jean quickly began preparing for the journey. It had been nearly three years since he had left Riobamba, and now his return was just a matter of sailing upriver. He figured that it would take him six or eight months—he would be back in Riobamba by August or September. He hurriedly wrote to the governor in Pará, informing him that he would be arriving shortly to pick up the passport that had been sent from Lisbon. But before Jean had time to depart, he received a stunning note from Pará. "I inquired of the governor of that place for news [of the passport]," Jean wrote, in a letter to La Condamine, "and he replied that he had no knowledge of them."

Faced with this rebuff from the governor in Pará, Jean—or so it seems in hindsight—should have considered other ways to return to Riobamba. The papers he needed for travel up the Amazon were lost in Portugal's bureaucracy, and prompting Lisbon into action from French Guiana would be nearly impossible. Two years of effort to secure a passport had gone for naught. And other possibilities did exist. He could have sailed on *L'Aventure* to France and made arrangements from there to return to Peru. Or he might have tried to make his way along the coast to Cartagena. Yet Jean, as evidenced by his writings, never gave such options much thought. Instead, he stubbornly clung to his plan to return via the Amazon. He now approached d'Orvilliers with a new proposal: He would make the trip upriver as a servant of the colony. He would chase down slaves in Brazil who had escaped from French Guiana, and he would, in the manner of a spy, gather "intelligence" on how the Amazon might be seized and on the riches that could be had by opening this trading route to Peru. He would also bring back shoots from cinchona and cinnamon trees, with the hope that these two species could be cultivated for great profit in French Guiana. In return, he asked that the colony provide him with a military boat staffed with a commanding officer and troops.

By any standard, Jean was proposing a far-reaching colonial adventure. While it might be possible for a boat to slip past Portugal's military forts on the lower part of the river, if it were discovered, Portugal would undoubtedly treat the incursion as an act of war. Yet both d'Orvilliers and his deputy, Lemoyne, while voicing some "reservations" about Jean's plan, wrote to Rouillé to request that France fund it. Godin, they noted, would bring back plants that if cultivated, "would be a source of riches," and France could also hope that he would find a method for "transporting gold and silver out of Peru." In a letter dated June 14, 1753, Lemoyne even pleaded with Rouillé for a quick reply: "I implore you, Sir, to indicate to me whether I can inform him that he will be reimbursed for the expenses that he may incur in doing research that would be useful for the colony."

The proposed "research" mission was clearly meant to serve the expansionist goal articulated by Godin in his earlier letter to Rouillé, in which he had urged France to consider seizing the northern banks of the Amazon. Although this was a startling pro-

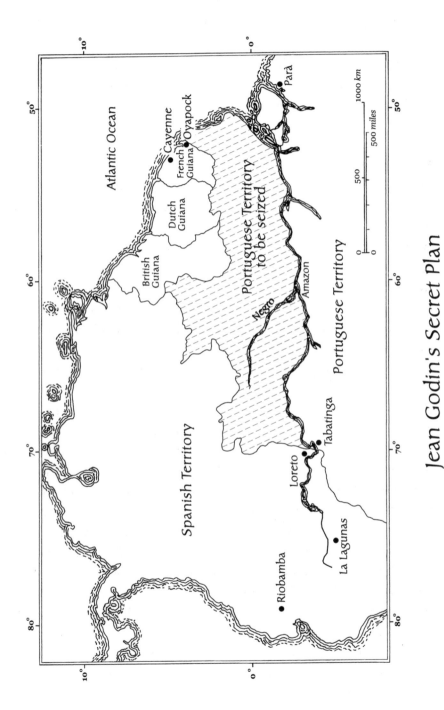

Jean Godin's Secret Plan

posal, geography did provide a rationale for it. During the seventeenth century, Guiana had been seen as a region that extended to the Amazon. Moreover, while Portugal may have established missions along the river, its colonization efforts had been focused mostly along the coastline south of Pará. The wild area north of the Amazon was still there for the taking, and the river could easily be seen as a natural dividing line between colonies. France and Portugal could share "ownership" of the Amazon. Portugal, for its part, had spent the last 150 years grabbing an ever greater part of the Amazon basin, at Spain's expense. Now it was France's turn to lay claim to more than just a tiny corner of the continent.

Having gained the support of d'Orvilliers and Lemoyne, Jean had reason to be newly optimistic. D'Orvilliers, in his June 19 letter, had even assured the minister that Crown expenses would be kept to a minimum. "Only a small portion of the costs for this expedition will fall on the King, who will cover the costs of the boat and of the officer and the troops that will accompany [Godin]. The cost for the outfitting will fall on those who have slaves to reclaim." It was no longer just Jean urging this bold plan on Rouillé. So too were the officials who governed French Guiana. Yet their letters were met with the same silence that had greeted Jean's earlier ones. A handful of ships from France sailed into Cayenne in 1753 and 1754, but none brought a reply from Rouillé.*

A sense of desperation came over Jean, prompting an even wilder idea: He would build a boat of his own, a small, single-masted vessel known as a tartan. He would sail this to Pará, and armed with his letters of recommendation, he would convince the governor of Pará to allow him to proceed without a passport. There was a touch of madness in this plan, but surprisingly, the military commander of Cayenne, Monsieur Dunezat, approved of it. In a May 10, 1755, letter to Rouillé, Dunezat explained his decision:

---

* Paris's silence toward its overseas possessions was apparently common. In 1757, the governor of Louisiana complained that he had written fifteen letters without having receiving a single response from Paris.

Godin asked me for permission to go to Pará to request passports from the Court of Portugal and to make the necessary contacts for his trip to Quito. His requests, together with the protests of colonists who have fugitive Negroes in Pará, have convinced me to give him permission and to charge him with capturing the fugitive Negroes of this colony which may be in the province of Maragnon, where he will go from Cayenne, before going on to Quito.

Jean set sail toward the end of 1755, and he made it as far as the "mouth of the Amazon" in his small craft. But there, with waves spilling over his boat and the wind blowing him out to sea, he lost his courage and hope. His vessel was in a "poor state," he was still a good distance from Pará, and he no longer could see how this plan could possibly succeed. The Portuguese might well throw him into prison as a spy, just as they had done to Father Fritz. Even if he were allowed to continue his trip, Dunezat expected him to round up slaves who had escaped from French Guiana. None of this seemed likely to bring him to Isabel and the child he had never seen. Overwhelmed by a sense of defeat, he turned his leaky boat back toward Cayenne. Nothing had worked as he had hoped, he had tried again and again to get back upriver, and he no longer had the slightest idea how to set things right.

WHEN JEAN LEFT RIOBAMBA in March 1749, Isabel expected him to be gone for at least two years. She had promised Jean that she and their child, soon to be born, would be waiting patiently for his return. In August she gave birth to a girl, Carmen del Pilar, and by all accounts, she focused all of her attention on her. Upper-class mothers in colonial Peru typically left much of the daily nurturing of an infant to servants, but not Isabel. She doted on Carmen, determined that her baby would survive the scourges that had taken their first three children. Carmen was living proof that a *family* was waiting to be reunited, and as she grew into a toddler, Isabel spent hours telling her about her father, that he had come to Peru as part of a great scientific expedition, and that they would all one day be moving to France. This was the dream she constantly wove for her daughter, and as Carmen turned three and then four years old, Isabel tutored her in French—the language, Isabel was certain, that Carmen would eventually be schooled in.

Events unfolded slowly in eighteenth-century Peru, and so at first it was not too surprising to Isabel that Jean did not reappear in 1751 or 1752. Gossip had filtered back into Riobamba that Jean had safely passed through the Jesuit missions in the Peruvian Amazon. But after that? Nothing. Jean had simply disappeared. Every time her brother Juan came to town—he was a priest at a church in Pallatanga now—she would look to him for news, hoping that a bit of information had perhaps made its way up the missionary grapevine. But he never had any. No letter from Jean ever arrived,* and when four years of separation turned into five, and then five into six, Isabel's doubts grew. So did her loneliness. At times, she would walk to the top of the hill and look to the east, toward Mount Altar and Mount Tungurahua, as though she expected Jean to appear at any moment, climbing up out of the jungle. But other times she felt overwhelmed by her melancholy and remained for long hours in the darkness of her house. She heard too the crueler whispers in town, that the handsome Jean Godin, he of the great La Condamine expedition, had surely long since returned to France, having forgotten all about his Riobamban wife.

* This seems surprising until one considers how difficult it would have been for Jean to send a letter from French Guiana to Riobamba. He could not send one to Pará in the hope that it would be passed upriver, for the border between Portugal and Spain on the Amazon was closed. One possibility would have been to send a letter from French Guiana to France, with the thought that it could then be passed on to Spanish officials, who could place it in the care of a Spanish trading vessel, which could carry it to Cartagena or Lima; from there the letter could somehow be taken overland to Riobamba. This was a postal system that was almost certain to break down, and even if it did not, a letter could take years and years to be delivered. Jean's father died in 1740, and yet his siblings' letter informing him of the death did not arrive until 1748, and that letter had originated in France.

During this period, the Gramesón family as a whole suffered one setback after another. Their old way of life was slipping away. The decline in the textile industry caused by the flood of cheap imports from Europe was having a domino effect. Obrajes closed, and that meant the market for wool suffered, which in turn depressed trade throughout the colony. The Gramesóns kept their hacienda near Guamote, where Indian laborers harvested potatoes and fattened animals for slaughter, and family finances were good enough that in 1756, Isabel's mother, Doña Josefa, was able to buy several homes in town, next to La Concepción Church. But that same year, in a legal filing dated July 20, Doña Josefa informed the town council that the wealth she had inherited was nearly gone. Her husband, "el General Don Pedro de Gramesón y Bruno," had squandered her extensive dowry.

She died the following year, and Isabel was thrust into the role of the family matriarch, helping her father run Subtipud. She also had to manage the properties that she and Jean owned. But her mother's death came just as she sent Carmen off to a convent school in Quito, and suddenly her house overlooking the town square seemed emptier than ever. Her family's financial problems deepened in those years, too. In 1755, her father and her brother had won at auction a five-year right to collect (and keep) taxes from seven local villages, promising to pay 775 pesos annually for this privilege. But as a result of the economic depression that settled over the area, they were unable to recoup even this modest amount in 1758 and 1759. The final straw came when a former corregidor of Riobamba, Bruno de Urquizu, died owing them 1,200 pesos. Antonio and his father applied to audiencia authorities for relief, requesting that their annual fee of 775 pesos be lowered, but their plea was turned down, and Don Pedro was forced to cover the shortfall. Yet even this setback did not convince Antonio to give up the tax collection business, and in the early 1760s, as the economy continued to falter, he was forced to declare bankruptcy and beg the court for mercy: "I will always better your fortune and will have property [in the future] with which I can do that," he declared. But the court decreed that such promises of future payment would not do and sent him to jail, his imprisonment an example of just how far the family's fortunes had fallen.

Social unrest was also increasing throughout the central highlands. There had been eleven armed uprisings by Indians in the 1750s in colonial Peru, and in the early 1760s, such rebellions began occurring every six months or so. The Indians wanted better working conditions in the mines and an end to the mita system of forced labor. This was the early stage of a rebellion that would eventually claim the lives of more than 100,000 Indians, and in 1764, it erupted full-blown in Riobamba. Armed Indians from the countryside stormed into the city from the south and took over the Santo Domingo and San Francisco plazas, which became the scene of trench warfare. Blood spilled across bricked squares that were normally filled with boys playing ball, and everyone took the rebellion as a sign that the colonial order that had reigned for 200 years, one that had served the elite so well, was perhaps coming to an end.

As these many years passed, Isabel naturally came to think less often of Jean. She turned thirty-six in 1764, the year of the Indian rebellion. By colonial standards, she was no longer a young woman. Carmen had returned from convent school and was now of a marriageable age. Her childhood had passed, and with it their dream of moving to France. But they did have each other, theirs a mother-daughter bond that brought great comfort to them both. They attended mass daily, their servants always a step behind. Isabel's faith had always sustained her: She recited her Hail Mary's and felt reassured by the presence of the Virgin of Sicalpa, the statue high on the mountain, looking out over her town. And deep in her heart, she never gave up all hope that Jean would return. She knew that miracles could occur; she had even witnessed proof of that a few years earlier. In 1759, the image of a patron saint had suddenly appeared before the parishioners of San Sebastián Church. The apparition triggered a great celebration, the town council ordering candles to be lit in every square. Isabel felt the presence of God in her life, which gave her the strength to renew her prayers.

．　．　．

AFTER JEAN'S ABORTIVE TRIP to the Amazon, he settled down in French Guiana in a way that he had not previously. He needed to earn a living. He moved from Cayenne to Oyapock, a tiny village on the river that marked the boundary between French Guiana and Brazil. He built a house on stilts and hunted manatee, a large sea mammal that feeds on sea grasses and was abundant in the Oyapock estuary. The animal was highly prized for its meat, and it also gave a valuable oil. In addition to his manatee enterprise, he drew up plans for a timber business, which he put into operation in 1763.

Archival records provide only a smattering of details about his life during this period. Oyapock was a miserable frontier town, with only a few other white colonists, and Jean lived there isolated from most of the world—even Cayenne was several days away by boat. He appears to have given up any hope of gaining recognition for his scientific investigations or for his grammar of the Incan language, and there are hints, in a letter written by Governor Fiedmont (who had replaced d'Orvilliers), that he became somewhat quarrelsome, bitter over his fate. This was not a life that he had ever imagined for himself, staring night after night across the river at the dark forest that separated him from his family. He would stew like that for months on end, and then he would take out his feather pen and once again plead for help: "I renewed my letters every year, four, five, and even six times, for the purpose of obtaining my passports," he wrote years later, "and constantly without effect."

Not even La Condamine wrote back. The silence of his friend and mentor was almost too much to bear. Perhaps, Jean reasoned, La Condamine's failure to write was due to the war that had erupted on three continents. France and the other European powers were battling over their colonial territories, a fight that was also taking place on the open seas. His letters must have been getting "lost or intercepted," and La Condamine later confirmed that such had been the case. During the Seven Years' War, which concluded with the Treaty of Paris, signed on February 10, 1763, La Condamine did not receive a single one of Jean's many missives. Jean was writing letters that disappeared into a void, and yet he continued to take pen in hand, as though by sheer obsessive persistence he could get someone to respond to him.

France exited from the war a humiliated nation. In the Paris accord, it was forced to cede Canada and all of its territory east of the Mississippi to Great Britain, and it also lost several of its islands in the West Indies. Great Britain had emerged as the world's foremost colonial power, while France's overseas empire had dramatically shrunk. The bitter defeat demanded that France do something to regain its pride, and in 1763, Étienne-François de Choiseul, who had replaced Rouillé as minister of foreign affairs, decided that new resources should be devoted to French Guiana, which was one of its few remaining colonial possessions in the New World.* He sent 12,000 colonists to settle the mouth of the Kourou River, northwest of Cayenne, but this enterprise was so badly planned—and the arriving settlers so naive—that they brought ice skates instead of farm tools. Within two years, most had died from fever and starvation.

The arrival of the new colonists, however, stirred Jean's hopes. France was in need of a triumph and a way to reassert its power and influence. It held just a tiny corner of South America, a mere speck on the map, while lowly Portugal was the master of the Amazon. There was a new and compelling reason to dust off his old plan for seizing the Amazon, and this time, in a letter he wrote to Choiseul on December 10, 1763, he was very blunt about what it would require. As he later confided to Fiedmont,

---

* Étienne-François de Choiseul served as France's minister of foreign affairs from 1758 to 1761 and from 1766 to 1770. He was minister of the marine from 1761 to 1766, and during this period his cousin, Cesar-Gabriel, Duc de Choiseul-Praslin, was minister of foreign affairs. However, Étienne-François retained his authority to formulate foreign policy while his cousin served in that position.

I provided [Choiseul] with a very detailed account of how, in the blink of an eye, without giving [the Portuguese] the time to know what had happened, one could take over one side of the river, taking precautions to keep it. I also gave him the means of doing this according to the nature of the place. I would intercept the navigation of this river and all communication with the city of Pará until peace has been made.

Jean, of course, had an ulterior motive. France's seizure of the northern banks of the Amazon would enable him to go upriver to get Isabel. But no sooner had he sent the letter than he started feeling nervous about it. He lived on the border with Portugal; what if his neighbors discovered his plan? He had entrusted the letter to a missionary who was returning to France, and he had begged the man to deliver it "by hand to Choiseul." But he knew well that letters crossing the Atlantic had a way of not arriving at their destination, and when the king's vessel returned to Cayenne five months later, without a word of reply from the minister, his worries flared. On June 1, 1764, he begged Choiseul for a reply:

Sir,
In December 1763, I had the honor of writing you a letter, which contained a project that might be of interest to you. Not having received any news, I am anxious to know if you received it, as it may have had the misfortune of taking another route and falling into the hands of foreigners, which would be most unfortunate for the trip I have to make, and for the project itself. If you have received the letter, you will understand why I have taken the liberty to send you this and why I also dare to ask that you inform me as to its status.
Respectfully,
Your most humble and obedient servant, Godin

Over the next several months, his fears grew into full-blown paranoia. He began to cast about for someone new to write to, anyone who might comfort him, and in his desperation, he seized upon a bit of idle gossip he had heard. There was a certain Count d'Herouville who was said to be "in the confidence of Monsieur Choiseul." On September 10, 1764, Jean wrote to d'Herouville, and for once, he succinctly summarized his plight:

> I was, Sir, associated with the gentlemen of the Academy of Sciences who, in 1735, undertook the mission in Peru. I went down the Amazon in 1749 in order to reach Cayenne. Mr. De La Condamine, of the same Academy, and whom you surely know, will speak on my behalf. It is necessary that I go back up this river to fetch my family in the province of Quito and to bring them here. Dare I, Sir, hope for the good fortune of a moment of your attention?

There was little reason for Jean to believe that this letter would elicit a response. D'Herouville did not know him; he was just grasping at yet another flimsy straw. He had urged France to seize the northern banks of the Amazon, he had volunteered to lead a military boat up the Amazon in order to do "research," he had offered himself as a spy and a bounty hunter, and he had built his own boat—all to no avail. His letter to d'Herouville was little better than tossing a bottle containing a message into the ocean.

Yet a year later, Governor Fiedmont hurriedly called him to Cayenne. A Portuguese boat had arrived in port with a story that Jean would want to hear—and one that Fiedmont did not at all trust.

The boat, a decked galliot with sails and "manned with thirty oars," was commanded by a captain of the garrison at Pará. His name was Rebello, and he had come, he said, upon the order of the king of Portugal, to transport Jean up the Amazon "as high as the first Spanish settlement," where he would wait until Jean returned with his family. He would then bring them back to Cayenne. Fiedmont had listened to this and, as he reported to Choiseul, concluded the obvious: Rebello was a spy. "This behavior by our touchy and cruel neighbor on behalf of [Godin] did not surprise me, as I am persuaded that it is nothing more than a pretext to cover up their curiosity about what is going on here and to prevent us from using a similar pretext for going there to learn about their side. I thought it was my duty, nevertheless, to receive this officer."

Fiedmont laid out his doubts to Jean. The arrival of the 12,000 settlers in Kourou, he said, was causing "much suspicion and distrust" among all of French Guiana's neighbors. Jean could go with Rebello, but he should know that nobody in France had told him to expect the Portuguese boat. How could the king of Portugal order such a thing without first informing Paris?

The galliot departed from Cayenne in late November 1765 with a nervous Jean on board. Perhaps, he thought, his letter to d'Herouville had finally borne fruit. Perhaps the "generous nobleman" had gone to Choiseul and that had set off a chain reaction: Choiseul had written to the Portuguese ambassador, the ambassador to Portugal's king, and the king to Pará. That was certainly possible. But on the way to Oyapock, where they planned to stop for a short while so that he could tie up some loose ends, Fiedmont's suspicions fed his own, and he began to panic. He was alone among the Portuguese, "in the midst of a nation against which I have worked so hard," he told himself. He would engage Rebello in talk, and it seemed that the Portuguese captain responded with slightly malevolent double entendres. "Something is going on in this boat," Jean worried, and then, just before they reached Oyapock, he and the captain had a conversation that seemed to confirm his worst fears. He had told Rebello that in Oyapock he would like to pick up "a Negro and a couple of whites" to accompany him on the journey, and yet the captain had refused. There might be room for a Negro or two, but not for a white. What was Jean to make of this?

"The whites that I would have brought along are not great persons," Jean told Rebello. "They would have found enough space."

Jean did not know what to do. When they docked in Oyapock, he decided to stall for time. He tried to keep his suspicions from Rebello—he did not dare chase this boat away—and yet he feared that if he went upriver, his life would be in danger. It all made sense. "I've worked against this nation and I must scrutinize the tiniest things," he confided to Fiedmont in a letter. "I fear my letter [to Choiseul] has not been delivered; it has fallen into foreign hands and I am lost. Who will assure me that some evil soul has not turned this to his profit in the [Portuguese] Court?" Jean feigned that he was ill, and told Rebello that he had suffered a "nasty fall in the woods while going to the lumberyards of my Negroes." It could be a month or more before he could travel.

While waiting for Fiedmont to reply, Jean came up with a new strategy to divine Portugal's true motives. Rebello was eager to depart—a number of his oarsmen had fled to the woods in a bid for freedom—so Jean suggested that Rebello proceed to Pará without him. When Jean recovered his health, he would come to Pará to "take advantage" of the king's "generous" offer to transport him up the Amazon. But Rebello's answer once again convinced Jean that something was amiss: "He'll hear nothing of going ahead, and responds that he must, at all costs, conduct me [to Pará] for that is why he came here," Jean told Fiedmont. "This man wants to overpower me here. What will they do when they are in their home territory?"

Jean wrote this last letter to Fiedmont on December 28, 1766. He felt utterly paralyzed. He feared that if he went with the Portuguese, he would be murdered or imprisoned as a spy. But if he let the galliot go without him, his hopes of ever seeing Isabel again would vanish. "Please do me the honor, Sir, of giving me your thoughts on this matter," he begged Fiedmont. The governor, though, was tired of the whole affair. He wanted the galliot gone from French Guiana. Jean needed to make a decision. Either go or not go. At last, Jean came up with a compromise proposal for Rebello. Since he remained too "ill" to go, could he instead send a friend of his, "to whom I might entrust my letters, and who might fill my place in taking care of my family on its return?"

Much to Jean's surprise, Rebello agreed. And once he did, Jean's fears began to vanish. He now saw everything in a different light.

He reasoned that he could thank d'Herouville for his change in fortune. It was due "to the kindness of this nobleman" that the ship had arrived. Quickly, he selected a long-time friend, Tristan d'Oreasaval, to go in his stead. He provided d'Oreasaval with money for the journey and a packet of documents, which included letters to his wife and the recommendation that he had obtained in 1752 from the father general of the Jesuits. He had safeguarded Visconti's letter for so many years, always praying that the day would come when he could use it. The plan was straightforward. Rebello would escort d'Oreasaval to Loreto, the first mission in Spanish territory. After dropping him off, Rebello would retreat across the border to Tabatinga, a Portuguese mission, and patiently wait there. From Loreto, d'Oreasaval would canoe 500 miles upriver to Lagunas, the capital of the Maynas district in the Quito Audiencia, and hand the letters to the father superior. The Jesuits would then carry the packet to Isabel in Riobamba.

Everything had fallen into place. Jean felt his hopes soar, and on January 25, 1766, the galliot sailed from Oyapock. In seven months or so, it would reach Loreto, and this vessel, as Jean now happily declared, was under the command of a military officer who was nothing less than a "knight of the order of Christ."

THE RUMOR THAT ARRIVED nine months later in Riobamba was so vague as to be almost cruel. Isabel's brother Juan had heard it first, that a vessel *might* be waiting for them at Loreto, and that Jesuits *might* be in possession of letters from her husband, who—or so it was rumored—was alive and living in French Guiana. Isabel and Carmen had clung to each other; could this be true? Juan went to Father Terol, the priest who had married Isabel and Jean, to find out what he could, and together the two priests called on Jesuits in Quito. With the Jesuits' assistance, they were able to piece together a trail of sorts. A man named Tristan had delivered letters to a Father Yesquen in Loreto, who had handed them off to a second priest, who had given them to a third, and now these documents

225

were quite lost. But while the Jesuits were certain that letters of some sort had been sent Isabel's way, they were of two minds about the vessel. Some, Juan told his sister, "give credit to [it], while others dispute the fact."

Isabel did the only thing she could. She sent a trusted family slave, twenty-three-year-old Joaquín Gramesón,* to investigate. He left in January 1767 and returned three months later, exhausted and with no news at all. Authorities had ordered him back to Riobamba because he lacked the proper papers for travel into the Amazon. After resolving that problem, Isabel sent him out once again. It was close to 2,000 miles to Loreto and back, and twenty-one months passed before Joaquín returned. But this time he brought back certain news: He had personally spoken to d'Oreasaval, a boat was indeed waiting for her and Carmen, and Jean was indeed anxious for them to arrive in Cayenne.

This was the news that Isabel had been waiting to hear for so long … and yet by the time Joaquin returned, it was bittersweet. While he had been gone, Carmen—in April 1768—had died of smallpox. Isabel's hope was always that she, Jean, and Carmen would *all* be reunited. When Joaquin had left on his journey, Carmen had asked Isabel to tell her once more the stories she had heard as a child about her father and about how he and her mother had met. And now Isabel knew for sure that Jean had come back to get them, yet Carmen lay buried in the local cemetery, her nineteen years framing the time that she and Jean had been apart.

The decision that Isabel now had to make was not a simple one. A boat may have been waiting for her, but if she were to go, she would be leaving behind all that she had ever known. Her father, her two brothers and her sister, and her nephews and nieces all lived in and around Riobamba. Her children were buried here. This was her home. And to leave meant going on a journey that no woman had ever dared undertake, and one that her family was insistent that she not attempt.

---

* Slaves often took the surname of their owners.

The skinning of an Amazon snake.
*From John Pinkerton, ed.*, A General Collection of the Best
and Most Interesting Voyages and Travels in All Parts of the World,
*vol. 14 (London, 1813).*

To the colonial elite living in the Andes, the jungle was a place populated by savage Indians, terrifying beasts, and deadly disease. The wild Indians in this region, Ulloa and Juan had written, "live in a debasement of human nature, without laws or religion, in the most infamous brutality, strangers to moderation, and without the least control or restraint of their excesses." There were also "tigers, bastard lions, and bears" to worry about, and poisonous snakes like the cobra and the maca. This latter reptile, Ulloa and Juan reported, was "wholly covered with scales and makes a frightful appearance, its head being out of all proportion to the body, and it has two rows of teeth and fangs like those of a large dog." Most frightening of all was a man-eating snake that the Indians called jacumama:

It is a serpent of a frightful magnitude and most deleterious nature. Some in order to give an idea of its largeness, affirm that it will swallow any beast whole, and that this has been the miserable end of many a man. … They generally lie coiled up and wait till their prey passes near enough to be seized. As they are not easily distinguished from the large rotten wood, which lies about in plenty in these parts, they have opportunities to seize their prey and satiate their hunger.*

As for the terrain, all of the routes to the Amazon were "extremely troublesome and fatiguing, from the nature of the climate and being full of rocks, so that a great part of the distance must be travelled on foot." These difficulties had scared Maldonado's family thirty years earlier when he had been contemplating his trip to the Amazon, and if anything, the trek had since grown more dangerous. Indians throughout the viceroyalty were rising up in protest and had fled in significant numbers into the jungle, emerging periodically to attack outlying Spanish towns. Equally problematic, the Jesuits had recently been expelled from Peru, and it was their mission stations that had been the lifeline through this wilderness.

The expulsion of the Jesuits had been a long time coming. They had come to the New World in 1549 to convert the "heathens," and this missionary work had often put them into conflict with colonists seeking to exploit or enslave the Indians. The Jesuits had also grown very wealthy in their two centuries in the New World, adding to their predisposition to ignore governmental orders.

---

* Today we know this snake, the jacumama, as an anaconda, which is the largest member of the boa constrictor family of snakes. The maca described by Ulloa was a pit viper of some type, perhaps the fer-de-lance or the bushmaster.

Portugal ordered them out of Brazil in 1759, and eight years later Spain did the same. While other clergy had replaced the Jesuits in the mission stations along the Amazon, these priests and monks were—as Ulloa and Juan wrote—often utterly shameless in their behavior. Those living in the cities kept concubines, held drunken revelries, and exploited the Indians for financial gain, and these were the religious men that a traveler to Loreto would now have to depend on.

To most in Riobamba, it was inconceivable that a woman would even think of making this trip. Not only did the many physical dangers cry out for Isabel to stay, but cultural norms were an even more powerful restraint. To go would violate values so deep in the Peruvian psyche that they could be traced back to the Reconquest. A woman ventured outside with a maid or a servant by her side or with her husband for an evening of entertainment, and then she scurried back inside. As a descendant of the Godin family would later write: "Her father and her brothers opposed her going with all their power."

On the other side of the equation, there was only this: The memory of a husband that Isabel had last seen and held twenty years before.

There was much that Isabel had to do before she could depart. She sold her house in Riobamba and her furniture, and made a gift of her other properties—"a garden and estate at Guaslen, and another property between Galté and Maguazo"—to her sister, Josefa. There were also supplies to buy and her many personal belongings to pack. This all took several months, and once her family understood that they could not dissuade her, they rallied to her side. Both of her brothers decided that they would accompany her to Loreto and travel on to Europe. Juan obtained permission from his superiors to go to Rome, while Antonio—newly freed from bankruptcy jail—saw the journey as an opportunity to start a new life. He would take his seven-year-old son Martín with him to France, and once they were settled, he would send for his wife and his other son. Joaquín, the family's most trusted slave, would go with them to Loreto—Isabel promised to give him his "card of liberty" as a reward once they reached that point. She would also be accompanied by her two maids, Tomasa and Juanita, who were eight or nine years old. Meanwhile, her sixty-five-year-old father decided that he would leave ahead of the others and arrange for canoes to be ready for them as they proceeded from mission station to mission station. He would travel all the way to Loreto and wait there until he knew that his daughter had reached the Portuguese galliot safely. Then he would return to Riobamba.

News of Isabel's trip quickly spread throughout the audiencia and beyond. Men and women alike began to gossip about the "lady" who was heading off into the Amazon, and in early September this brought to Riobamba an unlikely visitor: A French man named Jean Rocha, who claimed to be a doctor. He had been making his way up the Peruvian coast, with plans to cross Panama and return to Europe via that route, when, on a stop in Guayaquil, he had heard about Isabel's trip. He was accompanied by a traveling companion, Phelipe Bogé, and a slave, and in return for passage with Isabel, he promised "to watch over her health, and show her every attention." Isabel initially turned him down—her instincts said that he was not to be trusted—but her brothers convinced her otherwise, telling her that she "might have need of the assistance of a physician on so long a voyage."

The traveling party was now set: They numbered ten in all, and Isabel hired thirty-one Indians to carry their goods and supplies. The mules were loaded, the people of Riobamba came out to see them go, and Isabel—on the morning of October 1—picked up the hem of her dress and stepped into a waiting sedan chair. The sky was a brilliant blue, the air crisp and clear, and the group headed north out of town, toward snow-capped Mount Chimborazo. The road climbed to the top of a ridge, and once they had left the last houses behind, Isabel summoned up every bit of her will and turned her sights firmly to the east, toward the high cordillera and the jungle beyond.

# CHAPTER TWELVE

# Lost on the Bobonaza

I SABEL AND THE OTHERS knew that the most difficult and dangerous part of their journey would be the first 350 miles. They would travel overland down the steep eastern slopes of the Andes, from Riobamba to Canelos, and then they would canoe 225 miles down the turbulent Bobonaza River, from Canelos to Andoas. At that point, they would be on the broad expanses of the Pastaza River, and although the Pastaza below Andoas had its share of whirlpools and strong currents, canoes could traverse it fairly easily. They expected to take twelve days or so to reach Canelos and then another two weeks to make it to Andoas. Before the month was over, they hoped that the worst part of their journey would be behind them.

Isabel, who had traveled very little in her life, found the first few days delightful. Once they had turned their backs on Mount Chimborazo and headed east, they began following the Chambo River, one of a handful of rivers in the entire Andean valley that cut through the eastern cordillera and drained into the Amazon. They crossed the Chambo on their second day out, entering into the mountains, and with the river now on their left and far below them, they picked their way across a steep slope. Mount Tungurahua, its top half covered with ice and snow, loomed ahead. The summit of the great volcano topped out at 16,465 feet, and Isabel, who had seen it from afar so many times, was awestruck by its size and air of hidden power. The graceful and slender Tungurahua she had always known, the petite "wife" of Chimborazo, now seemed fierce and threatening, holding within the furious fires of the earth. As they worked their way north around its lower slopes, at an altitude of about 8,000 feet, they had to struggle to cross gullies cut by water tumbling down from the ice fields above. Each time they came to one, they had to climb higher up Tungurahua's slopes until the gully narrowed enough that their Indian servants could throw a small bridge across it. Then they would descend the mountainside on the other side of the gully, to where the slopes of the volcano were not quite so steep, and proceed on their way. Although this was slow going, the air was cool, and they were hit by only an occasional burst of icy rain. Each night the Indians built them a shelter of tree branches and cooked a hearty meal over a fire. They had brought along several live chickens and an ample supply of dried corn, beans, potatoes, and dried meats— llama, sheep, and pig. Most likely, this trip was the first time that Isabel had ever slept outdoors.

On the fourth or fifth day of their journey, Isabel and the others reached the small town of Baños, perched on a shelf of land at the base of Tungurahua, about 250 feet above the Pastaza River. The Pastaza is formed by the merger of the Chambo and Patate Rivers a few miles above Baños, and it is a violent, turbulent river, hurling its way out of the Andes with a fury.

Since leaving Riobamba, they had traveled about fifty miles and dropped 3,000 feet in altitude, and they had now entered the cloud forest that covers the eastern slopes of the Andes, a lush world of moss-covered trees, delicate orchids, and hanging vines. There is no other place on the planet where massive snow-capped moun-

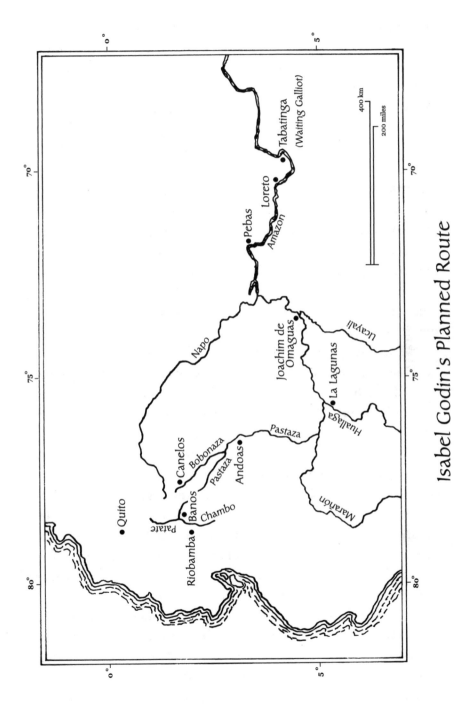

Isabel Godin's Planned Route

tains so closely overlook steaming tropical forest, the two disparate climates separated by less than 150 miles. In rapid order, the alpine world of the mountains turns into a dense forest perpetually bathed in clouds and fog, and then, at 3,000 feet above sea level, the cloud forest gives way to a rain forest, where although it may rain nearly every day, clouds are not constantly present. At an altitude of about 1,000 feet, the vegetation undergoes a further change, into lowland rain forest. For every 1,000-foot drop in elevation, the temperature rises about 4 degrees Fahrenheit, such that it will be fifty degrees colder on the slopes of Tungurahua than it is at the headwaters of the Amazon, only 100 miles away. As a result of these extremes in temperature, the terrain in between receives more than 160 inches of rain a year.

The airflow that drives this wet climate originates in the Amazon basin. Along the equator, heat builds up each day and the warm air rises. Evaporation fills these currents with moisture, and as the air rises, it cools, the water condensing and falling as rain. While this cycle keeps the Amazon basin well watered, prevailing air currents bring a double dose of rain to the eastern slopes of the Andes. Moisture-laden clouds ascending from the jungle floor are pushed by prevailing winds toward the west, where they run smack into the Andes, and as the clouds rise up the slopes, they cool and the rains come. The Andes act as a moisture trap for the entire Amazon basin, and this brings showers to the region more than 250 days a year. It also bathes the mid-level slopes of the Andes, where Baños is located, in a perpetual mist, except for brief periods in the morning, when dawn may break clear.

The constant watering produces a profusion of plant life, every tree covered with ferns, lichens, and other parasitic growth. The entire forest drips moss, and even the tree tops, as the nineteenth-century naturalist Alexander von Humboldt exclaimed, are "crowned with great bushes of flowers." Brightly colored birds, such as the golden tanager and the crimson-breasted woodpecker, find this world a paradise, as do bands of gibbering spider monkeys and such reclusive animals as the spectacled bear. But the thick vegetation, which is draped across the steep cliffs and crags of the Andes, makes this region almost impenetrable to humans. As travelers try to hack their way through the forest, they must cope with constant downpours that turn every path into a muddy quagmire. One stream after another has to be crossed, torrents racing down the mountainside, filled with snowmelt and the daily deluge of rain. This was the very region where Gonzalo Pizarro and his men got bogged down in 1541, when they set out for Canelos, the land of the cinnamon trees.

Isabel and her brothers did not tarry in Baños, stopping only long enough to purchase some additional food supplies and to enjoy a night of rest under a roof before plunging into the cloud forest. Barely had they started on their way before they had to confront the raging Pastaza. About three miles below the village, the river passed beneath two cliffs forty feet apart. They had to cross over on a bridge that consisted of three tree trunks that stretched from one cliff to the other. Thirty feet below, the river crashed against the rocks, throwing up a spray that kept the logs slick and wet.* Once they passed that peril, they began making their way along a narrow, muddy path that ran high above the river, just above the canyon cut by the Pastaza. Every few miles or so, they came to a stream cascading down from the mountains to the north. At times, the sheer beauty of the cascading waterfalls caught everyone's breath, one river after another spilling down the steep mountainside and then, at the rim of the canyon, leaping outward into a free fall, dashing onto rocks hundreds of feet below.

Each time they came to one of these rivers, they had to stop and find a way to ford it. A few were small enough that a log could be placed from bank to bank, but the Indians needed to cobble together bamboo bridges to navigate the wider ones. To do so, they would cut long poles of bamboo from the forest and drop one pole across the river. An Indian would shimmy along it, dragging a liana rope

---

* As a result of road construction, the river below Baños no longer passes through a channel this narrow.

Crossing a log bridge over a river in the jungle.
*Natural History Museum, London. Bridgeman Art Library.*

with him. Once on the other side, he would use the liana to bring a
second bamboo pole alongside the first. Then two or three more
would be positioned in this manner and lashed together. The sure-
footed Indians would cross the bridge loaded down with the goods
or carrying Isabel in her chair, the bamboo bending slightly under
their weight but never breaking.

Their progress was slow—they were lucky to make twenty miles
during the first two days. The trail was hopelessly narrow and slick
with mud, and, perched as they were high above the Pastaza, it
seemed to Isabel that at any moment her servants might slip and
they would all perish. At every step, she was pitched to and fro in
her chair, thrown backward one moment and forward the next,
leaving her bruised and battered. So uncomfortable was the ride
that she wished she could proceed on foot, like her brothers, but
that was out of the question for a woman, and she had to be carried,
no matter how unpleasant it was. As Jean later wrote, this road was

"impractical even for mules, and [those] who are able effect the passage on foot, but others"—and by this, he meant women—"are carried." The rains fell constantly, soaking the travelers and their goods, and there was never a chance to get dry. At night, the Indians hastily cut palm leaves and fashioned them into a shelter. The group made camp whenever they came upon the smallest patch of level ground, but the very air was wet, and all they could do each evening was cross another day off the calendar, thankful that they were twenty-four hours closer to Canelos.

Eighty-eight years later, the English explorer Richard Spruce made his way *up* this route, the first Englishman ever to traverse it. Although he was by then a seasoned traveler in South America, having spent ten years gathering plants from the forests, he was nearly defeated by this short sixty-five-mile trek from Canelos to Baños, which took him *seventeen days*. Every day, he complained, there was "rain from sunrise till nightfall. The sloppy ground, the soaked forest, and the unceasing rain kept us close prisoners." At one point, he and his companions had to wade through "fetid mud" for nearly a mile. At another, they were slowed by "beds of prickly bamboos." The path itself was "dreadful, what with mud, fallen trees, and dangerous passes, of which two in particular, along declivities where in places there was nothing to get hold of, are not to be thought of without a shudder." In places, he noted, "the track ran along the very edge of the cliff, and the projecting bushes menaced thrusting us over." He and his guides were constantly slowed by the charging rivers they had to cross, with one—the Topo—stymieing them for days. It "was one mass of foam, and the thunder of its waters against the rocks made the very ground shake to some distance from the bank." When he at last arrived in Baños, the end of a journey that had involved climbing up out of the Amazon via the Bobonaza River, he was completely spent. He was emaciated, his face shrunken from the difficult trek, and so sick that he vomited up blood. He called the seventeen days from Canelos "heart-sickening," and so filled with suffering that he could "hardly bear to think of it."

After five or six days of such travel, Isabel and her entourage reached a point along the Pastaza where the steepest slopes were behind them. They had dropped 3,000 feet over forty miles, and now they had to make their way across a series of lesser hills to Canelos. The Pastaza here is too turbulent for canoes, and so the path cut by Jesuits in the early part of the eighteenth century left the Pastaza watershed for the Bobonaza's, which was navigable starting at Canelos. This last stage of their overland journey was only twenty-five miles long, and they hurried across it. At Canelos, they knew, a priest and canoes would be waiting for them, as well as local Indians who would take them down the Bobonaza. This had all been arranged by her father Pedro, who had come through a month earlier. They would spend a night or two there, just long enough to get dry and refresh their spirits. Such thoughts quickened their pace, and late in the afternoon of October 12 they reached the banks of the upper Bobonaza, which—as Spruce would later write—was "crossed with difficulty and risk, as the turbid swollen waters careened violently among and over rocks and stones." The mission station, they had been told, was only a little further downstream, located on a high bluff above the river. There was a chance now to delight in the trill of the forest birds, the bright-colored splash of a passing toucan or a purple-throated fruit-crow. But when at last the village came into view, they all came to a halt. Plumes of smoke were rising from the huts, every dwelling except for the bamboo church having been set to the torch.

*Smallpox.* And they found the village, as Jean would later write, "utterly abandoned by its population."

ALTHOUGH THEY COULD NOT KNOW for certain, Isabel and her brothers guessed that it was their father's party that had brought the plague into Canelos. Few people visited this village, and it was likely that Pedro Gramesón had been the last to come through. Many of the Indians living in the village had apparently died, and others, they surmised, "had hid in the woods, where each had his own hut." Those fleeing had burned the huts to drive out the evil spirits, a sight that spooked Isabel's thirty-one Indian servants, who, in "dread of the air being infected," immediately dropped all of the supplies and fled toward their homes in the Andes. Isabel's journey had just begun—she could still see the snow-capped mountains of her home in the distance—and already she and the others were in peril: Their servants were gone and they did not have the canoes they needed to proceed further.

They camped that night on the outskirts of the village, uncertain what to do. Their only option seemed to be to go back, but Isabel, as Jean would later write, was unwilling to think of it: "The desire of reaching the vessel waiting her, together with her anxieties to rejoin a husband from whom she had been parted twenty years, were incentives powerful enough to make her, in the peculiar circumstances in which she was placed, brave even greater obstacles." The next morning, Isabel's prayers were answered. Scouting around the village, they found two Indians who were free from the contagion. Isabel spoke to them in Quechua and quickly hired them to build a canoe and guide her party to Andoas.

As the Indians worked, fashioning a cedar tree into a dugout canoe with their machetes, Isabel and the others got their first extended exposure to a tropical forest. They could hear birds everywhere, even though these creatures were often hard to spot. They heard the rat-a-tat-tat of woodpeckers and the squawking calls of macaws and parrots, and spotted a number of hawks and falcons darting through the sky. Such sights and sounds were comforting, for they made the rain forest seem less foreign and threatening. Even the mosquitoes were not too nettlesome, at least within the village's cleared area.

But the nights were a different matter. As dusk fell, the shrieks of howler monkeys living among the treetops across the river rattled their nerves. This bearded simian has a hollow and much-enlarged hyoid bone in its throat. As air passes over this cavity, it produces a plaintive call that some say resembles the sound of a human baby crying. Every evening at Canelos this piercing moan arose from the forest at the same time that a thick cloud of bats flew up from their roosts. Isabel and the others had heard all about the sinister habits of vampire bats, which abounded in this region. The furry creatures will creep into a hut at night, tiptoeing on their hind legs (rather than descending beneath noisy beating wings), and then climb onto their sleeping prey. Their incisors are so sharp that they can open a vein without waking their victims. When dining on human blood, they favor the face or feet, and although this blood sucking generally does not do much physical harm, newcomers to the jungle find it a deeply unnerving thought.

The Canelos Indians finished the canoe in about two weeks. It was nearly forty feet long, and toward the stern they had erected a small shelter with a thatched roof for Isabel, to protect her from the equatorial sun. Her only disappointment was that the canoe was too small for all their goods. She and her brothers had expected to have two or three canoes at their disposal, but now they had only one, and they were forced to leave some of their precious supplies behind. They stepped into the canoe uneasily—none of them knew how to swim—and then the two Indians, who had been steadying the craft, leapt from the sandbank and pushed off into the swift current. It was October 25, and in two weeks or so, Isabel and the others could hope to be in Andoas.

The Bobonaza drops about 100 feet over the course of the first twenty miles below Canelos, this stretch of river marked by more than a dozen small rapids that have to be carefully navigated. One of the Indians stood in the front of the canoe, using a long pole to push them away from the rocks, all the while employing hand signals and a sharp whistle to chart a course for the second Indian, who was seated in the rear and steering with a paddle employed as a rudder. They passed through several deep gorges, the stone walls rising more than seventy feet, and on each one, about twenty feet up, there was a high-water mark, the stone scoured clean to this line. Like all rivers that drained the eastern slopes of the Andes, the Bobonaza was a fickle beast. Should a storm of particular intensity break, it would rise with frightening speed, as much as fifteen feet in a single night. At such moments, a huge swell of water would descend downstream like a river tsunami, carrying with it a tangle of tree branches and other debris scoured from the banks.

When Spruce came to this stretch of the Bobonaza in 1849, he experienced this phenomenon. On his way from Andoas to Canelos, he was camped on a small spit of sand when, on May 21, a wave hit:

> We had scarcely resigned ourselves to sleep, at about nine o'clock, when the storm burst over us, and the river almost simultaneously began to rise. Speedily the beach was overflowed, the Indians leaping into the canoes, the waters continued to rise with great rapidity, coming in on us every few minutes in a roaring surge which broke under the canoes in whirlpools, and dashed them against each other. Floating trees now began to career past us like mad bulls. So dense was the gloom that we could see nothing while we were deafened by the pelting rain, the roaring flood, and the crashes of the branches of the floating trees, as they rolled over or dashed against each other, but each lightning flash revealed to us all the horrors of our position. Assuredly, I had slight hopes of living to see the day.

Two of Spruce's companions that night fled into the jungle to escape the raging river, which rose eighteen feet in twelve hours. They retreated "inland," Spruce wrote in his journal, "and when day broke it found them half dead with cold, and their clothes and bodies torn and wounded by prickly bamboos and palms."

Such was the Bobonaza. At first glance, the river could seem rather tranquil, and in fact, there were days when it could be negotiated with relative ease. But its true power rested in the skies, in the gray clouds that came marching westward from the Amazon basin each afternoon, slamming into the Andes and dropping a torrent of rain. When that process peaked, or turned more violent than usual, the Bobonaza awoke with a vengeance. And for those who were not of the forest, like Isabel, a retreat inland offered not refuge but a host of life-threatening dangers.

With the Canelos Indians piloting the canoe, their first two days went well. They passed through the upper narrows without mishap, and by the second afternoon, most of the rapids were behind them. The rock walls receded, replaced by a crush of trees and brush that cast shadows over the water's edge, creating a sensation of traveling through a cool, dark tunnel. The current had slowed, and with no big storm having hit above, the river seemed almost peaceful. As they floated downriver, new scenes of wildlife appeared at every turn. They could see a turtle riding on the back of a log, an alligator slipping into the water,* a family of capybaras playing on a muddy stretch of riverbank. (This last animal is the world's largest rodent, a 120-pound relative of the common rat.) There were too many river birds to count: black caracaras cruised overhead, letting out a loud raspy scream that sounded like "kra-a-a-a-a-a"; blue-throated piping-guans perched in the treetops, occasionally taking noisy wing to cross the river; and red-breasted kingfishers plunged suddenly into the water, emerging more often than not with a small fish. Isabel and the others were also certain to have come across a strange-looking bird with red eyes, blue face, and spiky blond crest, crashing through the underbrush, barking at the canoe as it passed by, and— if the bird dared to try—struggling mightily to fly. This was a hoatzin, one of the rain forest's more humorous creatures.

Each of those first two nights they camped on sandbars, their Indian guides building lean-tos to sleep in, and doing so with amazing speed. After tying up the canoe, they would plunge fearlessly into the jungle, apparently unconcerned about the poisonous snakes known to haunt these banks, emerging in a few moments with an armful of stout sticks and a bundle of palm fronds. After laying two sticks down on the sand, parallel to each other and about

---

* In South America, reptiles in the *Alligatoridae* family are more properly known as caimans. The caiman has a more heavily armored belly than the North American alligator.

nine feet apart, they would quickly lash the palm fronds to them. This "roof" was then propped up on two forked sticks planted upright in the sand. Isabel and the others ate well on those nights, their usual meal of dried meats and corn supplemented by whatever their Indian servants could take from the wilderness—perhaps a turtle one night and catfish the next, caught with a small net brought along for this purpose.

They retired the second evening with reason to feel optimistic. They were making good progress toward Andoas, and a beach could be a fairly pleasant place to sleep, the terrors of the jungle kept at bay by the sand between them and the brooding trees. The howler monkeys were in there, and not out here, and so too were the snakes, which liked to remain hidden in the brush. While vampire bats could still be a problem and jaguars might prowl a sandbar at night, the Indians kept a fire burning to keep the man-eating beasts away. Such skills comforted Isabel and the others. However, when they awoke the third morning, they looked upon a horrible sight. Their "pilots," as Jean later wrote, had "absconded."

Isabel realized her mistake at once. She had paid the Canelos Indians in full ahead of time. That was the custom, and they had demanded the advance pay, but the arrangement had removed any incentive for them to remain until they reached Andoas. Doing so would simply have led to a more arduous return journey to Canelos. She and the others were now alone on a river they knew nothing about. Their only salvation was that the Indians had left them the canoe, apparently choosing to make their way back to Canelos on foot.

There was little possibility that they might do the same. "We didn't know the path through the woods [to Canelos]," the French doctor Jean Rocha later told the priest at Andoas, "and it was even less possible to return by the river, since it was flowing very fast, filled with rocks and sticks. Even the Indians who were experienced in navigating the river found it terrible, and so we determined to lower ourselves on the river under the guidance of God, assigning to everyone a job."

Rocha took the place of the navigator up front. Joaquín, Isabel's slave, assumed the role of steersman in the rear, while Isabel's two brothers, Juan and Antonio, took paddles in hand and, seated in the middle, "rowed," hoping to propel them faster through the slower sections of the river. Isabel and the others—her nephew Martín, her two maids Tomasa and Juanita, the Frenchman's companion Phelipe Bogé, and Rocha's slave Antonio—sat scattered about the boat.

That day the river rose, and they could see it was raining in the mountains. A large tributary, the Sarayacu, flowed into the Bobonaza, adding to their sense that the river was growing exponentially in power and force. As Rocha was to tell the priest in Andoas, "None of us had any skills, which put the canoe at every instant in a million dangers, now against a stick, then against a rock, with the canoe filling with water often in the rough spots, with evident risk of going under." At such moments, Isabel clutched the two gold chains around her neck and silently asked that the "Virgin hear their prayers." It seemed that they would not survive the day. But they did, and at noon on the following one, they came upon a most welcome sight: "We saw a canoe," Rocha related,

> and next to it footsteps, and following the path to a hut, we found an Indian convalescing from the smallpox. He appeared like death, but this man was alive, and we were overjoyed at seeing him. He was in a state of total abandonment, as all his family had been killed by the smallpox. He was content to get on board and take over management of the canoe. Although he was weakened by his illness, he was animated by his skill.

The rest of that day and the next two—October 29 and 30—passed without incident. The Bobonaza continued to widen after yet another large tributary, the Rutunoyacu, flowed into it from the north. The landscape changed here as well. They were now more than 100 miles below Canelos, and the river had spilled out into a floodplain, snaking back and forth across the flat land, creating a swampy landscape of oxbows and lagoons. They were not moving at any great speed—indeed, at times it seemed they were just drifting along at a leisurely pace—and yet they could see the river pushing along huge logs and branches, a great force that kept them on edge. No one said much; they were all alone in their thoughts. Then, late on October 31, a gust of wind blew Rocha's hat into the water, and their pilot, "stooping to recover it," as Jean later wrote, "fell overboard, and not having sufficient strength to reach the shore, was drowned."

Everyone was too stunned to move. One moment the Indian was there, behind them, safely steering the canoe, and the next he was slipping beneath the water, his arms flailing as the current carried him off. And now the canoe was "again without a steersman, abandoned to individuals perfectly ignorant of managing it." They were adrift in the current, Joaquín trying to scramble past Isabel to the rear without upsetting the boat. In very short order, the canoe was turned sideways by the current, and, striking a log, was "overset."

They spilled into the river, and so too did the woven baskets with all of their goods. Isabel, pulled under by the weight of her heavy silk garments, came up gasping for air and grabbing for the overturned canoe, as did everyone else. They were not far from the river's edge, and by clinging to the upside-down boat, they were able, "with great work, to arrive at a beach."

They were now in a dire predicament. Although they were able to retrieve most of their supplies, Isabel and her two brothers were so spooked by the Indian's drowning and their own near escape that they resisted getting back into the canoe. They built a hut that night as far up on the beach as possible, planning to wait there for a day or two, to see whether the river would drop. But it did not. "Each day," Rocha said, brought "greater dangers." At last—on their third day on the beach—Rocha "proposed to repair to Andoas" and seek help. By everyone's reckoning, they were "five or six days journey from Andoas," and Isabel and her two brothers, with the river at such a height, were still not willing "to trust themselves on the water without a proper pilot." Rocha laid out his rescue plan: He, Bogé, and Joaquín would take the canoe, and since it would no longer be so loaded down, they should be able to steer it fairly easily. They would hurry to Andoas, where they would gather "a proper complement of natives" to come back upriver and rescue those left behind. Isabel and the others could expect to see a well-supplied canoe return within two weeks, three at most.

At ten o'clock the next morning—the date was November 3—Rocha and the others left. Those remaining on the sandbar stood together as they paddled off, the canoe passing around a bend and slipping from their sight. Only then did they realize what they had done. They were now marooned on this spit of sand. They were miles from the nearest speck of civilization, alone in a fearsome wilderness, and they had to rely on the others to return. As they looked around the sand and took a quick inventory of their supplies, their panic rose. Although they had a fair amount of food left, enough for three weeks if rationed, they could see what was missing: Rocha, while packing up, had taken "especial care to carry his effects with him." He had left none of his belongings behind.

# CHAPTER THIRTEEN

# Into the Jungle

THE SANDBAR THAT ISABEL'S PARTY was stranded on was perhaps 200 feet wide and several hundred yards long. They had built their hut, as Rocha later told the priest at Andoas, "at the top of the beach, located in a way that it could not have been more insulated from the growing river." They had also woven palm fronds together into beds, which made their rancho, as such beach shelters were called, at least somewhat comfortable. They were, however, surrounded by a wilderness that they did not dare enter. They were now in the very part of the Amazon basin that is most inhospitable to humans.

Much of the Amazon rain forest is relatively benign and not overly difficult to walk through, as long as one is equipped with a compass or is on a path. The dense canopy blocks out so much sunlight that there is only a sparse amount of vegetation on the forest floor. Leaves and other plant debris that fall to the ground are quickly chewed up by hordes of ants and beetles, and while there are poisonous snakes and other dangers in a rain forest of this type, they are not so overwhelming as to chase all humans away. Even the mosquitoes and bugs are not too nettlesome in a mature rain forest. But the forests along the lower Bobonaza, where Isabel and her party were stranded, are a different case. At this point, the river's descent from the Andes is over, and as it spills into the huge lowland that is the Amazon basin, it turns the landscape into a marshy swampland.

The jacumama that Ulloa and Juan wrote about, cautioning that this "man-eating serpent delights in lakes and marshy places," is known today as the great anaconda. Growing to as much as thirty feet long and weighing as much as 500 pounds, it lies in wait along the river's edge and in lagoons, feeding—in the eighteenth century —on a bountiful supply of capybaras, large birds, peccaries (a piglike animal), 400-pound tapirs (a hoofed mammal), and young caimans. The constrictor kills by coiling itself around its prey and strangling it.

The poisonous snakes that haunt the banks of the lower Bobonaza are of two kinds: coral snakes and pit vipers. The corals are recognizable by their red and yellow bands warning predators to stay away. Their powerful venom can cause heart and respiratory failure. The poison from the fangs of pit vipers, which have distinctive triangular heads and catlike eyes, kills by rapidly destroying blood cells and vessels. Most pit vipers, such as the fer-de-lance, hide coiled beneath forest-floor debris. However, the palm pit viper likes to hang from a branch, looking for all the world like a dangling vine, remaining perfectly still until striking out at any passing bird or warm-blooded animal that mistakenly brushes up against it. During October and November, snakes on the lower Bobonaza also tend to be on the move, for this is the season in which they shed their skins and travel to new holes.

Jaguars still roam this region as well, although not in the numbers they did in the eighteenth century, when they were called "tigers" by the Spaniards. They prowl the rivers and marshes, hunting monkeys, tapirs, peccaries, capybaras, and juvenile caimans. Their prints are often found on sandbars. At times, in the early morning hours, a jaguar still full from a night of successful

An explorer fights a "tiger" in the jungle.
*From Jorge Juan and Antonio de Ulloa,* Relación histórica
del viage a la América Meridional *(1749)*.

hunting will stretch out on a log floating down a river, catching some sun.

Even the river harbors a host of threatening creatures. In the lower Bobonaza, there are electric eels that can deliver a 650-volt jolt, blood-sucking leeches, stingrays with venom-laced tails, and a bizarre catfish called the candiru. Thin as a catheter, the candiru has the nasty habit of swimming up body orifices—the human urethral, vaginal, or anal opening—where it fixes itself by opening an array of sharp fin spines, triggering almost unendurable pain.

Isabel and the others, having been warned about all these dangers, clung to the sandbar. They were prisoners of their little spit of beach, near a spot on the Bobonaza known today as Laguna Ishpingococha. Their days quickly settled into a routine. They would awaken at the first break of light, often to the sound of monkeys chattering in the nearby trees. This was the best hour of their day. The light was soft and the air relatively cool, the temperature having dropped to seventy-five degrees Fahrenheit or so during the

A hut on the lower Bobonaza.
*Drawing by Ingrid Aue.*

night. Herons, swallows, and other river birds swooped about, and across the way, there was a beautiful ceiba tree in flower. All of the leaves had dropped from its majestic crown, and its seeds would drift across the water, held aloft by silky, cottonlike fibers. Isabel and the others would eat upon rising, taking from their supplies a serving of dried potatoes or corn or a small piece of jerky.

As the sun rose, however, the air would turn humid and oppressive. By midday, the sand would be hot to the touch, so much so that it would be difficult to cross barefoot. There was nothing for them to do but hide out in shade of their hut, no one saying much of anything. More often than not, the heat would give way to an afternoon rain, and when the rain ceased, the sand flies, gnats, and mosquitoes would come out. These insects pestered them as they pestered all who came through here: Isabel and everyone else scratched their bites, which became infected, their legs in particular becoming covered with the painful sores.

At dusk, the jungle would begin to resonate with the nerve-racking shrieks of howler monkeys and the whoosh-whoosh of bats—sounds that had become familiar and yet were still unsettling. And as night fell, Isabel and the others would struggle to put down thoughts of caimans, jaguars, and snakes creeping through the darkened foliage, only a few yards away from their hut. They worried too that the Jibaros would discover their campsite and swoop down upon them while they were sleeping. Although the Quechua Indians in Canelos and Andoas were not to be feared, the Jibaros were, and they were known to haunt both sides of this river. When Spruce came to this region, his Quechua guides slept with "lances and bows and arrows at the head of their mosquito nets, so as to be ready in case of an attack," while Spruce would only "go ashore with firearms." The Jibaros were the "naked savages" that La Condamine had written about, a tribe said to "eat their prisoners."

Isabel and the others passed a week in this anxious manner, and then a second. As the days passed, they began to grow weaker, the heat sapping their strength. During the long midday hours, they would all rest in the shade of their hut, and even though their throats would become parched with thirst, nobody would stir, as though the trip across the sand to the river would be too taxing. The jungle, meanwhile, was *literally* closing in on them: The rising river had narrowed their beach. Their clothing was rotting and disintegrating in the humidity, their insect bites were turning into open, festering sores, and with each passing day it seemed increasingly evident that nobody was coming back for them. They were notching a stick to count the days, but after a while, they were no longer certain just how much time had passed. Had they remembered to cut a notch the day before? They could not be quite sure, for the days merged one into another. In their confusion, they would add another notch to their stick, and in this manner—as later became clear—they became too quick with their calendar. As a result, sooner than they should have, they lost all "confidence that help would come."

By their count, that moment of total despair arrived "five and twenty days" after the others had left. Rocha had promised that he would return in two weeks, three weeks at most, and yet their cal-

## Lost on the Bobonaza

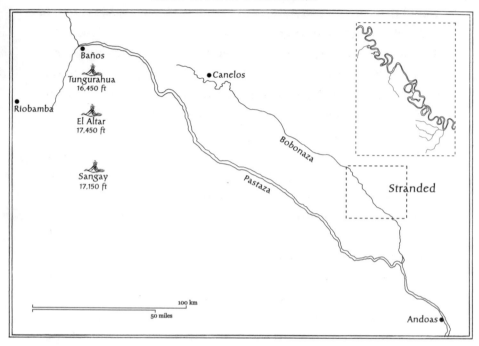

endar stood at November 28. They remembered too that he had
taken all his things with him. Their food supplies were nearly
gone—clearly, they could not stay on the sandbar much longer.
Faced with such facts, Isabel and her two brothers made a fateful
decision: They would build a raft. They had both a machete and an
ax, and fighting now for their lives, they entered the jungle, hacking away at the few slender trees they could find and dragging
them to the sandbar. After cutting the poles to the same length,
they lashed them together with lianas. This fragile craft would
have to carry them more than ninety miles to safety.

The raft, however, was not big enough to take everyone. Again,
they decided to split up. Isabel, her two brothers, and her nephew
Martín would go ahead, while Rocha's slave Antonio would stay
behind with Isabel's two maids, Juanita and Tomasa. The two girls
were only eight or nine years old, and Antonio would watch over
them, with the hope that a rescue party would soon arrive. Either

Rocha and Joaquín would finally return, or Isabel and the others would make it safely to Andoas and send a canoe back upriver.

Neither option—staying or going—had much to recommend it. This was a plan born of utter desperation and perhaps delirium. Everyone had grown weak and confused on the beach, and things quickly went awry. No sooner had Isabel and the others clambered onto the raft than it began swirling out of control in the river, Juan and Antonio struggling desperately with their two long poles to keep it headed in the right direction. Then disaster struck: "The raft," as Jean would later write, "badly framed, struck against the branch of a sunken tree, and overset, and their effects perished in the waves, the whole party being plunged into the water."

This time, there was no overturned canoe to grab onto. Isabel, still in her heavy dress, gulped for air and went under, her arms flailing as she struggled to keep from drowning. Those who had been left behind on the beach were screaming, helpless to do anything. Then Isabel felt a hand grab the back of her dress, pulling her momentarily to the surface. A burst of air flew into her lungs, then she plunged once more beneath the water, into a tangle of branches and debris. Her mind exploded in panic until yet again she felt a hand reaching for her, pulling her up and toward the bank. "No one was drowned," Jean wrote, "Madame Godin being saved, after twice sinking, by her brothers."

Frightened and muddy, they made their way back to the sandbar. The provisions they had placed aboard the raft were gone, putting them "in a situation still more distressing than before." Although the wise decision surely would have been to resume waiting there, they felt they had to do something. "Collectively," they "resolved on tracing the course of the river along its banks." Isabel, her two brothers, and Martín would try to walk to Andoas. Antonio, Juanita, and Tomasa would once again stay behind, and if rescue of any kind happened by—perhaps a Quechua Indian would come downriver, or perhaps a search party from Andoas would indeed at last be sent—they could tell it to look for Isabel and her brothers, who planned to stay close to the river's edge.

In preparation of the long trek ahead, Isabel changed out of her dress and into an extra pair of her brother's pants. Even in that desperate hour, the sight of Isabel wearing a pair of men's pants was startling: No one had ever seen a woman so dressed. They packed up the ax, the machete, and a portion of the remaining provisions. Their supplies were so low that they would only have enough food for a few days, and then they would have to forage for something to eat. Their minds were set, and without any further hesitation, Isabel, her two brothers, and Martín—all of them already weak and exhausted—plunged into the jungle.

HAD ISABEL AND HER BROTHERS possessed a map and a compass, along with supplies, it would have been feasible for them to walk to Andoas. They would have needed to walk away from the river, out of its swampy environs to slightly higher and drier land, and then make a beeline to Andoas, which was about seventy-five miles away as the crow flies. But their plan to follow the river—something that only a mountain-dweller would think of trying—was doomed to fail. The lower Bobonaza twists and turns as it makes its way across this lowland, heading north one moment and south the next, the river carving out huge, slow oxbows, such that one could walk several miles along its banks and end up only a few hundred yards further to the east. Even worse, the vegetation was so thick that they had to hack through it with their machete, which wore them out and slowed their progress. "The banks of the river are beset with trees, undergrowth, herbage, and lianas, and it is often necessary to cut one's way," Jean Godin wrote. "By keeping along the river's side, they found its sinuosities greatly lengthened their way, to avoid which inconvenience they penetrated the wood."

Although they were now out of the swampiest areas, they found it impossible to orient themselves in the darkened rain forest. The thick canopy of trees filtered out most of the light. They could not see more than twenty or thirty feet in any direction, the landscape a

A nineteenth-century illustration of a primeval forest in the Amazon.
*Private collection/Bridgeman Art Library.*

chaotic mix of shadows and otherworldly shapes. Many of the trees
rose from a tangle of aboveground roots, as though they were ready
to begin walking around on stilts. Vines and creepers were everywhere, climbing up tree trunks and dripping from the canopy.
Even the palm trees had whorls of sharpened spikes around their
trunks, a form of armor in this fierce landscape. This gloomy, foreign place was the very world that haunted their imaginations—
this was where they had "lost themselves"—and every night, as
dusk fell, mosquitoes, flies, and other insects came out in droves,
tormenting them in a most physical way.

Nineteenth-century explorers who spent any length of time in
this type of Amazonian terrain—wet jungle away from the con-
fines of a river—inevitably complained of how utterly intolerable
it was. When Spruce explored the forest bordering the Pastaza, in
the area around Andoas, he could bear it only for a few hours.
"The very air my be said to be alive with mosquitoes. ... I con-

stantly returned from my walk with my hands, feet, neck and face covered with blood, and I found I could nowhere escape these pests." Similarly, Humboldt, while traveling through landscape of this kind in the early 1800s, reported that the insects could drive one mad:

> Without interruption, at every instant of life, you may be tormented by insects flying in the air. ... However accustomed you may be to endure pain without complaint, however lively an interest you may take in the objects of your researches, it is impossible not to be constantly disturbed by the moschettoes, *zancudoes, jejens,* and *tempraneroes,* that cover the face and hands, pierce the clothes with their long sucker in the form of a needle, and, getting into the mouth and nostrils, set you coughing and sneezing whenever you attempt to speak in the open air.

As pervasive as the flying insects can be, the insects that march on the forest floor—the many species of ants—are even more so, their vast numbers sustained by the voluminous leaf litter. Ants are so numerous in a lowland rain forest that collectively they may outweigh all the vertebrates inhabiting it. As the American biologist Adrian Forsyth found, ants in this environment never leave a person alone:

> No matter where you step, no matter where you lean, no matter where you sit, you will encounter ants. There are ant nests in the ground, ant nests in the bushes, ant nests in the trees; whenever you disturb their ubiquitous nests, the inhabitants rush forth to defend their homes.
>
> One of the most painful nonlethal experiences a person can endure is the sting of the giant ant *Paraponera clavata*. These ants, with their glistening black bodies over an inch long, sport massive hypodermic syringes and large venom reservoirs. They call on these weapons with wild abandon when provoked, and they are easily offended beasts.

The catalog of bothersome insects in a lowland rain forest is endless. There are giant stinging ants, ants that bite, and ants that both bite and sting. People who have been attacked by the notorious "fire ants" describe the pain as exactly like "reaching into a flame." The sting from one of Forsyth's "bullet ants" is said to be like a "red-hot spike" that produces hours of "burning, blinding pain." Colonies of wasps and bees abound, and there are many scorpions and tarantulas. Chiggers fasten onto the legs of passersby who brush against the vegetation, and their saliva contains a digestive enzyme that dissolves the surrounding flesh, producing, as one traveler wrote, "raging complex itches that come and go for days on end." The assassin bug is a nasty bloodsucker that bites people around the mouth or on the cheek (and thus is sometimes known as the kissing bug), and even caterpillars in his lowland forest can be menacing. Many, the naturalist John Kricher writes, "are covered with sharp hairs that cause itching, burning and welts if they prick the skin, a reaction similar to that caused by stinging nettle."

This was the landscape in which Isabel, her two brothers, and her nephew were now stranded. During the daylight hours, they tried to keep moving, usually in single file, with either Juan or Antonio in the lead, the other at the rear, and Isabel and Martín in the middle. They would walk and walk, and then they would have to stop to rest, drained by the heat and humidity. They would drink their fill of water at a stream, and at last they would pull themselves to their feet and wander some more, until their throats thickened again with thirst. They were not trying to go in any particular direction, they were just trying to keep moving, hoping that they would stumble back upon the Bobonaza. Then, as dusk fell, the insects would come out, and there was absolutely nothing they could do to protect themselves from this onslaught. They had no ointments, no mosquito nets, no tents—only the clothes they were wearing and several shawls, which they would desperately wrap around their faces and hands. But it was futile. The insects feasted on them, and even the full darkness of the night did not bring them relief. They would huddle together in the blackness, perhaps leaning against a fallen branch or against a large tree trunk, and hordes of ants would begin their onslaught, crawling over them, under their pants and over every inch of exposed skin. This would be their lot for twelve nightmarish hours, and then the pitiless cycle would begin all over again.

During these awful days, they were plagued in particular by mosquitoes laden with botfly eggs. A botfly will stick its eggs to a passing mosquito, and when the mosquito feeds on an animal, the animal's body heat causes the eggs to hatch. The larvae then burrow beneath the skin. A botfly maggot has two anal hooks that anchor it firmly in its new nest, and there it grows for more than a month, causing discomfort in its host every time it turns because its body is covered with sharp spines. At last, it emerges as an inch-long worm, ready to pupate and begin its life as a botfly. Monkeys in the lowland rain forests of the Amazon can be so parasitized by botflies that they die from them. And that was now happening to Isabel, her two brothers, and young Martín. They were taking their turn as food for the botflies of the Bobonaza forest, even as they were slowly starving to death.

THE FERTILITY OF THE RAIN FOREST, with its profusion of plants and wildlife, suggests that it should be an easy place to forage for food. Orellana and Acuña, after their voyages down the Amazon, reported that Indians living along the banks had bountiful supplies of food, raising turtles in pens, growing manioc, fishing, and hunting the abundant game. But their mastery over the environment had been achieved over the course of 10,000 years, and in a part of the Amazon basin that was much more habitable than the swampy lowlands near the Bobonaza. Wild Jibaros of the eighteenth century may have hunted in these lowlands, but they built their villages on drier ground, further upriver. Even in that more hospitable environment, nearly all of the available food—other than game—is out of reach, in the top part of the canopy. At ground level, there is little to harvest. Trees and plants are in such fierce competition for light and space that they are armed with a panoply of defenses to prevent their leaves and bark from being consumed.

The foremost of these are chemical toxins, mainly phenolics, tannins, and alkaloids; this last group is experienced by humans as analgesics, stimulants, and hallucinogens. In the wild, they serve to discourage insects from feeding on a plant's leaves. As one naturalist has written, the caffeine that we find stimulating and enjoyable "is in reality a form of insecticide." Indigenous tribes in the Amazon use these compounds in their shaman medicine and also, as La Condamine discovered, as poisons with which they hunt and fish. In addition to an array of chemical defenses, tropical plants may have spiny leaves and jagged stilettos on their trunks to ward off insects. These daggers are in turn covered by lichens and microbes that can easily cause an infection.

As a result of this plant warfare, the food cycle in the rain forest is an unusual one. High up in the canopy, there may be an abundance of fruit and nuts that can be consumed, since plants may depend on animals to spread their seeds. The fruits and nuts are feasted on by monkeys, sloths, bats, birds, insects, and other denizens of the treetops. But lower down in the rain forest, there is little food available for ground-dwelling herbivores. Most of the ground animals either consume dead vegetable matter, as ants and termites do, or feed on fish, birds, monkeys, and other meat-eaters, with the jaguar at the top of this particular food chain. The American biologist Victor von Hagen, who lived among the Jibaros in the upper Amazon during the 1930s, described how impossible it is to forage for food in this environment:

> All that the primitive has, he has cultivated from indigenous plants in the forest. These he has grown since time immemorial. The jungle yields, in its wild state, practically nothing. To be explicit, there are only four or five foods that may be obtained, irregularly from bountiful nature, and none of these can sustain man, brown or white, over an extended period of time.

One of the few edibles that can be found in the Bobonaza watershed is the palm cabbage, and that is what Isabel, her two brothers, and Martín were "fain to subsist on," along with "a few seeds and wild fruit." After their food ran out, they spent all their daylight hours in search of something to eat. They would fall upon a palm cabbage as though it were a feast, and then they would resume their hunt. Yet they were growing ever more gaunt, and each succeeding day their "fatigue" and their "wounds" increased. "Thorns and brambles" tore at their flesh and clothing, and the insects never let up; every inch of their bodies was covered with bites, which were horribly infected. The jungle was killing them in a thousand small ways.

They struggled in this way for three weeks, and then a fourth. They were still on their feet in late December. They kept on finding just enough food to keep going a little longer, wandering for a few hours each day to hunt for palm cabbage and then moving on to a new spot, until at last, "oppressed with hunger and thirst, with lassitude and loss of strength, they seated themselves on the ground without the power of rising, and waited thus the approach of death."

THE PROCESS OF DYING from starvation is fairly well understood. At first, the body is able to draw on stored carbohydrates and fats as a source of energy. Liver glycogen, which is how the body packs away carbohydrates for emergency use, is broken down to maintain blood glucose levels. Once the glycogen stores are depleted, the body begins to break down muscle tissue to extract amino acids that can be used to make glucose. At the same time, with glucose in such short supply, the body begins to utilize an emergency energy source, ketones synthesized by the liver from fatty acids. The body's metabolism slows down as well, and the starving person becomes ever more lethargic. Toward the end, speech becomes slurred, and all of the senses start to fail: Hearing dims, eyesight fades, and smell disappears, the body progressively consuming itself until death arrives.

This was the point of near-death that the Gramesóns had reached. As they lay on the forest floor, too weak to move, all except Isabel, who retained a certain strength, slipped in and out of consciousness. Isabel did what she could to care for her brothers and her nephew, whose pain during these final hours came not from their hunger but from their thirst. The humidity of the jungle drew water from their parched bodies just as it drew moisture from plants, and there, in a rain forest of all places, their agonies were increased by the torments of dehydration. As their saliva dried up, horrible lumps formed in their throats, which they were unable to dislodge no matter how many times they swallowed. Their tongues thickened so much that they gasped for breath. It was as though they were dying not from hunger or even, in the very end, from thirst but from suffocation.

Martín was "the first to succumb." Isabel cradled him in her arms, for she still had the energy to sit, with her back against a tree. Their unlucky fate was such that hardly any rain came in those last days, but when it did, Isabel soaked up the water with her shawl and used it to moisten Martín's forehead and his lips. Her nephew looked so *old*. His skin had turned purplish, and his eyes had sunk ever deeper into his skull. He seemed to be pleading with her, but he was too weak to speak, the only sound escaping from his lips a low moan. At last his eyes closed, he groaned slightly as his lungs fought for one more breath, and he was gone. His father Antonio and his uncle Juan expired in similar pain over the course of the next couple of days, and then Isabel, having "watched as they all died," awaited "her own last moments."

Because women have a higher percentage of body fat, they tend to outlast men in starvation situations.* Isabel was also short and middle-aged, both factors that affect metabolism in ways that allow a

* Perhaps the best-known example of this phenomenon occurred in the winter of 1846, when the infamous Donner Party became trapped in the Rocky Mountains. More than two-thirds of the twenty-five men in the group died, mostly from starvation, while only four of fifteen women died, and they succumbed only at the very end of the ordeal.

starving person to live a little while longer. And for two days more, Isabel lay "stretched on the ground by the side of the corpses of her brothers [and her nephew], stupefied, delirious, and tormented with choking thirst." All of the flies and insects of the forest had descended on the three rotting bodies, and they swarmed over her too. She was little more than a living corpse, and she desperately wanted to die. Yet even as she prayed to God for relief, for an end to her suffering, images of Jean began to flit in and out of her mind. At one point, she thought she could hear him calling to her. She was hallucinating, of course, yet it seemed so vivid, and in those moments she felt a surge of willpower, a desire to live. God was sparing her, it seemed, and a boat was waiting to take her to her husband. She was thirsty, she needed to "look for water," and suddenly a single thought was pushing loudly to the front of her mind: *Get up.*

At last, as Jean would later write, Isabel gathered the "resolution and strength" to stand. Her "clothing was in tatters" from the many weeks in the jungle, her blouse so torn to shreds that she was nearly naked from the waist up. Her shoes too were gone. After steadying herself, she saw clearly what she had to do. Taking the machete in hand, she knelt next to the decaying corpses. Antonio's shoes would now be hers. She "cut the shoes off her brother's feet," and hacked away until she had converted them into sandals. Seeing that her clothing was "all torn to rags," she "took her scarf and wrapped it around herself." And then Isabel Godin, who only three months earlier had departed from Riobamba dressed in silk, disappeared into the forest.

BY THIS TIME, a rescue canoe had long since come and gone from the sandbar where Isabel and the others had been stranded. The scene that Joaquín had found there was as gruesome as the one in the forest. He, Rocha, and Bogé had successfully reached the mission station in Andoas on November 8, "at four in the afternoon." The resident priest, Juan Suasti, was not there when they arrived, as he was off visiting a village further downriver called

Pinchis, and it took Joaquín at least two days, and possibly three, to pull together a crew of Indians willing to go upriver to rescue those left behind. Rocha and Bogé declined to go back, seemingly indifferent to the fate of Isabel and the others, which caused Jean to later write bitterly that Rocha thought "more of his own affairs than forwarding the boat which should recall his benefactors to life."

Because they had to row against the current, it took Joaquín and the Andoas Indians fourteen days to reach the sandbar, more than twice as long as it had taken Joaquín, Rocha, and Bogé to come downriver. Suasti described what happened next:

> Filled with hope, they jumped onto the land, the slave [Joaquín] with greater energy than the Indians. But they found no one living. The slave entered the rancho where they had left everyone, and found there the beds of straw strewn about, the clothes scattered about the beach, some human bones without meat on them in the forest, and a cadaver in a dip in the river, without much vestige of a person. There was a balsa raft leaning on the side of the river, and on the bank they could find perhaps the footsteps of three persons.

Joaquín and the Indians arrived at the sandbar on November 25, and thus the tragic timeline: Isabel and her family must have departed just a few days earlier, and then those staying behind— Juanita, Tomasa, and Antonio—were killed by marauders of some kind from the jungle. Although the cadaver in the river was badly decomposed, Joaquín thought that perhaps it was Antonio, Rocha's slave. But he also found reason to hope that not all had died. The pile of human bones in the forest was not very big, and there were footprints in the riverbank by the raft, suggesting that several in the group had tried to go on. He ordered the Indians to scour the woods "on both sides of the river to see if they could find some trail," and he too went in search of his beloved mistress. He was a slave but also a Gramesón—in the culture of eighteenth-century Peru this was his *family*—and he walked through the wilderness for four days, calling out Isabel's name every few seconds. He and the Indians searched five or six miles inland, on both sides of the river, but, as Suasti wrote, "all these efforts were in vain."

Before departing from the sandbar, Joaquín took an inventory of the items strewn about the beach. Everything that had been there when he had left on November 3 was still to be found, except for the "ax and machete" and a pair of "old trousers." But Isabel's jewelry and silverware were still there, as were her fancier clothes, such as a "velvet petticoat," and these items he gathered up, intending to bring them to her father, who was waiting in Loreto. On the way back to Andoas, they traveled slowly, regularly stopping so that the Indians could hunt for footsteps or any sort of trail in the woods. They spent two weeks making their way downriver in this halting manner, arriving back in Andoas shortly before December 15. Joaquín and the Indians told Suasti what they had found, and he, in turn, summed up the "sad" news for authorities in Quito:

> They were not able to verify the cause of such a lamentable event because they had not found even one person of the [Grameson] family, and with the countryside being so harsh, with forests empty of all human commerce. The most reasonable Indians formed some ideas of what had happened. They believed that three or four days after the family had been left behind on the beach, they were ravaged either by barbaric Indians or by the fierce tigers that are abundant in these woods. To support the first judgment, they note that they had found in the hut all of their clothing and even their undergarments, which led them to conclude that the infidels killed them during the night, while they were sleeping, killing them all and throwing them into the river.* Plus they found a body torn to pieces in the river. The same

---

* The reasoning here seems to be that if it had been daytime when they were attacked, they would have been wearing their undergarments. But since these items of clothing were found in the hut, the Indians concluded they must have been killed while in their sleep wear.

facts could support the second possibility. Being terrorized by tigers, or something else preying on them, they were filled with dread and shock and inadvertently they threw themselves into the river [and drowned], and some of them could also have fled, taking the balsa raft, getting on it and also drowning. All of the Indians and the Negro that went to look for the señora answered with this declaration and swore on the cross that it was true.

Having written up his report, Suasti told Joaquín to carry it to his superior in Lagunas and to the governor of the Maynas district, Antonio Peña, who was located in Omaguas, near the border with Brazil. Suasti entrusted Isabel's belongings to Rocha, requesting that the Frenchman deliver the jewelry, silverware, and other items to Isabel's father. Rocha, Bogé, and Joaquín arrived in Lagunas on January 8, 1770, where the priest, Nicolás Romero, declared that "knowing what I know about these mountains and its inhabitants, it is not at all difficult to imagine these deaths." They reached Omaguas on January 30, and Peña was similarly convinced, although he thought it most likely that Isabel and the others left behind on the sandbar had been killed "by the Jibaros Indians." He then commanded Joaquín to take the papers to officials in Quito in order to inform them of this "tragic happening."

Joaquín reached the audiencia capital in early May, traveling back to Quito via the Napo River rather than retracing his steps up the Bobonaza. Among the papers he carried was a letter from Rocha and Bogé, which they had signed on December 16 in Andoas, stating that Isabel had promised that she would give him his "card of liberty" once they reached Loreto, where her father was waiting. Although her voyage had come to an awful end, Joaquín had done his part—should he not get the promised card? Joaquín spent three weeks trying to deliver the documents to the audiencia president, Joseph Diguja, but each time he came to Diguja's office he was turned away, told by Diguja's assistant that the president was too busy to see him. Then, as Diguja wrote, on May 28, Quito authorities came to him:

It became known that walking in this city was a fugitive Negro who had come from the province of Maynas. He was apprehended and put in jail. There they found in his possession papers and a letter that was for the head of this Audiencia, which give an account of the extraordinary happenings of the disappearance of the Gramesón family that was traveling by the Río Bobonaza in that province.

With Joaquín's arrest, Spain's colonial bureaucracy began to turn in its usual tortured way. Joaquín, Diguja concluded, was to be blamed for "having been the one that was conveying the said family." This slave had even tried to "hide" the various reports "indispensable for verifying" what had happened, Diguja wrote, and yet he now had the nerve to ask for "his liberty." The audiencia court quickly took up the matter, and it decided that Joaquín was not the only one who should be jailed. The court decided to send to Omaguas a warrant for the arrest of the two Frenchmen on the grounds that they had never obtained a permit for travel to the Maynas province.

The audiencia's investigation continued for another three months. Joaquín was interrogated, and he confessed that as far as he knew, Isabel and her brothers had left Riobamba without proper travel papers. Although Jean Godin, in 1740, may have secured permission from the viceroy of New Granada authorizing him to travel this route, that permit, the court decided, hardly applied to Isabel and her family in 1769. "These roads," wrote a Quito official, are "closed because of their being a route to the Portuguese colony." The law did not "permit commerce or even communication" across this border, and anyone who traded "with a foreigner without a license" could "lose his life." Because Joaquín was one of the "accomplices in this sinful behavior," it was only right that he be imprisoned.

Even members of Isabel's family in Riobamba were asked to explain themselves. Fearful of being fingered as "accomplices," they did their best to wiggle out of any possible blame. Did Isabel and her brothers have a proper license for this travel? No, admitted Isabel's brother-in-law, Antonio Zabala. However, Isabel had left "upon the orders of Jean Godin"—she was obeying her husband, as Peruvian law expected a woman to do. Nor was it conceivable, he and others swore, that Isabel planned to engage in any illicit trading. She had become very poor in the previous years, they said, and had departed with but a few personal things and a paltry "100 pesos." The caravan of thirty-one Indian servants and countless mules was conveniently forgotten, and this seemed to mollify the stuffy bureaucrats.

At the end of August, the Quito court wrapped up matters by ordering villages and cities in the mountains of the audiencia— places that might serve as departure points to the Amazon—to post a public warning. Everyone was to understand that travel into the Amazon was prohibited without a permit and that anyone who traded with a "foreigner" there risked being put to death. One town after another—Ambato, Patate, Riobamba, and Baños— dutifully nailed up the warning, and the sudden appearance of this government advisory might have perplexed people had they not been quick to read between the lines. And thus did the news spread throughout the audiencia and to points beyond, as surely as if a town crier had stood in every village's *plaza mayor* and bellowed out the headline.

Madame Godin, dead.

# CHAPTER FOURTEEN

# Deliverance

WHEN ISABEL LEFT THE SCENE of her brothers' death, she was so weak that she was able only to "drag herself along." That was around the first of January, or possibly a little later, which meant that Isabel had been wandering in the jungle for at least six weeks. In more than 200 years of Amazon exploration, no solo traveler had been lost in the forest for any length of time and emerged alive, and as anyone who was familiar with the jungle could attest, there was little reason to believe that Isabel would be the first. Many years later, when two of Spruce's companions fled into the woods in order to escape a storm, a single night left them "half dead with cold, and their clothes and bodies torn and wounded by prickly bamboos and palms." But Isabel, drawing on an almost unfathomable inner strength, was still putting one foot in front of the other.

At first, she was able only to walk a few hundred yards away from where the bodies of her brothers and nephew lay rotting. Water was her foremost concern, and frequently she stopped to sip drops of the precious liquid from plant leaves, moistening her lips and throat. Early on the second day, she came upon a stream and dropped thankfully to her knees. Her cupped hands trembled as she brought the water to her lips, her throat so dry that swallowing was difficult. But after two or three handfuls, her throat opened up, and she "drank as much as she could."

Isabel was not thinking at all about the best direction to head in. She had stumbled upon water, which was good, and with her thirst at least temporarily allayed, she could focus on finding something to eat. Water, food—all she thought about was how to stay alive. On her third day of wandering alone, her prayers were answered. In a low-lying bush, she came upon a nest that was filled with fresh eggs, a rare find in the rain forest. They may have been partridge eggs, and these, Jean would later relate, she swallowed "with the greatest difficulty ... her esophagus, owing to the want of aliment, having become so much parched and straightened." This was the most Isabel had eaten in weeks. There were seven or eight eggs, "green and about the size of duck eggs," in the nest. The following day she came upon some wild fruit, and this, along with "other food she accidentally met with, sufficed to support her skeleton frame."

These days were not so different from the many that she had spent wandering with her family. She and her brothers had given up all thought of finding their way and had instead spent every moment thinking about food and water. This was still Isabel's lot. Only now, she was much weaker than she had been before, and she was alone. The loss of companions in a survival situation can break even the strongest person, and as bad as it was for Isabel during the day, it was many times worse at night. When dusk fell, she would find a large tree to lean against, usually one with buttressed roots that flared out from its base, and she would draw her shawl around her for the long vigil. Although she was in a tropical jungle, where the temperature rarely dropped below 75 degrees Fahrenheit at night, in her dilapidated condition she would feel chilled. Ants would begin crawling over her, and so too would the flies and mos-

quitoes come, and then she would be engulfed in the noisy blackness of the night.

These moments, as Jean would later write, were the worst for
Isabel. "The remembrance of the shocking spectacle she'd witnessed, the horror of her solitude and the darkness of the night in a
wilderness, and the perpetual apprehension of death, which aug-
mented with every instant, had such effect on her spirits as to cause
her hair to turn gray." While the color of her hair probably turned
because of a lack of food, the metaphor was apt, for it captured the
fact that Isabel, in those long hours, was surely as alone as a human
being could be.


IN HIS 1963 BOOK *They Survived: A Study of the Will to Live,*
the English writer Wilfrid Noyce concluded that in desperate situations, where people are confronted with extremes of thirst and
hunger, "often the apparently strong do not come off best in the
end." What seems to count most is an inner psychological strength,
which is nurtured by purpose, hope, and spiritual beliefs. These
Isabel Godin had in abundance, and she was also experienced in a
humble act that Noyce found was practiced by nearly all survivors:
prayer.

Survivors of long ordeals regularly report that their will to live
was sustained by the *thought* of a specific goal or task they needed to
achieve—with such unfinished business, they could not allow
themselves to die. The British survival psychologist John Leach
found that even a seemingly small task could provide a sense of
purpose that would help one live. "It is surprising the large number
of survivors who come through their ordeal with a message for
loved ones from their friends who have perished, and with the
thought that they must get this message through at all costs."
Similarly, even the most humble hope can provide fuel for the will
to live. One survivor of the death camps at Auschwitz reported that
early on, he had made a date with a woman prisoner, with the

promise that they would go on the outing after they were free, and that it was the hope of that future date that kept him alive.

Prayer, Noyce found, can provide people in desperate situations with a remarkable resilience. He discovered that this was true even for people who were not religious prior to their ordeal. In addition to fostering hope, prayer gives people a palpable sense that they are not alone and, perhaps more important, helps them escape their physical suffering.

Ensio Tiira, a Finn who in 1953 spent thirty-two days on a raft in the Indian Ocean, including fourteen days alone after his companion died, reported, "For the whole voyage I'd had the strange feeling that someone else was with me, watching over me and keeping me safe from harm." After his mate perished, he said, "I felt it more strongly than ever." Similarly, Ernest Shackleton, the English explorer who in 1916 led a crew of twenty-seven men through seventeen months of cruel Antarctic conditions, declared that as he and two of his men crossed South Georgia Island on foot, the last leg of their desperate journey to find help, a "fourth walked beside them." His two companions also spoke of this mysterious "fourth." The story told in 1972 by sixteen Uruguayans who spent ten weeks marooned in the Andes after an airplane crash was much the same. "I can assure you that God is there," one of the survivors told the press. "We all felt it, inside ourselves, and not because we were the kind of pious youths who are always praying all day long. Not at all. But there one feels the presence of God. One feels, above all, what is called the hand of God, and allows oneself to be guided by it."

At the same time, prayer enables people in dire straits to "turn their thoughts to the outside," Noyce discovered. They must escape their physical suffering, and prayer is a vehicle that helps that happen. "Energy which but for prayer would be bound," Noyce wrote, "is by prayer set free." Moreover, as this occurs, survivors report that a "second self" seems to emerge, one that is disassociated from their suffering self. They find refuge in their daydreams and in their thoughts of their loved ones, and in this manner they are able to catch what Leach calls a "spiritual second wind." Those who are able to reach this state, both Leach and Noyce concluded, may endure in ways that defy imagination.

This is what happened to Isabel Godin. After the deaths of her two brothers and her nephew, for two days she waited for God to take her. But then, in some mysterious way, she was called to her feet by the image of her husband and a voice calling out to her. And as she wandered alone in the jungle, "in search of deliverance," as Jean would later write, she was able to escape from the awful torments of the night through prayer. Had she kept her thoughts on the terrors surrounding her as she settled up against a tree, surely she would have gone mad. She would have felt the ants crawling relentlessly up her neck, imagined poisonous snakes rustling through the bush, and dug her nails into her face to get at the botflies hatching there … her mind needed to be elsewhere, and prayer was what allowed it to fly free. As she huddled within her shawl, she would finger the two gold chains that hung from her neck, as though they were a rosary, and begin to say her Hail Mary's, over and over again, just as she had learned to do as a child. Such moments of meditation would give way to fitful sleep, and when she awoke, she would begin her daily search for food and water, convinced—as she later told a priest in Lagunas—that the "Almighty had preserved her" another night, that it was his will that she continue on.

ON WHAT ISABEL COUNTED as her eighth day of wandering alone, she stumbled upon a river of some size, which she took to be the Bobonaza. She spent that night on a small sandbar, and at dawn she "heard a noise at about two hundred paces from her." There, in clear sight, were "two Indians and their wives pushing a canoe into the water." Isabel hurried to hide behind a tree. What if they had spotted her? She was only half-clothed and defenseless … were these the man-eating savages that she had been warned about? "Her terror occasioned her to strike into the wood," Jean wrote, but after observing the two men and their wives for a moment, Isabel had a change of mind. What worse "could possibly befall her than to continue in her present state?"

The Indians were from Canelos. One was named Antonio, and—as he later told others in Andoas—Isabel stepped out of the forest like a ghost. She was wearing a flimsy pair of sandals and "the pants of a man and a shawl," and she spoke to them in Quechua. Would they take her to Andoas? She was so weak that she could barely get these words out, and when the Indians gave her some meat, she was unable to swallow it. The two Indian women then prepared a broth for her, and this she was able to get down.

The Indians also took care of her many wounds. They put a jungle balm on her cuts, and Antonio, as the Andoas Indians would later attest, "took out from her head the worms that had dug into her in the forest." This required some skill, for the maggots, as the Indians well knew, cannot simply be pulled out. The worm is too firmly anchored in the flesh; if it is tugged at, a part will simply break off, inevitably causing an infection.

One way to get rid of the botfly maggot, which breathes through a tiny tube that pokes through the host's skin, is to coax it out with meat. If its breathing tube is covered, the maggot will migrate upward into the meat in its search for air. Another remedy, which the Indians with Isabel probably used, involves rubbing the toxic oil from a green cashew nut over the air hole. This suffocates the maggot, and once its anal hooks loosen their grip, it can be dug out.

The Indians remained with Isabel on the riverbank, nursing her back to health, for an uncertain length of time—perhaps just a few days or perhaps as long as a few weeks.* On their trip to Andoas,

---

* According to Jean's account, Isabel arrived on the riverbank around January 10, 1770. However, she did not reach the mission station of Andoas until mid-February at the earliest. This would mean that the Indians had stayed with her on the riverbank for about a month before they all departed. But Jean's account also suggests that Isabel and the four Indians, following their chance encounter, departed almost at once for Andoas. If so, Isabel had wandered much longer than she believed—either with her brothers or alone—and it was around the first of February when she stumbled back upon the Bobonaza. The true timetable probably lies somewhere in between.

they treated her with "kindness truly affectionate," Jean wrote, devoting "every attention to her wants." They cooked her soups and other easy-to-eat foods and made her a bed of palm fronds to lie down on, for she was too weak to sit for any length of time. To drive the insects away, they kept a clay pot of grass and charcoal constantly smoldering, and from time to time, one of the women would sit by her head, fanning her to keep her cool. As the Bobonaza flowed into the Pastaza, they were even greeted by leaping dolphins, which the Indians took as a sign of good luck.

After about a week of travel, they reached the small mission station. As Isabel stepped from the canoe, nobody—neither the Andoas Indians nor the village priest, Juan Suasti—could believe their eyes. Isabel had been given up for dead nearly *two months* earlier. Suasti had written up his account of the tragedy, and everyone had concluded that she and the others had been set upon either by tigers or by savage Indians and that anyone who had not been killed in this way had drowned or died in the woods. Yet here she was, so gaunt that her bones were nearly poking through her skin, strangely dressed in a soiled pair of men's pants and with a torn shawl wrapped around her naked shoulders. "Doña Isabel," the Andoas Indians later told authorities, had arrived "many days" after having been declared dead, around the "time of Lent." [*]

Suasti ordered the mission-station Indians to bring her a dress and shoes, but "her feet were so swollen and covered with cuts that she was not able to wear them." As the Indians crowded about Isabel, tears welled in her eyes, and she turned to Antonio and the three others who had rescued her:

> Madame Godin, stripped of almost every thing, not knowing otherwise how to testify her gratitude to the Americans who had saved her life, took from her neck two chains of gold, such as are

[*] In 1770, Ash Wednesday—the start of the forty days of Lent—fell on February 28. Thus, at the very earliest, Isabel reached Andoas in mid-February, which might still be seen as the "time of Lent." That date also fits with documented dates of her arrival in villages further downriver.

usually worn in this country, of about four ounces weight, and gave one to each of [the couples], whose admiration at the richness of the present equalled that they would have experienced had the heavens opened before them.

This, however, was not a scene that particularly moved Suasti. He was, as Jean would write, an example of what had been lost in the missions when the Jesuits were expelled and replaced by secular priests. Many of these secular priests were accustomed to extracting a profit from the natives; giving gold to Indians made as much sense as giving it to mules. Even as Isabel looked on, Suasti "took possession of the chains, and gave the poor Americans in their place about three or four yards of coarse cotton, such as is manufactured in the country."

Isabel, "worn out as she was," did not say anything in protest. He was a priest, and she had been taught to obey the clergy. She also desperately needed to rest, to regain her strength before traveling on. But she could not stay here now. The two Indians and their wives had stayed with her and given her water, fed her and tended to her wounds, nursed her at every moment on their journey to this village. She owed her life to them. Nor did she believe it was chance that had brought her to the Bobonaza at the moment they were passing by. That was an act of Providence. As Isabel would later explain, to remain would be to dishonor God.

Isabel departed from Andoas the next morning. She told Suasti that she would need a canoe and rowers to take her to Lagunas, 250 miles downriver, and the priest—who was stunned by her insistence on leaving—did help to arrange this transportation. Seven Indians agreed to take her there, and just before she left, a native woman handed her a white cotton dress, which she had apparently made during the night. This was yet one more act of kindness from the "Americans," and Isabel, who would cherish this simple dress the rest of her life, later sent back a gift to thank her.

It took them eight days to travel to Lagunas. The Pastaza flowed into the Marañón, and they proceeded on this section of the upper

Amazon for a short stretch until they came to the Huallaga, the tributary where Lagunas was located. Isabel's condition worsened during this trek, and she arrived "with a high fever and very upset." The village priest, Romero, who was the superior for all the missions in the Maynas district, immediately put her to bed, where she remained for most of the next six weeks.

Just as everyone in Andoas had been, Romero was astonished to see Isabel arrive, and he quickly sent out a canoe to carry the joyous news downriver. Madame Godin, alive! Four weeks earlier, Joaquín and Rocha had brought the news of her death to Omaguas, and that information had reached Pedro Gramesón in Loreto sometime in early February. Devastated, he had begun making plans to return to Riobamba. Captain Rebello, who had been waiting patiently in Tabatinga for nearly four years, had similarly started preparing to head back to Pará. It was essential that this missive from Romero, sent out from Lagunas in late February, make its way downriver rapidly. Fortunately, it arrived before Rebello departed.

In his letters to the Portuguese captain and to Isabel's father, Romero requested that d'Oreasaval, who had remained in Tabatinga all this time, come to Lagunas. If Isabel were to travel any further, she would need an escort. However, d'Oreasaval never showed up, yet one more instance of Jean's friend failing him. But Rocha did appear in Lagunas; he had been in Omaguas when he learned of Isabel's survival. He must have been disconcerted as well as surprised by this news, for he had not been the most faithful caretaker of Isabel's goods, which Joaquín had collected from the sandbar. He handed over what he had—"four silver dishes, a silver saucepan, a velvet petticoat, one of Persiana and one of taffety, some linens and other trifles"—and awkwardly muttered that "all the rest was rotten."

Already Isabel had felt the sting of seeing Suasti grab the two gold chains from the Indians. Hers was a world in which people were supposed to behave with honor, and yet here was Rocha—who had failed her and everyone else on the sandbar by not returning with a rescue canoe in the promised time—telling a story that could mean only one thing: He had stolen her precious things. Perhaps he had already sold them, or perhaps he still had them. But clearly, once it seemed that she had perished, he had seen an opportunity for profit. How, Isabel asked, was it that "bracelets, snuffboxes, rosaries of gold and earrings set with emeralds were subject to rottenness?" Or "silverware and powdered gold?"

He could only pretend that he knew nothing of such items, and Isabel finally let loose in fury: "Go your way, Sir. It is impossible that I can ever forget that, to you, I owe all my misfortunes and all my losses. Manage henceforth as you may. I am determined you shall make no part of my company."

By the end of March, Isabel had recovered to the point that she could resume her travels. But since she was adamant about not traveling with Rocha, she had no escort to take her further downriver other than the Indians from Andoas, and Romero advised her to return to Riobamba. "You are at the beginning of a long and tedious voyage," he told her, "and if you go ahead, you are likely to incur fresh danger." He would see to it that she could return "in perfect security" to her home in the Andes. It was in response to this plea that Isabel—who had been reluctant to talk about her ordeal—provided a hint of the faith that had sustained her during her wanderings in the jungle. As Romero recounted in a letter to the governor in Omaguas, Madame Godin was "surprised by his proposal":

She said that the Almighty had preserved her even when she was alone amid perils that had led all her former companions to perish, and that the first of her wishes was to rejoin her husband, and it was for this purpose that she had begun her journey, and were she to cease to prosecute her intention, she would consider herself guilty of counteracting the views of Providence, and render useless the assistance that she had received from her two dear Americans and their wives, and for which God alone could recompense them.

Jean, upon hearing of this, was understandably moved: "My wife was ever dear to me," he wrote, "but sentiments like these add veneration to tenderness."

ALTHOUGH ISABEL HAD REQUESTED that Rocha be sent away, Romero—unable to talk her out of going ahead—begged her to allow Rocha to accompany her. Otherwise, he said, Rocha would be stranded. Isabel felt a deep gratitude toward Romero, and thus she departed from Lagunas with the man she held responsible for the death of her brothers, her nephew, and the others left behind on the sandbar. The seven Andoas Indians took them downriver, and although theirs was a silent canoe, Isabel refusing to say a word to Rocha, they encountered no "fresh dangers." In truth, they were now on the part of the Amazon that had been tamed by the Spanish. The 500 miles to Loreto could be traveled in three weeks or so, and an escort, it turned out, was coming upriver, the governor of Omaguas having dispatched a canoe "loaded with refreshments" to meet her. Rebello too had sprung into action. He had brought his galliot to Loreto, where Pedro Gramesón was waiting, and from that village he had sent out a well-stocked canoe, which met Isabel in Pebas on April 21, 1770. There Isabel paused long enough to take care of one final task, which was of great importance to her.

She wrote this letter to the lieutenant corregidor of Riobamba:

> Don Domingo Zapater:
> Dear Sir, with all my esteem: always considering your health and with my best wishes for its continuation, from this great distance, and offering once more what your Grace has awarded me, so that regardless of the distance my wishes may be fulfilled.
> Whilst I found myself in the difficult and sorrowful situation in the mountains after that fatal event which your Grace is aware of and resulting from my having ignored the wise advice which had been given to me with regard to my unfortunate voyage,

Juachín* went downriver to inform the Governor of our mission, and once he had been informed of everything he sent Juachín on to Quito which is why I was unable to give him his freedom as I had promised, which is why I am begging your Grace to take the necessary steps to fulfill said promise as that is my will.

I was not able to use the letter which your Grace had given me addressed to the Governor because I did not have the opportunity to give it to him. Please let me know if there is any way I can serve your Grace and trust that I will do so. May God keep your Grace for many years.

Pebas, April 21 of '70. From this mission of Maynas.

I kiss your Grace's hands and remain your most devoted and trusted servant.

Doña Isabel Gramesón

This is the only document written in Isabel's hand that history has preserved, and in it, she asks that her loyal slave be freed.

ISABEL WAS NOW IN THE CARE of the Portuguese, and a few days later, she met her father in Loreto. Theirs was a tearful reunion, and the general, who had always planned to return to Riobamba, decided that he would accompany Isabel to Oyapock. He had lost two sons and a grandson, which left him "penetrated with the most lively grief," and he could not bear the thought that anything more might happen to Isabel, whom God, it seemed, had miraculously spared.

In order to speed their trip, Rebello "doubled the number of oars." He also regularly sent out canoes to hunt for fish and game. During the ten-week journey, Isabel "wanted for nothing to render her comfortable, not even the nicest delicacies." Isabel regained some of her strength during this time, although at one point her thumb swelled to a hideous size, apparently from a thorn that had been lodged

---

* An alternative spelling for Joaquín.

inside for months and had finally erupted into an infection. "It was proposed to take off the thumb," Jean later reported, but "care and fermentation" finally brought the swelling down, sparing the need for amputation, although Isabel never regained full use of it.

When they reached Fort Curupa, Rebello was relieved of his duty and replaced by a Captain Martel. Rebello had proven himself to be a man of uncommon patience and generosity, deserving in every way of Jean's gratitude. Now the party only had to exit the Amazon and scurry along the coast to Oyapock. But as the galliot entered the Atlantic, it lost one of its anchors, "at a spot along the coast where the currents are very violent," and Martel decided that it was unsafe to go any further. Fate had thrown up one final obstacle to Isabel and Jean's reunion. Martel, who had moored his galliot in a bay, sent ahead a canoe to Oyapock, where Jean had been waiting for more than five years for the Portuguese to return.

With the galliot stalled, Isabel began to feel quite anxious. Twenty-one years had passed since she and Jean had last seen each other, and she was no longer the young woman he remembered. She was thin, her face had been permanently scarred by the botflies and other insects of the jungle, and her hair was gray. Would her husband flinch when he saw her? More than a week passed while the galliot bobbed in the gentle waters of the bay, and then, on July 18, a small boat, with sails up and several men at the oars, rushed toward them. This was the very craft that Jean had built sixteen years earlier, hoping to travel up the Amazon, and then suddenly he was climbing up the galliot's rope ladder:

> On board this vessel, after 20 years absence, and a long endurance on either side of alarms and misfortunes, I again met with a cherished wife, whom I had almost given over every hope of seeing again. In her embraces I forgot the loss of the fruits of our union, nay, I even congratulated myself on their premature death, as it saved them from the dreadful fate which befell their uncles in the wood of Canelos beneath their mother's eye, who certainly could never have survived the sight.

Later, in a letter to La Condamine, Jean marveled at the wonder of it all:

> Were it told in a romance that a female of delicate habit, accustomed to all the comforts of life, had been precipitated into a river; that, after being withdrawn when on the point of drowning, this female, the eighth of a party, had penetrated into unknown and pathless woods, and traveled in them for weeks, not knowing whither she directed her steps; that enduring hunger, thirst, and fatigue to very exhaustion, she should have seen her two brothers, far more robust than her, and a nephew yet a youth expire by her side and she yet survive; that, after remaining by their corpses two whole days and nights, in a country abounding in tigers and numbers of dangerous serpents, without once seeing any of these animals or reptiles, she should afterwards have strength to rise, and continue her way, covered with tatters, through the same pathless wood for eight days together till she reached the banks of the Bobonaza, the author would be charged with inconsistency; but the historian should paint facts to his reader, and this is nothing but the truth. The truth of this marvelous tale is attested by original letters in my hands, from many missionaries on the Amazon, who felt an interest in this event, and by other proofs.

Jean and Isabel reached Oyapock on July 22, 1770. This was not long after Joaquín had returned to Quito, and such was the flow of time and information in colonial Peru that even as people throughout the Quito Audiencia were learning of her tragic death, the long-suffering couple was at last joyfully reunited.

# CHAPTER FIFTEEN

# Saint Amand

F OR TWO WEEKS AFTER THEY ARRIVED in Oyapock, Jean and Isabel did all they could to show their gratitude to Martel and to his country. The Portuguese vessel needed a new keel and repairs to its sails, and while this work was being done, the Godins entertained Martel. Even Governor Fiedmont traveled from Cayenne to join in the festivities, bringing refreshments and other delights for the dinner table. His arrival also signaled that he was holding out an olive branch to Jean, ending a feud that had been simmering for several years. After Jean had refused to go with Captain Rebello in 1766, Fiedmont—while sharing Jean's suspicions of the Portuguese at the time—had come to distrust him, and a year later he had written harshly about Jean in a letter to Choiseul in Paris. He had accused Jean of getting rich by cutting down the "king's forests" in Guiana and trading in rum, along with a few other sins. But now all seemed to be forgiven. This was a time for goodwill, and when Martel departed, Jean sailed alongside the Portuguese galliot in his own boat until they had passed Cape Orange, his way of offering a final salute: "I took my leave of him with those feelings which the polite attention and noble behavior of that officer and his generous nation were so well calculated to inspire in me."

However, those initial euphoric days soon gave way to a difficult period for Isabel and Jean, one that lasted nearly three years. Isabel fell ill. Those who came to Guiana often became sick, but she was also still recovering from her ordeal. Emotionally too she struggled, as survivors of disasters so often do. She was visited regularly by bouts of melancholy, "her horrible misfortunes being ever present to her imagination," Jean confessed. He wanted to whisk her away to France, to a new life there, but he was now broke. Far from having made a fortune from his timber and fishing operations, or from the rum trade that Fiedmont had accused him of operating, Jean owed 3,700 francs to the king's treasury, a debt that he had incurred to fund d'Oreasaval's trip upriver.

Once again, Jean appealed to the Crown for relief. Toward the end of 1770, he wrote César-Gabriel de Choiseul-Praslin, minister of the marine, detailing all that had happened to Isabel in the jungle. "Might we, Your Grace, ask you to cancel our debt? We find ourselves, after all these hardships and sorrows, unable to fulfill this obligation. Please, my lord, cast your eyes on our painful situation and we shall not cease, both of us, to pray for your good health." Although this letter found its way into French archives, it did not elicit any relief. By the time it arrived in Paris, the Choiseuls—both the Duc de Choiseul-Praslin and his powerful cousin, the Duc de Choiseul—had fallen into disgrace and were no longer in a position to help.

At the same time, Jean sought to recover the 7,000 francs he had given d'Oreasaval at the start of the trip. Although Isabel advised him not to do it—she had "compassion even for that wretch," Jean wrote—he sued d'Oreasaval, who he felt had betrayed him. D'Oreasaval had failed to take his letters to Lagunas, and that dereliction of duty had led to the loss of the letters and, from Jean's point of view, the subsequent tragic turn of events. His friend had stayed all the while in Tabatinga, trading away the 7,000 francs. It was this "infidelity and neglect," Jean told the court, that had "caused the death of eight persons, including the American who was drowned, and all the misfortunes which befell my wife."\*

Although one could understand Jean's ire, this was a rather impractical battle to wage. D'Oreasaval had no money. He had arrived back in Cayenne without a cent. The most that Jean could hope for was that the court would agree that he had been wronged, and naturally the lawsuit dragged on and on, delaying his and Isabel's departure to France.

Over the next two years, however, Jean was able to raise the funds they needed to leave South America. Precisely how is not clear, but a 1772 census of Oyapock reports that the Godin household included seven slaves and their four children, and the fact that he owned so many slaves meant he had a commercial business of some type. They would have provided the labor for whatever timber or fishing operation he had kept going.

Jean also managed to bring his lawsuit against d'Oreasaval to a successful end of sorts. On January 7, 1773, the Superior Court of Cayenne ruled that d'Oreasaval had indeed failed to fulfill his obligations to Jean and ordered him to repay the 7,000 francs. However, as expected, he could not. If Jean had asked the authorities to imprison him for nonpayment of the debt, Jean would have been required, under the law, to pay for d'Oreasaval's upkeep in jail. "For my part," Jean later wrote, "I judged it unnecessary to augment the losses I had already sustained."

On April 21, 1773, Jean, Isabel, and her father sailed from Cayenne. After thirty-eight years, Jean was at last returning home. They were leaving South America behind, and although they could not have known it, back in Riobamba there was a matter close to Isabel's heart that had come to the happy end she desired. Not only had Joaquín been released from prison, but on May 29, 1771, Isabel's sister Josefa and her husband Antonio Zabala, acting at

---

\* Jean was mistaken here. Including the Indian pilot, the correct number of deaths was seven.

Isabel's request, had given him his "card of liberty," the Zabalas avowing all "love and good will" toward him.

After arriving in La Rochelle on June 26, Jean, Isabel, and her father traveled straight to Saint Amand, Jean's home in the center of France. Jean had left a young man and come back an old one—he was sixty now. Many in his family had passed away. Both of his parents were dead, his mother having died in 1750, and his two sisters were widows. But his brother Carlos was still living, and the warmth of his three siblings, who "tenderly received" Isabel and her father, made him happy to be home. They moved into a family house on Rue Hotel-Dieu, near the center of the small town.

They had barely had time to finish unpacking their trunks before a letter from La Condamine arrived, welcoming Jean back. In many ways, Jean's return brought the expedition to a conclusion, with Isabel's ordeal being the final chapter in that history, and La Condamine wanted to know all of the details. Rumors about her travails had been circulating in Parisian salons for some time—the idea of a high-society woman lost in such a frightening wilderness was almost beyond comprehension—and La Condamine requested that Jean provide him with a narrative of her journey.

Jean replied on July 28, 1773. His was a lengthy letter, nearly 7,000 words, and it was replete with vivid details. Hailing it as a story that showed what "miracles may be effected by resolution and perseverance," La Condamine promptly prepared it for publication. His 1745 account of his travels down the Amazon, *Relation abrégée d'un voyage fait dans l'intérieur de l'Amérique Méridionale,* was in the process of being republished, and he added Jean's letter to the text. When this updated edition of *Relation abrégée* appeared and was translated into other languages, Isabel's story left readers throughout Europe mesmerized. An English printer declared that it presented "as extraordinary a series of perils, adventures, and escapes, as are anywhere to be found on record."

· · ·

By the end of 1773, only three other members of the expedition besides La Condamine and Jean Godin were known to be still living. Collectively, the fates of the expedition members had played out in ways both admirable and tragic.

Three of the members, of course, had died in South America: Couplet, Senièrgues, and Morainville. Hugo, the instrument maker, simply disappeared there. He had last written to La Condamine in the early 1750s, telling once more of his homesickness for France, and then he was never heard from again. Verguin enjoyed a prosperous career as a naval engineer after his return to France and was still alive in 1773, living in Toulon, when Jean finally made it back home.

Bouguer was the first of the three academicians to die. Unfortunately, his envy of La Condamine soured their relationship for good, and the two never reconciled. But he remained a productive scientist until his death in 1758, at age sixty. In his last decade, he wrote about navigation, invented an instrument called the heliometer for measuring the diameters of planets, and studied the properties of light. This last work earned him posthumous recognition as the "father of photometry." He never married, reserving his deepest attachment for the Academy of Sciences, where he was the resident astronomer until his death. Because he lacked heirs, he gave most of his money to friends and servants before he died, and in his will, he allocated what remained of his wealth to the poor.

Louis Godin died two years later, and by the end he was something of a broken man. During his years in Lima, while waiting for Peru to give him permission to leave, he had taught math at the University of San Marcos and had overseen the reconstruction of the port of Callao after it was destroyed in a massive earthquake. Upon his return to Paris in 1751, he resumed living with his wife and two grown children, whom he had not seen for sixteen years. For the next twelve months, he petitioned the academy to give him back his seat and his pension. Clearly, he had been unfairly expelled—the academy had done so thinking that he had willingly taken a position with a university in Lima—yet his plea went unheard. Disappointed, he and his wife moved to Cadiz, where Ulloa and Juan had secured an appointment for him as director of Spain's naval academy. In 1756, the French Academy of Sciences finally readmitted Godin as a member with "veteran" status, but this bit of justice came too late. His son had recently died from smallpox, and his daughter perished shortly thereafter, which crushed his spirit. Although he had been the nominal leader of the Peruvian expedition, he never published his account of it. In 1760, at the age of fifty-six, he died from an attack of apoplexy.

Jussieu took even longer to return to Paris. After traveling south from Lima in 1748 to La Paz and Lake Titicaca, where he collected plants and aquatic birds, he lived for six years in the famous silver mining town of Potosí. There he taught, practiced medicine, rebuilt the public works system, and oversaw the construction of a bridge. His skills were deemed so valuable that, much as had been the case in Quito, authorities in Potós did all they could to prevent him from leaving. He moved to Lima in 1755, where he provided medical care to the poor but slipped into an ever deeper despondency.* For the next fifteen years, his family constantly begged him to return. Finally, his friends in Lima, alarmed at his deteriorated state, arranged for him to go. Unfortunately, he left behind most of his papers and much of his life's work was lost.

Jussieu reached Paris on July 10, 1771, and fell weeping into the arms of his brother, Bernard. He moved in with Bernard, but his mind was shattered, and for the next eight years, until his death at age seventy-four, he rarely ventured outside. He never visited the Academy of Sciences, which had elected him a member in 1743. His memory went, as did his eyesight and the use of his limbs, and he died a painful death from gangrene. At his funeral, he was eulogized as a "martyr to botany," a melancholy man who had never garnered the recognition he deserved.

---

* In addition to his usual melancholy, Jussieu began to suffer headaches and dizziness in Potosí, which may have been due to poisoning from the mercury used in the processing of silver from the mines in this notoriously unhealthy town.

Juan enjoyed a fairly tranquil life after his return to Spain. The publication of his and Ulloa's book on their voyage to South America made him well known throughout Spanish society, and he was appointed the squadron commander of the Spanish Royal Armada. For the next twenty years, he devoted his energies to writing about navigation, improving the operations of Spain's shipyards, and developing the sciences in Spain. He founded an astronomical observatory at Cadiz and established the Friendly Literary Society, which met each Thursday at his house to discuss scientific questions. This group later gave rise to the Royal Society of Sciences of Madrid. He died in 1773 at age sixty.

Ulloa's post-expedition life was filled with drama. He had been the principal author of *Relación histórica del viage a la América Meridional,* and after it appeared, Spain sent him on a tour of Europe to study the roads, canals, and factories of France and other countries. Spain wanted this information to support its modernization plans. At the same time, Ulloa mined his notes from Peru in order to write a second report, this one on the colony's dark underside. He did not hold back a thing, describing at length the venality of colonial officials, the exploitation of Indians by greedy village priests, and the awful abuses of the mita system. The report, which he titled *Discurso y reflexiones políticas sobre el estado presente de los reynos del Peru,* was a reformist manuscript meant for the Crown's eyes only. Juan contributed in small ways to the document, which was indeed kept secret until 1826, when an English merchant in Cadiz, David Barry, obtained a purloined copy and published it under the title *Noticias secretas de América* (Secret news of America). The book's appearance created a storm in Europe similar to the one Las Casas's book, *A Short Account of the Destruction of the Indies,* had generated in 1542, and the book proved to be of similarly lasting historical importance.

Perhaps in response to his report, Spain appointed Ulloa governor of the troubled Huancavelica province in Peru in 1757. The province contained an important mercury mine and was known to be rife with corruption, with the miners and local officials colluding to cheat the monarchy out of its royalties. This was an opportunity for Ulloa to put into practice his reformist ideals, but six years later he had reached a point of total defeat, writing the Crown to ask to be rescued from a situation made impossible by "vexations, mortifications, and rebuffs." However, rather than allowing him to come home, Spain asked him to assume the post of governor of Louisiana, which Spain had recently obtained from France in the Treaty of Paris. Naturally, the French-speaking Creoles deeply resented this new Spanish rule, and in 1768, they rose up in revolt, forcing Ulloa and his Peruvian wife to flee.

As a colonial administrator, Ulloa had failed utterly. However, once back in Spain, he resumed a productive life as a naval officer, writer, and scientist. He published *Noticias Americanas,* a concise natural history of Spanish America, established a natural history museum in Madrid, and—while fathering nine children—gradually turned himself into a Spanish Benjamin Franklin. He studied electricity and artificial magnetism, observed the circulation of blood in fish and insects, introduced innovations into the printing and paper-making industries, designed surgical instruments, and improved weaving techniques for making fine cashmere woolens. An English visitor to his home in the 1780s told of meeting a humble man surrounded by books, instruments, fossils, guns, and various antiquities—all the clutter of a life of science and adventure, enjoyed by a man with a most curious mind. Ulloa died in 1795 at age seventy-nine.

La Condamine penned an update on the members of the expedition in 1773, and by that time he too was nearing the end of his life. He was almost totally deaf and had suffered from paralysis in his legs for nearly a decade, leading him to quip that he doubted whether he and Jussieu together could be "reckoned equivalent to one living being." But while his body may have been giving out, his mind remained as alert as ever.

Partly as a result of his skills as a writer, much of Europe had come to think of the Peruvian mission as the "La Condamine expedition." In the 1740s and early 1750s, he published three volumes on the voyage. One was a diary of his ten years abroad, *Journal du voyage fait par ordre du roi à l'équateur*. The second was his account of his exploration of the Amazon, *Relation abrégée d'un voyage fait dans l'intérieur de l'Amérique méridionale*, and the third was a scientific treatise on their arc measurements, *Mesure des trois premiers degrés du méridien dans l'hémisphere austral*. In the wake of the books' success, he became something of a statesman for science, happily corresponding with scholars throughout Europe and lobbying for two pet projects: the establishment of a universal standard of measurement and the use of inoculation practices to protect against smallpox. Inoculation involved deliberately exposing children to mild cases of the disease, which many people thought was mad. Indeed, his relentless advocacy on this topic earned him the nickname "the Don Quixote of inoculation" from those who thought he was surely tilting at windmills with this idea. However, he gradually won over the skeptics, and by the early 1770s the practice was being adopted throughout Europe.

In 1756, La Condamine traveled to Italy, where he researched the ancient measurements of Rome and visited Vesuvius. He also returned from that trip with a papal dispensation to marry his twenty-five-year-old niece. The adventurer who had always thought that his smallpox scars rendered him unlovable had finally found a mate. In 1760, he was elected to the select Académie Française, whose forty members were often described as France's immortals. His physical infirmities began to slow him down after that, and as his leg paralysis set in, he offered a prize to the scholar who could best explain his illness. He gladly offered himself up as a guinea pig for experiments with electricity that were designed to ease his pain, none of which worked. But he was ever the curious man, and in early 1774, as he prepared to undergo a risky hernia operation, he told the surgeon to perform it slowly because he wanted to make mental notes and report on his experience to the academy. This was before the invention of anesthesia, and yet he was willing to lengthen the operation in order to learn from it. He died on February 4, shortly after this final scientific quest.

Buffon, one of La Condamine's long-time friends in the academy, eulogized him in this memorable way:

La Condamine may have had faults and shortcomings, but he had the advantage that his faults tended toward respectable qualities and his shortcomings were more than compensated for by his virtues. His faults and shortcomings will be soon forgotten and what will remain will be the memory of all the good he has done for mankind. He was a philosopher and scholar who loved his fellow man, who had a zeal for truth, and who spoke about what he loved.

In the months before he died, La Condamine had indeed shown those words of praise to be true, for he had performed one final act of kindness on behalf of Jean Godin, his faithful signal carrier on the expedition.

IN SAINT AMAND, Jean and Isabel had settled into a peaceful life. While Isabel may have dreamed as a young girl about Paris, that fancy had long since passed, and now she and Jean stayed close to their home in rural France. Jean managed family properties in Odonais and at Epourneaux, and he acquired other lands adjacent to those, which he put to use as vineyards. He also maintained an interest in French Guiana and dashed off more than one letter to Louis XV's ministers, urging them to develop a cattle industry there. This proposal was seen as having some merit, and for once Jean even received a polite letter thanking him for his recommendations. The correspondence with the Crown reflected the fact that Jean had found a place in society, so much so that his name was known to King Louis XV.

Shortly after Jean's return to Saint Amand, La Condamine had gone to Louis Phélypeaux de Vrillière, who oversaw the operations of the Academy of Sciences for the king, to request that Jean be given a pension. This was an award, La Condamine told the duke, that Jean had "well earned by his zeal and toil" in Peru. In an order dated October 27, 1773, the king granted Jean an annual sum of 700 francs, and while the money was important, Louis XV's words were more so: The pension was for Jean's service on the expedition "as official geographer to the King." *Geographer.* Not signal carrier, not assistant, but "official geographer." At last, Jean had a title that he could carry to his grave.

Content now in a way that he had never been before, Jean resumed working on his grammar of Quechua. Isabel, with her linguistic skill, presumably helped him with this task. According to a nineteenth-century French historian, the manuscript Jean produced included a substantial lexicon, "which he prepared in St. Amand up until his death." However, he was not able to get it published. In the last rejection letter he received, dated July 22, 1787, one of the king's ministers gently informed him that it would be impossible to have it "printed at the expense of the King."

Details about the years that Jean and Isabel spent together in Saint Amand are sparse. They managed their properties and lived quietly, out of the public eye, even though their story had become so well known. Isabel bore physical scars from her ordeal, her face badly pocked, and that led some in Saint Amand to wonder whether her emotional wounds could ever heal. Isabel rarely spoke about her sufferings in the jungle—she was enigmatic in that regard—and the diary that she kept in Saint Amand, which might have revealed her feelings, was later lost. But there were many aspects of her life in Saint Amand that surely brought her much comfort. Her father, who was ever so dear to her, lived with them until his death in 1780, at age seventy-six. Four priests attended the burial, evidence of the high esteem in which he—and the Godins— were held. Then too there was the solace that she drew from Jean's enduring love, which he publicly professed when he made out his will in 1776:

I owe to Madame Isabelle Godin, my wife, much regard, both thanks to the happy union that has always existed between us, and because of the suffering she endured in her travels to find me in Cayenne. I give her full title to one quarter of all my goods, with no exception of anything, according to what custom allows me, and am sorry that I cannot give her more.

There was one other joy that enlivened the Godin home on Rue Hotel-Dieu in their final years. At some point—the date is unknown—Isabel's nephew Juan Antonio came from Riobamba to live with them.* He was Martín's younger brother, and Jean and Isabel raised him as their own. He quickly adapted to his new country, changing the spelling of his name to Jean-Antoine Grandmaison, and on February 21, 1792, he married a local woman, Magdeleine Picot. They moved into a house on Rue Cheval Blanc, and in the years ahead, they often told their son Gilbert Felix about his famous great-aunt, Isabel Godin.

Jean was too ill to attend the wedding of Jean-Antoine and Magdeleine, and he died nine days later, on the first of March, at eleven in the evening, with Isabel by his side. He was seventy-nine years old. He was buried in a local cemetery, and once he was gone, Isabel's health quickly began to decline. Her whole life had been entwined with his. She had been eight years old when the French arrived in Quito, and she had married Jean when she was only thirteen. Although they had lived apart for twenty-one years, she had spent much of that time imagining their reunion; he had never been far from her thoughts. The world they had known together for the last nineteen years in Saint Amand was ending too, the monarchy tumbling before revolutionary mobs in Paris. Yet her last months were peaceful. Jean-Antoine visited her often, she was not alone, and—as Jean-Antoine would later relate—from time to time she would take out an ebony box and prop it open on her lap, softly running her fingers over the cotton dress and sandals stored inside.

* There is no record of how he traveled from Riobamba to France. The most common route at the time would have been overland to Cartagena and from there to Spain.

Isabel died on September 27, 1792, at age sixty-five, and was buried in the same parish cemetery as Jean. Jean-Antoine and his wife Magdeleine had their first child two months later, and the descendants of one of their sons, Gilbert, can still be found living today in the Berry region of France. Isabel's sandals were handed down as an heirloom, and not long ago, a distant relative of Isabel's, Marc Lemaire, recalled that as a child he would visit his great-aunt Emma and she would show them off, the sandals "completely flattened and made of some kind of raffia, grey and dusty." Isabel and Jean's house in Saint Amand still stands as well, and in the town library there is a copy of the famous letter Jean wrote to La Condamine, telling of his wife's wanderings in the Bobonaza wilderness.

# Characters

## Members of the Expedition

*Members of the French Academy of Sciences*
Charles-Marie de La Condamine
Louis Godin
Pierre Bouguer

*Assistants*

| | |
|---|---|
| Couplet | General assistant |
| Jean Godin | Signal carrier |
| Hugo | Instrument maker |
| Joseph de Jussieu | Botanist and physician |
| Morainville | Engineer |
| Jean Senièrgues | Physician |
| Jean Verguin | Engineer and draftsman |

## Isabel Gramesón's Family

| | |
|---|---|
| María Josefa Pardo de Figueroa | Isabel's mother |

| | |
|---|---|
| Pedro Manuel Gramesón y Bruno | Isabel's father |
| Juan Gramesón | Isabel's older brother, an Augustinian priest |
| Antonio Gramesón | Isabel's younger brother |
| Josefa Gramesón | Isabel's younger sister |
| Carmen del Pilar Godin | Isabel's daughter |
| Martín Gramesón | Isabel's nephew, son to Antonio |
| Juan Antonio Gramesón | Isabel's nephew, son to Antonio |
| Joaquín Gramesón | Family slave |
| Pedro Pardo de Figueroa | Isabel's uncle |
| José Augustín Pardo de Figueroa | Isabel's uncle |
| Antonio Zabala | Isabel's brother-in-law, married to Josefa |

*Other Members of Isabel's Traveling Party*

| | |
|---|---|
| Jean Rocha | Frenchman, who claimed to be a doctor |
| Phelipe Bogé | Rocha's traveling companion |
| Antonio | Rocha's slave |
| Tomasa | Isabel's servant |
| Juanita | Isabel's servant |

## Others

ALSEDO Y HERRERA, DIONESIO DE. President of the Quito Audiencia in 1736 when the French expedition arrived

ARAUJO Y RÍO, JOSEPH DE. Replaced Alsedo y Herrera as president of the Quito Audiencia on December 28, 1736

ARMENDÁRIZ, JOSÉ DE (MARQUÉS DE CASTELFUERTE) Viceroy of Peru, 1724–1736

BERNOULLI, JOHANN. Belgian mathematician who devised mathematical equations supporting the idea that Cartesian vortices would cause the earth to be elongated at the poles

BUFFON, GEORGES LOUIS LECLERC DE. Naturalist and keeper of the Jardin du Roi in Paris; member of the French Academy of Sciences

CASSINI, JACQUES. Son of Jean Cassini; director of the Paris Observatory of the French Academy of Sciences from 1700 to 1740; directed the measurement of a meridian in France that supported the conclusion that the earth was elongated at the poles

CASSINI, JEAN-DOMINIQUE (BORN GIAN DOMENICO CASSINI). Astronomer who directed the Paris Observatory from 1669 until 1700, when his son Jacques took over this position

CHOISEUL, ÉTIENNE-FRANÇOIS (DUC DE CHOISEUL). French minister of foreign affairs, 1758–1761 and 1766–1770; French minister of the marine, 1761–1766

CHOISEUL-PRASLIN, CÉSAR-GABRIEL (DUC DE CHOISEUL-PRASLIN) French minister of foreign affairs, 1761–1766; French minister of the marine, 1766-1770. Jean Godin wrote a letter to him in 1770 in which he described Isabel's ordeal in the Bobonaza wilderness.

CLAIRAUT, ALEXIS-CLAUDE. Mathematician in the French Academy of Sciences who was a Newtonian; member of expedition to Lapland

DESCARTES, RENÉ. Seventeenth-century French philosopher and mathematician. In *Principles of Philosophy* (1644), he set forth a theory that planets were held in their orbits by a swirling vortex of particles, a cosmology that came to be known as Cartesian physics.

D'HEROUVILLE. A friend of the Duc de Choiseul to whom Jean wrote for help in 1764 and who helped bring a Portuguese galliot to Cayenne

DIGUJA, JOSEPH. President of the Audiencia of Quito, 1767–1778; directed an investigation into Isabel Godin's voyage

D'OREASAVAL, TRISTAN. Jean's friend who went in his stead with the Portuguese galliot to pick up Isabel

D'ORVILLIERS, GILBERT GUILLOUET. Governor of French Guiana in 1750, when Jean Godin arrived in the colony

FIEDMONT, GOVERNOR. Replaced d'Orvilliers as governor of

French Guiana and was in that position during Jean Godin's last decade in the colony

Louis XIV. King of France, 1643–1715. The French Academy of Sciences was established during his reign.

Louis XV. King of France, 1715–1774

Maldonado, Pedro. Native of Riobamba and governor of the Esmeraldas province when the La Condamine expedition arrived in 1736; traveled down the Amazon with La Condamine in 1743

Maupertuis, Pierre-Louis Moreau de. Mathematician who led the revolt by the Newtonians against the Cartesians in the French Academy of Sciences; led the expedition to Lapland

Maurepas, Jean-Frédéric Phélypeaux de. French minister of the marine, 1723–1749, who oversaw the La Condamine expedition for Louis XV

Mendoza, José de (Marqués de Villagarcía). Viceroy of Peru, 1736–1745

Newton, Sir Isaac. English mathematician who published a theory of gravity in 1682 that contradicted Cartesian physics. According to his theory, the earth would be flattened at the poles, rather than elongated, as the Cartesians believed it was.

Philip V. King of Spain, 1700–1746

Picard, Jean. French astronomer who measured a degree of arc in France in the late 1660s

Rebello, Captain. Captain of the Portuguese galliot sent by the Portuguese king to French Guiana in 1765 with orders to help Jean Godin bring his wife from Riobamba

Richer, Jean. French astronomer who discovered in 1672 that a pendulum clock beat more slowly in French Guiana than in Paris, which suggested that gravitational forces were not the same at all points on the globe

Romero, Nicolás. Superior of the Maynas district who tended to Isabel in Lagunas

Rouillé, Antoine-Louis (Comte de Jouy). France's minister of the marine in 1750, when Jean arrived in French Guiana; minister of foreign affairs, 1754–1757

SUASTI, JUAN. Priest in Andoas

VOLTAIRE, FRANÇOIS-MARIE AROUET DE. French philosopher and writer who was ardent champion of Newtonian physics

VRILLIÈRE, LOUIS PHÉLYPEAUX (DUC DE VRILLIÈRE). French minister who in 1773 approved a pension for Jean Godin

# Notes

See the bibliography for the sources referred to in these notes. For additional information on the Bobonaza River, go to www.themap-makerswife.com.

### Chapter One: A Sunday in 1769
La Condamine wrote in his journal of Maldonado's family and friends advising him not to go into the Amazon. Jean Godin described Isabel's departure from Riobamba in a sedan chair in his 1773 letter to La Condamine. The *Archivo Nacional de Historia (Arnahis)* documents also provide information about Isabel's departure from Riobamba.

### Chapter Two: Not Quite Round
Berthon and Robinson's *Shape of the World* and Brown's *Story of Maps* were particularly useful regarding historical efforts to determine the size and shape of the world prior to the La Condamine expedition. Greenberg's *Problem of the Earth's Shape from Newton to Clairaut* and LaFuente and Delgado's *La geometrizacion de la tierra* provide accounts of the debate within the French Academy of Sciences over the earth's shape.

8. "an unclouded and attentive mind," A. Wolf, 644.

8. "Science was the true passion," Hahn, 57.

14. "Plato, Aristotle, and the old philosophers," Berthon and Robinson, 102.

19. "has cost me a major portion of my realm," Berthon and Robinson, 109.

20. "the success of this work," Cassini, 245–257.

21. "Nothing in our research," Cassini, 245–257.

21. "emits from itself," Hall, 262.

24. "to entertain a notion," Westfall, 51.

24. "How these Attractions," Westfall, 258.

25. "the axes of the planets," Jones, 45.

25. "spheroid prolonged toward the poles," Jones, 57.

26. "It is suspected that this resulted," Berthon and Robinson, 108.

26. Huygens's "absurd" letter to Newton, Westfall, 193. Also see Boss, 59.

26. "It is obvious that the current measurements," LaFuente and Delgado, 21.

26. "gibberish … I tried to understand it," Greenberg, 12.

27. "badgered, intimidated, cajoled," Greenberg, 87.

27. "justify the English at the expense," Greenberg, 87.

28. "Who would have ever thought it necessary," Paul, 30.

28. "being scandalous, and offensive to religion," Brandes, 266.

28. "Apparently a poor Frenchman," Brandes, 365.

29. "this senseless and ridiculous phantom," Brandes, 389.

29. "most eminent geniuses of Europe," Juan and Ulloa, *A Voyage to South America,* 5.

29. "cannot have any determinate shape," Greenberg, 12.

29. "inconceivably exact," LaFuente and Delgado, 26.

29. "sectarian" and "indiscreet," Harcourt Brown, 174.

29. "facts of the matter," Greenberg, 80.

## Chapter Three: A Daughter of Peru

The best biographical information about Isabel Gramesón can be found in a book published by the municipality of Riobamba in 2000, *Una historia de amor.* The author, Carlos Ortiz Arellano, is a local historian who relied on archival documents in Ecuador. Similarly, Marc Lemaire in France, who is a distant relative of Isabel's, unearthed helpful information through his research into the genealogy of the Godin family.

31. "equipped with a considerable fortune," *Le Magasin Pittoresque,* 371.

33. "the most splendid appearance," Juan and Ulloa, *A Voyage to South America,* 156.

33. "everywhere so level," Juan and Ulloa, *A Voyage to South America,* 154.

33. "300 loads of wheat," Arellano, 32.

33. "didn't let pass by any business," Arellano, 32.

34. "she was quite precocious," Lemaire, "Mais ... qui etait Dona Isabelle Godin des Odonais?"

35. "kept their women sequestered," Rowdon, 36.

36. "most distinguished and blessed day," Kamen, *Spain: 1469–1714,* 35.

37. "mirrored with sufficient fidelity," O'Connor, 8.

37. "for our rulers would not commit so great a crime," Leonard, *Books of the Brave,* 30.

38. "We went along the coast," Leonard, *Books of the Brave,* 46.

38. "because it is said that there are people," Leonard, *Books of the Brave,* 46.

39. "If there be any so craven," Prescott, 183.

39. "We were amazed," Leonard, *Books of the Brave,* 43.

40. "at given times men from the mainland," Leonard, *Books of the Brave,* 48.

40. "eat and drink out of gold vessels," Prescott, 309.

42. "We protest that the deaths," Burkholder and Johnson, 37.

44. "These women are very white and tall," Leonard, *Colonial Travelers in Latin America,* 52. The text in *Colonial Travelers* is an excerpt from *The Discovery of the Amazon according to the Account of Friar Gáspar de Carvajal,* as translated into English by Bertram Lee in 1934.

45. "it is considered a shame," Martín, 154. This quote is from Amedée Frezier, a Frenchman who traveled to South America in 1712.

45. "spend almost whole days in this manner," Leonard, *Colonial Travelers in Latin America,* 167. The text is an excerpt from Frezier's *Voyage to the South Sea and along the Coasts of Chili and Peru in the Years*

*1712, 1713, and 1714;* an English translation of his work first appeared in 1717.

45. "If sometimes I had put my hands on her," Martín, 148.

## Chapter Four: The Mapmakers

The eulogies in *Histoire et memoires de l'Académie Royale des Sciences* provide excellent biographical information on La Condamine, Bouguer, Louis Godin, and Joseph de Jussieu. I also relied on information from Gillispie's *Dictionary of Scientific Biography.* See Pierre Godin's "Génealogie de la famille Godin" and Boyer's *Nouvelle biographie generale* for biographical information about Jean Godin. Jacques Charcellet, a local historian in the Berry region of France, also provides some biographical information about Jean Godin's family in his "Histoire fantastique de Jean et Isabelle Godin des Odonais," as does Felix Grandmaison in "Un drame inconnu: Voyage de Madame Godin des Odonnais," his 1830 account of Isabel's adventure. Felix was the son of Isabel's nephew.

48. "He knew how to intersperse humor," eulogy for Louis Godin, which was composed by Jean-Paul Grandjean de Fouchy.

49. "dislike for sea voyages," Bouguer, 271.

50. "extensive scarification of his face," eulogy for La Condamine, which was composed by Jacques Delille and included remarks by Georges Louis Leclerc de Buffon.

51. "an apostle of Newton and Locke," LaFuente and Delgado, 25.

52. "sensed that his zeal," eulogy for La Condamine.

52. Several who have written about the La Condamine expedition claim that there was an eleventh member, Mabillon, and a few even report that he went crazy on the expedition. But La Condamine does not list Mabillon as a member of the expedition, he does not write about him in his journal of the voyage, and there is no Mabillon listed on the expedition's passport. The confusion seems to have arisen because La Condamine, when he provided an update on the expedition members in 1773, stated that Jussieu had lost his memory, much like the "famous Mabillon." But in that passage, La Condamine was not stating that Mabillon was on the expedition. Instead, he was simply comparing Jussieu to a person who would be known to eighteenth-century French readers (perhaps Jean Mabillon, a seventeenth-century French scholar

and Benedictine monk). Victor Von Hagen, in his 1945 book *South America Called Them,* wrote that Mabillon went "mad" on the voyage, an invention subsequently repeated by others.

52. "vivid imagination," eulogy for Jussieu, which was composed by Marie-Jean-Antoine-Nicolas Caritat de Condorcet.

53. "born a traveler," Grandmaison.

53. "study at their source," Boyer.

54. "By the abundant treasure of that country," Means, 230.

54. "ravening wolves among gentle lambs," Las Casas, xl.

54. "a moral pestilence which daily consumes," Las Casas, xx.

55. "I testify that I saw," Las Casas, 113.

56. "they rain[ed] down from the sky," Leonard, *Colonial Travelers in Latin America*, 73. This is an excerpt from Carletti's *My Voyage around the World*, translated by Herbert Weinstock and reprinted in 1964.

56. "themselves together by their tails," Leonard, *Colonial Travelers in Latin America,* 75.

57. "eyes in their shoulders," Alexander, 172.

57. "far exceeds any of the world," Gheerbrant, 42.

58. "three and four hundred bars and ingots of silver," Leonard, *Colonial Travelers in Latin America,* 83.

59. "They always go dressed very fine," Leonard, *Colonial Travelers in Latin America,* 130. The text in *Colonial Travelers* is an excerpt from Biscay's *Voyage à Buenos Aires et delá au Perou,* which was published in Paris in 1672 and translated into English in 1698.

59. "that should oppose their pleasures," Leonard, *Colonial Travelers in Latin America*, 161.

59. "wear three or four buff-waistcoats," Leonard, *Colonial Travelers in Latin America*, 134.

59. "display themselves strolling about," "the part which men do in France," and "proposals which a lover would not dare to make," Leonard, *Colonial Travelers in Latin America*, 160–174.

59. "where the rivers ran inland," Las Casas, xl.

60. "persons who have never been induced," Bouguer, 272.

61. "while abroad there is progress in physics," Kamen, *The Spanish Inquisition*, 250.

61. "sharp voice," LaFuente and Delgado, 37.

61. "to study the country and bring back a detailed description," Trystram, 35.

61. "which would be advantageous not only for," La Condamine, *Journal du voyage*, 272.

62. "be made at the equator itself," and "useful for navigation in general," La Condamine, *Journal du voyage,* 273.

62. "give them all assistance, favors and protection," and "above suspicion of any illegal commerce," La Condamine, *Journal du voyage,* 274–276.

## Chapter Five: Voyage to Quito

La Condamine wrote about the voyage to Quito and their scientific work in the Andes in *Journal du voyage fait par ordre du roi à l'équateur.* Juan and Ulloa described the journey in *Relación histórica del viage a la América Meridional;* the page numbers cited here are from the Adams's 1806 translation, *A Voyage to South America.* Ulloa was the principal author, and in passages where it is apparent that it is Ulloa writing, I have at times attributed the quote only to him.

65. "large and long waves," Juan and Ulloa, *A Voyage to South America*, 13.

66. "Mr. Amonton's sea barometer," La Condamine, *Journal du voyage,* 9.

66. "be of Use, where the Motion of the Objects," Lloyd Brown, 194–196.

67. "far beyond the usual limits," La Condamine, *Journal du voyage,* 9.

67. The account of a dog biting Jussieu is from Trystram, 38.

68. "700 toises above sea level," La Condamine, *Journal du voyage,* 9.

68. "determine their heights geometrically," La Condamine, *Journal du voyage,* 9.

69. "ill, bled, purged, cured," La Condamine, *Journal du voyage,* 3.

71. "youngbeard without experience," Trystram, 43.

72-5. Descriptions of daily life in Cartagena, Juan and Ulloa, *A Voyage to South America*, 19–87.

76. "the knowledge and the personal merit," La Condamine, *Journal du voyage,* 5.

76. "great fatigue, time and expense," La Condamine, *Journal du voyage,* 5.

76. "four, five, six thousand crowns," Juan and Ulloa, *A Voyage to South America*, 104.

77. "these verifications were so precise," La Condamine, *Journal du voyage*, 275.

77. "cursed by nature," Juan and Ulloa, *A Voyage to South America*, 99.

77. "without treading on them," Juan and Ulloa, *A Voyage to South America*, 103.

78. "the most fertile imagination," Juan and Ulloa, *A Voyage to South America*, 111.

78. "When dead, [the monkeys] are scalded," Juan and Ulloa, *A Voyage to South America*, 110.

79. "of the thermometer, the barometer," La Condamine, *Journal du voyage*, 10.

79. "I see that this trip," LaFuente and Delgado, 43.

80. "and sometimes another in their mouth," Juan and Ulloa, *A Voyage to South America*, 129.

80. "wraps its fins around a man," Juan and Ulloa, *A Voyage to South America*, 129.

80. "Tomorrow we are to see," LaFuente and Delgado, 41.

81. "easier to provide for the subsistence," LaFuente and Delgado, 38.

81. "extremely mountainous and almost covered," Juan and Ulloa, *A Voyage to South America*, 143.

82. "of all this coast, the most westerly," La Condamine, *Journal du voyage*, 11.

82. "an emerald the size of an ostrich egg," Bouguer, 276.

83. "of labour painful to excess," Bouguer, 276.

83. "discordant stunning noise," Bouguer, 278.

83. "Palmar, where I carved," La Condamine, *Journal du voyage*, 12.

84-8. The trek from Guayaquil to Quito is described by Juan and Ulloa, *A Voyage to South America*, 150–211.

89. A number of writers have reported that Maldonado and La Condamine traveled together from Esmeraldas to Quito. This mistaken version of events appears to have originated with Von Hagen's *South America Called Them*. Historians at a 1985 colloquium in Paris pointed out the error.

89-91. La Condamine describes his trip from Esmeraldas to Quito in *Journal du voyage*, 13–15.

## Chapter Six: Measuring the Baseline

93. "tropical paradise," Bouguer, 285.

95. "transcendental matters of science," Vera, 10.

96. "seemed to vie with each other," Juan and Ulloa, *A Voyage to South America*, 208.

96. "breathing an air more rarified," Bouguer, 286.

96. "Nature has here scattered," Juan and Ulloa, *A Voyage to South America*, 276.

96. "vast quantities of wrought plate," Juan and Ulloa, *A Voyage to South America*, 255.

96. "white and fibrous, but infinitely delicate," Bouguer, 299.

97. "affected great magnificence in their dress," Juan and Ulloa, *A Voyage to South America*, 264.

97. "Every part of their dress is," Juan and Ulloa, *A Voyage to South America*, 265.

98. "Seventy mules used to carry cargo," La Condamine, *Journal du voyage*, 16.

99. "watch that the said astronomers," *Colloque International.* Article by Jorge Salvador Lara, "La Biblioteca Americana de Don Antonio de Alcedo y Bejarano y la expedición de los académicos franceses," 81.

100. "within the boundaries," Zúñiga, 26.

100. "I will always be suspicious," *Colloque International,* 82.

100. "would be found near or next to the equator," Zúñiga, 27.

100. "the first time that I had emerged," La Condamine, *Journal du voyage*, 17.

101. "I completely satisfied the President," La Condamine, *Journal du voyage*, 17.

101. Zúñiga details how many of the elite in Quito bought goods from La Condamine.

102. "operations alone without needing to refer," La Condamine, *Journal du voyage*, 39.

104. "as a pessary, composed of gun-powder," Juan and Ulloa, *A Voyage to South America*, 219.

104. "the base of whole work," Juan and Ulloa, *A Voyage to South America*, 212.

106. "Such dreadful whirlwinds," Juan and Ulloa, *A Voyage to South America*, 212.

107. "was always open for all the French men," Zúñiga, 38.

107. "the practice of astronomy and trigonometry," La Condamine, *Journal du voyage*, 269–270.

107. The story of the connection between the Gramesóns and the expedition can be put together from information in Zúñiga, 's *250 Años,* Arellano's *Una historia de amor,* genealogical research by Lemaire, and La Condamine's journal. Martín's *Daughters of the Conquistadores* provides a wonderful account of daily life inside eighteenth-century convent schools in Peru.

## Chapter Seven: High-Altitude Science

112. "cabelleros del punto fijo," Krousel, 6.

112. "no employment or calling to occupy," Juan and Ulloa, *A Voyage to South America*, 269.

112-113. Arthur Whitaker detailed the dispute between Ulloa, Juan, and Araujo.

115. "considerably incommoded by the rarefaction," Bouguer, 287.

115. "I remained a long time without sense or motion," Juan and Ulloa, *A Voyage to South America*, 216.

115. "No one before us, that I know of, had seen the mercury," La Condamine, *Journal du voyage*, 35.

116. "rolling large fragments of rock," Juan and Ulloa, *A Voyage to South America*, 217.

116. "When the fog cleared up," Juan and Ulloa, *A Voyage to South America*, 217.

117. "that they would rather have suffered," Juan and Ulloa, *A Voyage to South America*, 220.

117. "we were continually in the clouds," Bouguer, 287.

117. "Our feet were swelled and so tender," Juan and Ulloa, *A Voyage to South America*, 218.

118. "The mountains in America are in comparison," La Condamine, *Journal du voyage*, 47.

119. "He was always in movement," Pierre de La Condamine, 1314. Although some of the biographical details about Jean in Pierre de La Condamine's article are wrong, his description of Jean's harsh life in the mountains fits with what Charles-Marie de La Condamine wrote about Jean's work as a signal carrier.

120. "strongest and most convincing proof," LaFuente and Delgado, 42.

120. "Mr. Godin des Odonais preceded us," La Condamine, *Journal du voyage*, 52.

121. "from this sad situation," La Condamine, *Journal du voyage*, 55.

122. "clothes, eyebrows, and beards covered in icicles," La Condamine, *Journal du voyage*, 58.

122. "and we could guarantee the accuracy," La Condamine, *Journal du voyage*, 58.

122. "alter in a geometrical progression," Bouguer, 288.

124. "They retired with all the marks of extreme sorrow," Juan and Ulloa, *A Voyage to South America*, 226.

124. "Even those of the best parts and education," Juan and Ulloa, *A Voyage to South America*, 224.

125. "the little cabins of the Indians," Juan and Ulloa, *A Voyage to South America*, 223.

125. "completely imprudent enterprise," La Condamine, *Journal du voyage*, 43.

125. "one might even come to believe that the earth," LaFuente and Delgado, 50. (Modern surveys have determined that at the equator, a degree of longitude is 1,948 feet longer than a degree of latitude.)

126. "Do the observers have some predilection," LaFuente and Delgado, 27.

126. "it is evident that the earth is considerably flattened," LaFuente and Delgado, 258.

126. "flattener of the earth and the Cassinis," Jones, 93.

126. "The arguments increased," LaFuente and Delgado, 17.

127. "This flatness [of the earth] appears even more considerable," James Smith, 94.

127. "choose to stay [neutral] till the French arrive," Jones, 93.

128. "agreeable reception provided us," La Condamine, *Journal du voyage*, 66.

128. "She possessed every talent," La Condamine, *Journal du voyage*, 66.

129. "contrary to all received opinion," Bouguer, 275.

129. "Nature has here continually in her hands," Bouguer, 306.

130. "I spent eight days wandering," La Condamine, *Journal du voyage*, 75.

130. "sleep was continually interrupted," Bouguer, 306.

130. "the most beautiful horizon," La Condamine, *Journal du voyage*, 78.

130. "whole side of the mountain seemed to be on fire," La Condamine, *Journal du voyage*, 77.

130. "suffering too much from the heat," La Condamine, *Journal du voyage*, 80.

133. See James Smith and LaFuente and Delgado for details about the expedition's measurements around Tarqui and about the accuracy of their work in the Andes.

133. "our geometric measurements were completely finished," La Condamine, *Journal du voyage*, 84.

## Chapter Eight: Death in the Afternoon

La Condamine wrote at length about Senièrgues's murder, in the form of a "Lettre à Madame ***," which he published in his *Relation abrégée d'un voyage fait dans l'intérieur de l'Amérique Méridionale,* pages 215–260. I have relied on a Spanish translation of that letter, published in *Relación abreviada de un viaje hecho por el interior de la América Meridional* (Madrid: Calpe, 1921), 133–192.

Ulloa and Juan wrote about the abuse of the Indians in their confidential report to the Spanish Crown, published in 1826 under the title *Noticias secretas de América;* Ulloa is believed to be the principal author. I have used a more recent translation of that book, titled *Discourse and Political Reflections on the Kingdoms of Peru.*

136. "Senièrgues stopped Leon at a street corner," La Condamine, *Relación abreviada de un viaje,* 138.

138. "Work in the *obrajes,*" Juan and Ulloa, *Discourse and Political Reflections,* 135.

139. "commanded to stretch out on the ground," Juan and Ulloa, *Discourse and Political Reflections,* 145.

139. "so that the sparks fall on the victims," Juan and Ulloa, *Discourse and Political Reflections,* 145.

140. "all their efforts to enriching themselves," Juan and Ulloa, *Discourse and Political Reflections,* 103.

141. "there were times when there would not be a week that passed," La Condamine, *Journal du voyage*, 55.

141. "stabbed by a mulatto in broad daylight," La Condamine, *Journal du voyage*, 56.

142. "bullfights are in the blood of the Spanish people," Carrión.

143. "did not have any virtue," La Condamine, *Relación abreviada de un viaje,* 139.

143. "This was the first time," La Condamine, *Relación abreviada de un viaje,* 141.

143. "There was nothing that could infuriate," La Condamine, *Relación abreviada de un viaje,* 143.

144. "give them a spectacle," La Condamine, *Relación abreviada de un viaje,* 145.

144. "Seeing himself surrounded," La Condamine, *Relación abreviada de un viaje,* 145.

144. "up in his arms the wounded," La Condamine, *Relación abreviada de un viaje,* 148.

145. "Senièrgues alone has paid for all of us," *Colloque International.* Article by Gabriel Judde, "Recherches sur Joseph de Jussieu botaniste (et médecin) de l'expedition La Condamine," 28–42.

146. "It seems that they were shewing some French gallantry," Jones, 113.

147. The Cuenca church that La Condamine and Louis Godin used as a triangulation point is still standing; San Sebastián Plaza where Senièrgues was murdered is about one-half mile away from that spot.

148. "series of sad and difficult observations," La Condamine, *Journal du voyage,* 87.

148. "They had the talent of mimicking," La Condamine, *Journal du voyage,* 88.

## Chapter Nine: Marriage in Quito

For a description of marriage practices in colonial Peru, see Socolow's *Women of Colonial Latin America,* Lavrin's *Sexuality and Marriage in Colonial Latin America,* Martín's *Daughters of the Conquistadores,* and Descola's *Daily Life in Colonial Peru.*

151. "Creole women recognize the disaster," Juan and Ulloa, *Discourse and Political Reflections,* 220.

152. "Don't marry an old man," Descola, 116.

152. "stir up immoral and lascivious desire," Leonard, *Books of the Brave,* 88.

153. "so utterly absorbed in reading," Leonard, *Books of the Brave,* 22.

153. "She was always dressed," Martín, 281.

153. "an amatory conversation through the Venetian blinds," and "frantic desire to marry," Descola, 116.

154. "little kisses, raise the old-man," Socolow, 102.

154. "after four years of a traveling life," La Condamine, *Journal du voyage,* 92.

155. "I love my country," La Condamine, *Relación abreviada de un viaje,* 156.

156. "Only the French members of the Academy," *Journal du voyage,* La Condamine, 245–246.

156. "a new comedy by Molière," La Condamine, *Journal du voyage,* 269.

157. "put his affairs and his conscience in order," La Condamine, *Journal du voyage,* 103.

158. "the most famous in all South America," and "never hazarded without the utmost dread," Bouguer, 295–296.

159. "reconnoitering the ground," Jean Godin, 1773 letter to La Condamine, as translated into English in *Perils and Captivity.*

160. "His duties regarding the objective," La Condamine, *Journal du voyage,* 132.

160. Dowry information is from Arellano, 41.

162. "At a time when I was flattering myself," La Condamine, *Journal du voyage,* 131.

163. "for the same purpose we use waxcloth," Wolf and Wolf, 28.

163. "It matters not on what place of the earth we stand," Bouguer, 311.

164. "One wishes that it would be universal," Vera, 21.

164. "I tried in vain to keep moving," La Condamine, *Journal du voyage,* 151.

165. "no one obeyed it," La Condamine, *Relación abreviada de un viaje,* 153.

165. "insulted the nation of Spain," La Condamine, *Journal du voyage,* 242.

166. "justice in Quito is constant," La Condamine, *Journal du voyage,* 270.

166. "attracted the attention of the ladies," La Condamine, *Journal du voyage,* 164.

167. "series of labors and hardships," Juan and Ulloa, *A Voyage to South America,* 229.

## Chapter Ten: Down the Amazon

169. "I reckoned on taking the same road," Godin, 1773 letter to La Condamine.

170. Arellano describes the financial difficulties of Jean Godin in Quito.

171. "Riobamba is situated," *Ecuador: Insight Guide,* 251.

171. "very careful not to diminish their wealth," Juan and Ulloa, *A Voyage to South America,* 311.

171. "tallest in the viceroyalty," Mejía, 9.

172. "landscape elegantly adorned," Juan and Ulloa, *A Voyage to South America,* 312.

173. The folklore regarding Chimborazo, Altar, and Tungurahua is recounted by Anhalzer.

174. "There are a great number of young people," Mejía, 52.

174-175. Details about the Gramesón family during this period are from Arellano's *Historia de amor.*

175. The fact that Jean and Isabel's first three children died shortly after birth is from research by Saint Amand librarian Hélène Touzel.

175. Pierre Godin's "Génealogie de la famille Godin" provides the date for the death of Jean's father.

177. "They were like madmen, without sense," Hanson, 154.

177-184. Hemming's *Red Gold* provides a very thorough and disturbing history of the exploration of the Amazon River and the slave trade that depopulated it.

181. "most intelligent, the best governed on the river," Anthony Smith, 150.

181. "settlements are so close together," Hemming, 231.

182. "They killed them as one kills mosquitoes," Hemming, 411.

184. "As for the discomforts," La Condamine, *Journal du voyage,* 123.

185. "The famous straight known under the name," La Condamine, *Journal du voyage,* 174, and "Abridged Narrative of Travels through the Interior of South America," 215.

186. "should die en route," La Condamine, *Journal du voyage,* 187.

186. "on rafts constructed on the spot," La Condamine, "Abridged Narrative of Travels," 216.

187. "Ever since, secluded in accessible woods," La Condamine, "Abridged Narrative of Travels," 219.

187. "The waters seem to hurl," La Condamine, "Abridged

Narrative of Travels," 219.

187. "I found myself," La Condamine, "Abridged Narrative of Travels," 220.

189. "grows in the flesh of men," La Condamine, "Abridged Narrative of Travels," 247.

189. "By a strong puff of the breath," La Condamine, "Abridged Narrative of Travels," 225.

190. "nothing but a thirst for gold," La Condamine, "Abridged Narrative of Travels," 238.

190. "probably exaggerations or inventions," La Condamine, "Abridged Narrative of Travels," 234.

191. "While thus torpified," La Condamine, "Abridged Narrative of Travels," 245.

192. "On the banks of the Marañón," La Condamine, "Abridged Narrative of Travels," 229.

192. "The chief decoration," La Condamine, "Abridged Narrative of Travels," 229.

192. "Of all the savages," La Condamine, *Journal du voyage,* 189.

192. "to make them more perfectly resemble," La Condamine, "Abridged Narrative of Travels," 226.

193. "without coming across any signs of life," La Condamine, *Journal du voyage,* 190.

193. "native women all clad in Britany linen," La Condamine, "Abridged Narrative of Travels," 230.

194. "In dull, distant places," Jones, 153.

194. "furnishes a new argument and demonstration," La Condamine, *"Relation abrégée de un voyage,"* iii.

196. "By all appearances," LaFuente and Delgado, 285.

197. "Bouguer could not disguise," eulogy for La Condamine.

197. "One of the best and most useful," Hanke, 169.

198. "No other wish but," La Condamine, *Journal du voyage,* 218.

199. "heart covering itself with a black veil," eulogy for Jussieu.

200. "never hazarded without the utmost dread," Bouguer, 296.

200. "Anyone but you, Sir," Godin, 1773 letter to La Condamine.

201. "With no other recommendation," Godin, 1773 letter to La Condamine.

201. "He received me with open arms," Godin, 1773 letter to La Condamine.

202. "a large pirogue of fourteen oars," Godin, 1773 letter to La Condamine.

202. "by following the same route," Froidevaux, 95–96.

202. "It doesn't appear that his time," Froidevaux, 96.

## Chapter Eleven: A Continent Apart

206. The two memoires by Jean Godin cited in this chapter were published in a nineteenth-century book, *Extraits des auteurs et voyageurs qui ont écrit sur la Guyane de 1596 à 1844,* edited by Victor de Nouvion.

206. "France's interest in navigation along the Amazon," Godin, "Mémoire sur la navigation de l'Amazone," in *Extraits,* 88–91.

208. "owing to it being light and pliable," Godin, "Mémoire sur différents bois dans l'ile de Cayenne," in *Extraits*, 91–93.

209. "He was well regarded," Froidevaux, 103.

209. "I had the honor," letter from Godin to Rouillé, April 8, 1751. Froidevaux, 125–126.

210. "We have not yet responded to him," Froidevaux, 98.

211. "facilitate, on my account," letter from Ignatius Visconti, January 16, 1754. Copy obtained from the municipal library in Saint Amand-Montrond.

211. "I write, Sir, to Monsieurs d'Orvilliers," letter from Rouillé to Godin, March 19, 1752. Froidevaux, 98.

211. "I inquired [about the passport] of the governor of that place," Froidevaux, 98.

212. "would be a source of riches," and "I implore you, Sir," letter from Lemoyne to Paris, June 14, 1752. Froidevaux, 127.

214. "Only a small portion of the costs," joint letter from Lemoyne and d'Orvilliers to Paris, June 19, 1752. Froidevaux, 128.

215. "Godin asked me for permission," letter from M. Dunezat to Paris, May 10, 1755. Froidevaux, 129.

215. "mouth of the Amazon," and "poor state," Froidevaux, 141.

215. The name of Isabel and Jean's daughter does not appear in genealogical records; Carmen del Pilar is as cited by Arellano.

217. Arellano describes the financial problems of the Gramesón family during the 1950s in his *Historia de amor.*

217. "I will always better your fortune," Arellano, 55.

218. Information about Indian uprisings in the 1760s can be found in *Encyclopedia del Ecuador* and Mejía's *Riobamba: La villa peregrina.*

218. Mejía describes the importance of the Virgin of Sicalpa in Riobamba during this period.

219. "I renewed my letters every year," Godin, 1773 letter to La Condamine.

221. "I provided [Choiseul] with a very detailed account," letter from Godin des Odonais to Fiedmont, October 25, 1765. Froidevaux, 134–136.

221. "In December 1763, I had the honor," letter from Godin des Odonais to Choiseul, June 1, 1764. Froidevaux, 130.

222. "I was, Sir, associated with the gentlemen," letter from Godin des Odonais to d'Herouville, September 10, 1764. Froidevaux, 130–132.

222. "This behavior by our touchy and cruel neighbor," letter from Fiedmont to Paris, October 18, 1765. Froidevaux, 132–133.

223. "in the midst of a nation against which," Godin, October 25, 1765, letter to Fiedmont.

223. "something is going on in this boat," letter from Godin des Odonais to Fiedmont, October 25, 1765.

223. "The whites that I would have brought," letter from Godin des Odonais to Fiedmont, October 28, 1765. Froidevaux, 137–139.

224. "I've worked against this nation," Godin, October 28, 1765, letter to Fiedmont.

224. "nasty fall in the woods," Godin, October 25, 1765, letter to Fiedmont.

224. "He'll hear nothing of going ahead," Godin, October 25, 1765, letter to Fiedmont.

224. "This man wants to overpower me," Godin, October 28, 1765, letter to Fiedmont.

224. "Please do me the honor," Godin, October 28, 1765, letter to Fiedmont.

224. "to whom I might entrust," Godin, 1773 letter to La Condamine.

225. "a knight of the order of Christ," Godin, 1773 letter to La Condamine.

226. "give credit to [it], while others dispute," Godin, 1773 letter to La Condamine.

226. The date for Carmen's death is from Arellano.

227. "live in a debasement of human nature," Juan and Ulloa, *A Voyage to South America,* 479.

227. "wholly covered with scales," Juan and Ulloa, *A Voyage to South America,* 362.

228. "It is a serpent of a frightful magnitude," Juan and Ulloa, *A Voyage to South America,* 397.

228. "extremely troublesome and fatiguing," Juan and Ulloa, *A Voyage to South America,* 370.

229. "Her father and her brothers," Grandmaison, "Un drame inconnu."

229. "a garden and estate," Godin, 1773 letter to La Condamine.

230. "to watch over her health," Godin, 1773 letter to La Condamine.

230. "might have need of the assistance," Godin, 1773 letter to La Condamine.

## Chapter Twelve: Lost on the Bobonaza

Jean Godin wrote twice about Isabel's ordeal. The first time was in a 1770 letter to the Duc de Choiseul-Praslin. The second was in his 1773 letter to La Condamine. While the two letters are generally consistent, they differ in a few details. The 1773 document is both longer and more specific, and Jean also could have expected it to be the "historical record" of his wife's journey. In contrast, his 1770 letter to the Duc de Choiseul-Praslin was sent as a private appeal for relief from a debt. Thus, in those instances where the details in the two letters are not quite the same, I have used the 1773 letter as the authoritative source. Rocha's descriptions of the voyage, as he related it to a priest at Andoas, Juan Suasti, can be found in the *Arnahis* documents.

For information on the rain forest, see Kricher's *Neotropical Companion.* Alexander Von Humboldt wrote a three-volume account of his travels in South America that appeared between 1814 and 1825. Spruce's 1857 trip up the Bobonaza, which he relates in *Notes of a Botanist on the Amazon and in the Andes,* provides a revealing foil for Isabel's journey. In some instances, descriptions of the river basin are based on observations I made while traveling this route in 2002.

234. "crowned with great bushes of flowers," Kricher, 4.

235. The description of this bridge is from Spruce, vol. 2, 163.

237. "impractical even for mules," Godin, 1773 letter to La Condamine.

237. "rain from sunrise till nightfall," Spruce, vol. 2, 142.

237. "dreadful, what with mud," Spruce, vol. 2, 148.

237. "the track ran along the very edge of the cliff," Spruce, vol. 2, 145.

237. "was one mass of foam," Spruce, vol. 2, 149.

237. "hardly bear to think of it," Spruce, vol. 2, 104.

238. "crossed with difficulty," Spruce, vol. 2, 135.

238. "utterly abandoned by its population," Godin, 1773 letter to La Condamine.

238. "had hid in the woods," Godin, 1773 letter to La Condamine.

239. "The desire of reaching the vessel," Godin, 1773 letter to La Condamine.

241. "We had scarcely resigned ourselves to sleep," Spruce, vol. 2, 121.

243. "We didn't know the path," and "none of us had any skills," letter written by Juan Suasti, December 15, 1769. *Arnahis*, 111–114.

244. "We saw a canoe," Suasti's letter, *Arnahis*.

245. "stooping to recover it," Godin, 1773 letter to La Condamine.

245. "with great work," Suasti's letter, *Arnahis*.

246. "especial care to carry his effects with him," Godin, 1773 letter to La Condamine.

## Chapter Thirteen: Into the Jungle

In his two letters, Jean Godin stated that all seven of those left behind on the sandbar went together on the raft. As a result, this became the accepted history. However, the documents published in *Arnahis* tell a different story, and conclusively so. The documents include statements made by Rocha, Joaquín, and the Indians who went with Joaquín on the rescue mission. Their accounts provide a precise description of the scene at the sandbar. In addition, the *Arnahis* documents include a statement by a priest from the Santa Rosa mission station, Luis Peñaherrera, who said that Isabel informed him that only her two brothers and her nephew went on the raft, while Juanita, Tomasa, and Antonio stayed behind.

247. "at the top of the beach," Suasti's letter, *Arnahis*.

251. "lances and bows and arrows," Spruce, vol. 2, 107.

251. "confidence that help would come," Peñaherrera's account, *Arnahis*, 149–150.

251. "five and twenty days," Godin, 1773 letter to La Condamine.

253. "The raft, badly framed," Godin, 1773 letter to La Condamine.

253. "No one was drowned," Godin, 1773 letter to La Condamine.

253. "resolved on tracing the course of the river," Godin, 1773 letter to La Condamine.

254. The description of Isabel dressed in pants is from testimony given by Andoas Indians, *Arnahis,* 141–147.

255. "The very air may be said to be alive with mosquitoes," Honigsbaum, 11.

256. "Without interruption, at every instant," O'Hanlon, 124.

256. "No matter where you step," Forsyth and Miyata, 108.

257. "reaching into a flame," O'Hanlon, 249.

257. "burning, blinding pain," Forsyth and Miyata, 108.

257. "raging complex itches," Forsyth and Miyata, 225.

257. "are covered with sharp hairs," Kricher, 380.

258. Descriptions of the botflies feasting on Isabel and her party is from testimony given by Andoas Indians, *Arnahis,* 141–147.

259. "is in reality a form of insecticide," Kricher, 145.

259. "All that the primitive has," Von Hagen, *Off with Their Heads,* 166.

260. "fain to subsist on," Godin, 1773 letter to La Condamine.

260. "fatigue" and "wounds," Godin, undated letter to the Duc de Choiseul-Praslin. *Arnahis*, 111–122.

260. "oppressed with hunger and thirst," Godin, 1773 letter to La Condamine.

260. See Whitney and Cataldo for a description of death from starvation.

261. "first to succumb," Godin, letter to Choiseul-Praslin.

261. "watched as they all died," Godin, letter to Choiseul-Praslin.

262. "stretched on the ground," Godin, 1773 letter to La Condamine.

262. "look for water," Godin, letter to Choiseul-Praslin.

262. "resolution and strength" to stand, Godin, 1773 letter to La Condamine.

262. "clothing was in tatters," letter to Choiseul-Praslin.

262. "cut the shoes off her brother's feet," and "converted them into sandals," Godin, 1773 letter to La Condamine.

262. "took her scarf and wrapped it around herself," letter to Choiseul-Praslin.

263. "more of his own affairs," Godin, 1773 letter to La Condamine.

263. "Filled with hope," Suasti's letter, *Arnahis.*

263. "on both sides of the river," Suasti's letter, *Arnahis.*

264. "ax and machete," letter written by Antonio de la Peña, January 30, 1770. *Arnahis,* 111.

264. "old trousers," declaration by Jean Rocha, January 30, 1770. *Arnahis*, 114–115.

264. "They were not able to verify," Suasti's letter, *Arnahis.*

265. "knowing what I know," declaration by Nicolás Romero, January 8, 1770. *Arnahis*, 114.

265. "by the Jibaros Indians," Peña's letter, *Arnahis.*

265. There is one confusing note in the *Arnahis* documents. Those who went back to the sandbar on the rescue mission described finding human bones and a cadaver in the river. However, nearly a year later, several Andoas Indians told of hearing a rumor that two of Isabel's servants had shown up alive in Canelos. One was said to be a small boy and the other a big woman. However, that rumor does not square with several facts, and thus I chose not to include it. There was no "big woman" servant on the trip. (Juanita and Tomasa were only eight or nine years old.) There was only a short period between the time that Isabel and the others left the sandbar and Joaquín arrived with the rescue canoe, making it unlikely that two of the three left behind would have been rescued during this time. Finally, the Indians and Joaquin found a corpse in the river and a pile of human bones stripped of their flesh, a scene consistent with multiple deaths.

266. "It became known that walking," declaration by Joseph Diguja, May 28, 1770. *Arnahis,* 115–116.

266. "These roads [are] closed," court documents, *Arnahis*, 126.

266. "permit commerce or even communication," declaration by Joseph Ferrer, a Quito judge, on June 1, 1770. *Arnahis*, 121–122.

266. "accomplices in this sinful behavior," statement by Doctor Galdeano, June 1, 1770. *Arnahis,* 118–120.

267. "upon the orders of Jean Godin," declaration by Antonio Zabala, June 26, 1770. *Arnahis,* 129.

## Chapter Fourteen: Deliverance

269. "drag herself along," Godin, 1773 letter to La Condamine.

269. "half dead with cold," Spruce, vol. 2, 123.

270. "drank as much as she could," Godin, letter to Choiseul-Praslin.

270. "with the greatest difficulty, Godin, 1773 letter to La Condamine.

271. "The remembrance of the shocking spectacle," Godin, 1773 letter to La Condamine.

271. "often the apparently strong," Noyce, 59.

271. "It is surprising the large number," Leach, 151.

272. "For the whole voyage," Noyce, 79.

272. "fourth walked beside them," Noyce, 192.

272. "I can assure you that God," Read, 338.

272. "turn their thoughts to the outside," Noyce, 196.

273. "heard a noise at about two hundred paces," Godin, 1773 letter to La Condamine.

273. "two Indians and their wives," Godin, letter to Choiseul-Praslin.

273. "Her terror occasioned her," Godin, 1773 letter to La Condamine.

274. "the pants of a man and a shawl," and "took out from her head the worms," statement by Joseph Macuca on October 9, 1770. *Arnahis*, 145.

275. "kindness truly affectionate," Godin, letter to La Condamine.

275. "time of Lent," statement by Pedro Nolasco Saruín on Oct. 9, 1770. *Arnahis*, 141–142.

275. "her feet were so swollen," Godin, letter to Choiseul-Praslin.

275. "Madame Godin, stripped of almost every thing," Godin, 1773 letter to La Condamine.

276. "took possession of the chains," Godin, 1773 letter to La Condamine.

277. "with a high fever," Godin, letter to Choiseul-Praslin.

277. "four silver dishes," Godin, 1773 letter to La Condamine.

278. "Go your way, Sir," Godin, 1773 letter to La Condamine.

278. "She said that the Almighty had preserved her," Godin, 1773 letter to La Condamine, recounting a letter written by Romero.

279. "My wife was ever dear to me," Godin, 1773 letter to La Condamine.

279. "Dear Sir, with all my esteem," Isabel Godin, letter written April 21, 1770. *Arnahis*, 147.

280. "penetrated with the most lively grief," Godin, 1773 letter to La Condamine.

281. "It was proposed to take off the thumb," Godin, 1773 letter to La Condamine.

281. "On board this vessel," Godin, 1773 letter to La Condamine.

282. "were it told in a romance," Godin, 1773 letter to La Condamine. As explained in the notes for chapter 13, Jean mistakenly wrote that everyone left behind on the sandbar stayed together, and that there were six or seven who died by Isabel's side. In order to avoid confusing the reader, I have edited from this passage his comment that Isabel's maids and Rocha's slave were with her when they died.

## Chapter Fifteen: Saint Amand

283. "I took my leave," Godin, 1773 letter to La Condamine.

284. "Might we, Your Grace, ask you to cancel our debt," Godin, letter to Choiseul-Praslin.

285. "infidelity and neglect," Godin, 1773 letter to La Condamine.

285. The 1772 census information is from Froidevaux, 111.

285. "For my part," Godin, 1773 letter to La Condamine.

286. "card of liberty," Arellano, 93.

286. "miracles may be effected," La Condamine, "Abridged Narrative of Travels," 258.

286. "as extraordinary a series of perils," Godin, *Perils and Captivity,* vi.

290. "vexations, mortifications, and rebuffs," Whitaker, 180.

290. "reckoned equivalent to one living being," La Condamine, "Abridged Narrative of Travels," 258.

292. "La Condamine may have had faults," La Condamine eulogy.

293. "as official geographer to the King," Lemaire, "À la recherche de la famille d'Isabel Godin."

293. "which he prepared in St. Amand," Boyer.

293. "printed at the expense," letter from a minister to Godin des Odonais, July 22, 1787. Froidevaux, 148.

293. Information about the funeral for Isabel's father can be found in Vannier.

293. "I owe to Madame Isabelle," Jean Godin's "Last Will and Testament." Copy provided by the Saint Amand-Montrond municipal library.

294. The description of Isabel stroking her sandals and cotton dress comes from Felix Gilbert Grandmaison, the son of Isabel's nephew Jean-Antoine.

295. Lemaire, in his article "À la recherche de la famille d'Isabel Godin," writes of seeing the sandals when he was a young man.

## Along the Bobonaza Today

There are several indigenous groups that live in the Bobonaza region today. Shuars, known as Jibaros in the eighteenth century, have settlements along the Pastaza. They long had a reputation for being skilled warriors, and became known for their custom of shrinking the heads of their victims. The Shuar population is about 40,0 today, and many live in towns that border the jungle, such as Puyo.

As was the case in 1770, Quichua live in Canelos and along the banks of the upper Bobonaza. They are the indigenous group that has always interacted the most with the Spanish. Canelos still has the feel of the mission town it once was, and Pacayacu, which is about twenty miles downriver from Canelos, also has Spanish-style buildings. Sarayacu, meanwhile, is a thriving Quichua village of perhaps 1,0. The people there live in traditional ways.

There are several Achuar communities along the lower Bobonaza. The Achuars are related to the Shuars, and for a long time the two groups fought regularly, with the victors carrying off women from the other tribe. Fiercely independent, the face-painting Achuars remain wary of intruders, and outsiders traveling through this stretch of river are advised to avoid stopping at their villages unless they come with someone who can provide an introduction. Achuars may still hunt with blowguns and curare-tipped darts. There are only about 5,0 Achuar alive today.

Like the Shuars, the Zaparos were known for their fighting skills. But this group was devastated in the first half of the twentieth century by contact with whites who came into the Pastaza region looking for rubber. Today there are fewer than twenty Zaparos who speak the Zaparo language.

Huaoranis live to the north of the Bobonaza, deep in the jungle. As recently as forty years ago, their members used stone axes and resisted contact with outsiders. Quichua called them "Aucas," meaning "people of the jungle, savages," because of their aggressive attitude toward other indigenous groups and white colonists. However, since that time, oil exploration in Ecuador's orient has put tremendous pressures on the Huaoranis, endangering their way of life. There are thought to be about 2,000 Huaoranis living in the Ecuadorian rain forest.

The people of Sarayacu and along the lower Bobonaza are currently struggling to stop oil exploration in this river basin, fearful that it will contaminate their lands and ruin their way of life. They point to the experience of indigenous groups in northeastern Ecuador, where Texaco began drilling in 1971, as reason for this concern. Texaco dumped millions of gallons of toxic waste fluids in open pits and streams from 1971 to 1991, and the indigenous people there maintain that the pollution has caused many to die from cancer.

Although oil companies initiated plans to explore the Bobonaza in 1989, opposition from indigenous groups stalled these efforts until late 2002, when an Argentinian oil firm, Compania General de Combustibles (CGC), established work camps on the upper section of the river. That led to several skirmishes between the oil workers and residents of Sarayacu, who at one point "detained" several oil company employees who came into their territory. Throughout 2003, tensions continued to escalate, and toward the end of the year, the Ecuadorian government announced that if the indigenous people living along the Bobonaza continued to resist, it would send in military troops to enable the oil drilling to proceed.

Marlon Santi, who was one of my guides on my trip down the Bobonaza, is now the president of the Sarayacu and a leader of this resistance. Several international environmental groups are supporting the indigenous people of the Bobonaza. They note that the region around Sarayacu is old-growth rainforest and one of the richest biological environments in the world. Updated news of this conflict can be found at www.sarayacu.com and www.mapmakerswife.com.

# Bibliography

## Primary Sources

*Archivo Nacional de Historia (Arnahis).* "Sobre la pérdida de la familia de Don Pedro Gramesón en la provincia de Mainas." Revista 18, Edición de la Casa de la Cultura, Quito, 1970, 111–150. This contains statements of witnesses to the Isabel Godin tragedy and other documents produced by authorities investigating it in 1770.

Bouguer, Pierre. *La figure de la terre.* Paris: C. A. Jombert, 1749. Translated into English as "An Abridged Relation of a Voyage to Peru," in John Pinkerton, ed., *A General Collection of the Best and Most Interesting Voyages and Travels in All Parts of the World.* Vol. 14. London, 1813.

Cassini, Jacques. "De la grandeur et de la figure de al terre." *Histoire et memoires de l'Académie Royale des Sciences,* 1718: 245–257.

"Eulogy for Pierre Bouguer." *Histoire et memoires de l'Académie Royale des Sciences,* 1758: 127–136.

"Eulogy for Jacques Cassini." *Histoire et memoires de l'Académie Royale des Sciences,* 1756: 134–146.

"Eulogy for Louis Godin." *Histoire et memoires de l'Académie Royale des Sciences,* 1760: 181–194.

"Eulogy for Joseph de Jussieu" *Histoire et memoires de l'Académie Royale des Sciences,* 1779: 44–53.

"Eulogy for Charles-Marie de La Condamine." *Histoire et memoires de l'Académie Royale des Sciences,* 1774: 85–121.

Froidevaux, Henri. "Documents inédits sur Godin des Odonnais et son séjour à la Guyane." *Journal de la Société des Américanistes de Paris* 1, no. 3 (1895–1896): 91–148. This article contains letters written by Jean Godin during his time in French Guiana as well as correspondence between the governors of French Guiana and authorities in Paris.

Godin, Jean. "Letter to de La Condamine, 1773." First published in *Relation abrégée d'un voyage fait dans l'intérieur de l'Amérique mériodionale,* by Charles-Marie de La Condamine. Maestricht: J. E. Dufour and P. Roux, 1778. An English translation of this letter appeared in *Perils and Captivity: Voyage of Madame Godin along the River of the Amazons in the Year 1770.* Edinburgh: Constable and Co., 1827.

———. "Mémoire sur différents bois dans l'ile de Cayenne." In *Extraits des auteurs et voyageurs qui ont écrit sur la Guyane de 1596 à 1844,* ed. Victor de Nouvion, 91–93. Paris: Béthume et Plon, 1844.

———. "Mémoire sur la navigation de l'Amazone." In *Extraits des auteurs et voyageurs qui ont écrit sur la Guyane de 1596 à 1844,* ed. Victor de Nouvion, 87–91. Paris: Béthume et Plon, 1844.

Godin, Pierre Amedée. "Génealogie de la famille Godin" (1890). Handwritten copy.

Grandmaison y Bruno, Felix de. "Un drame inconnu: Voyage de Madame Godin des Odonnais." Unpublished manuscript, 1830. Felix was the son of Isabel Godin's nephew, Jean-Antoine Grandmaison.

Juan, Jorge, and Antonio de Ulloa. "Discurso y reflexiones políticas sobre el estado presente de los reynos del Peru." Private report, 1749. Later published as *Noticias secretas de América sobre el estado naval, militar, y politico de los reynos del Peru y provincias de Quito.* London: R. Taylor, 1826. Translated into English as *Discourse and Political Reflections on the Kingdoms of Peru,* ed. John Tepaske, trans. John Tepaske and Besse Clement. Norman: University of Oklahoma Press, 1978.

——. *Relación histórica del viage a la América Meridional.* Madrid: Antonio Marin, 1748. Translated into English as *A Voyage to South America,* trans. John Adams, Piccadilly: John Stockdale, 1806.

La Condamine, Charles-Marie de. *Journal du voyage fait par ordre du roi à l'équateur.* Paris: Imprimerie royale, 1751.

——. *Mesure des trois premiers degrés du méridien dans l'hémisphere austral.* Paris: Imprimerie royale, 1751.

——. *Relation abrégée d'un voyage fait dans l'intérieur de l'Amérique méridionale.* Maestricht: J. E. Dufour and P. Roux, 1778. Translated into English as "Abridged Narrative of Travels through the Interior of South America," in John Pinkerton, ed., *A General Collection of the Best and Most Interesting Voyages and Travels in All Parts of the World.* Vol. 14. London, 1813.

——. *Supplément au journal historique du voyage à l'équateur et au livre de la mesure de trois premiers degrés du méridien servant de réponse à quelques objections.* Paris: Pissot, 1752.

——. "Sur l'arbre du quinquina." *Histoire et memoires de l'Académie Royale des Sciences,* 1738: 226–243.


## Secondary Sources


MAPPING THE EARTH'S SIZE AND SHAPE

Ashley, Maurice. *Louis XIV and the Greatness of France.* New York: Collier Books, 1962.

Berthon, Simon, and Andrew Robinson. *The Shape of the World.* Chicago: Rand McNally, 1991.

Boss, Valentin. *Newton and Russia.* Cambridge, MA: Harvard University Press, 1972.

Brandes, Georg. *Voltaire.* New York: Tudor Publishing Company, 1930.

Brown, Harcourt. *Science and the Human Comedy.* Toronto and Buffalo: University of Toronto Press, 1976.

Brown, Lloyd. *The Story of Maps.* New York: Bonanza Books, 1949.

Cobban, Alfred. *A History of Modern France.* London and New York: Penguin Books, 1985.

Gaukroger, Stephen. *Descartes: An Intellectual Biography.* Oxford: Clarendon Press, 1995.

Greenberg, John. *The Problem of the Earth's Shape from Newton to Clairaut*. Cambridge: Cambridge University Press, 1995.

Hahn, Roger. *The Anatomy of a Scientific Institution*. Berkeley and Los Angeles: University of California Press, 1971.

Hall, A. Rupert. *The Scientific Revolution, 1500–1800*. Boston: Beacon Press, 1954.

Jacob, James. *The Scientific Revolution*. Atlantic Highlands, NJ: Humanities Press, 1998.

Paul, Charles. *Science and Immortality*. Berkeley and Los Angeles: University of California Press, 1980.

Sound, Parry. *Science and the Human Comedy*. Toronto: University of Toronto Press, 1976.

Stroup, Alice. *A Company of Scientists*. Berkeley and Los Angeles: University of California Press, 1990.

Sturdy, David. *Science and Social Status*. Woodbridge, UK: Boydell Press, 1995.

Westfall, Richard. *The Life of Isaac Newton*. Cambridge and New York: Cambridge University Press, 1993.

Wolf, A. *A History of Science Technology and Philosophy in the Sixteenth and Seventeenth Centuries*. New York: Harper Torchbooks, 1959.

COLONIAL SOUTH AMERICA

Alexander, Michael, ed. *Discovering the New World: Based on the Works of Theodore de Bry*. New York: Harper and Row, 1976.

Burkholder, Mark, and Lyman Johnson. *Colonial Latin America*. New York: Oxford University Press, 1998.

Carrión, Mario. "Spanish *Fiesta Brave* … A History of Bullfighting." *The Mexico File,* November 1977. Online. Available: http://www.mexicofile.com/bullfightinghistory.htm.

Descola, Jean. *Daily Life in Colonial Peru*. New York: Macmillan, 1968.

Elliott, J. H. *Imperial Spain*. New York: Meridian, 1977.

Haring, C. H. *The Spanish Empire in America*. New York: Oxford University Press, 1947.

Kamen, Henry. *Spain: 1469–1714*. London and New York: Longman, 1991.

——. *The Spanish Inquisition*. New York: New American Library, 1965.

Las Casas, Bartolomé de. *A Short Account of the Destruction of the Indies* (1542). London and New York: Penguin, 1992.

Lavrin, Asunción. *Sexuality and Marriage in Colonial Latin America.* Lincoln: University of Nebraska Press, 1992.

Leonard, Irving. *Books of the Brave.* Cambridge, MA: Harvard University Press, 1949.

———, ed. *Colonial Travelers in Latin America.* Newark, DE: Juan de la Cuesta-Hispanic Monographs, 1986.

Lockhart, James, and Stuart Schwartz. *Early Latin America.* Cambridge: Cambridge University Press, 1983.

Martín, Luis. *Daughters of the Conquistadores.* Dallas, TX: Southern Methodist University Press, 1989.

Means, Philip. *Fall of the Inca Empire.* New York: Charles Scribner's Sons, 1932.

O'Connor, John J. *Amadis de Gaule and Its Influence on Elizabethan Literature.* New Brunswick, NJ: Rutgers University Press, 1970.

Parry, J. H. *The Age of Reconnaissance.* New York: Mentor, 1964.

———. *The Spanish Seaborne Empire.* New York: Alfred A. Knopf, 1966.

Prescott, William Hickling. *The Rise and Decline of the Spanish Empire.* New York: Viking Press, 1963.

Rowdon, Maurice. *The Spanish Terror.* New York: St. Martin's Press, 1974.

Shubert, Adrian. *Death and Money in the Afternoon.* New York: Oxford University Press, 1999.

Socolow, Susan Migden. *The Women of Colonial Latin America.* Cambridge and New York: Cambridge University Press, 2000.

## THE LA CONDAMINE MISSION

*Colloque International, La Condamine y la expedición de los académicos franceses al Ecuador, 250e aniversarios, 1735–1985.* IPGH-Mexico Universidad Paris X, 1987. Published talks given in Paris on November 22–23, 1985, about the La Condamine expedition.

Gillispie, Charles Coulston, ed. *Dictionary of Scientific Biography.* New York: Charles Scribner's Sons, 1981.

Hanke, Lewis. "Dos palabras on Antonio de Ulloa and the *Noticias secretas.*" *The Hispanic American Historical Review* 16 (November 1936): 479–514.

Jones, Tom. *The Figure of the Earth.* Lawrence, KS: Coronado Press, 1967.

Krousel, Hilda. *Don Antonio de Ulloa.* Baton Rouge, LA: VAAPR, 1986.

LaFuente, Antonio, and Antonio Delgado. *La geometrizacion de la tierra.* Madrid: Consejo Superior de Investigaciones Científicas, Instituto Arnau de Vilanova, 1984.

McBride, Barrie St. Clair. "Charles-Marie de La Condamine: Measurement at the Equator." *History Today* 15 (August 1965): 567–575.

Smith, Anthony. *Explorers of the Amazon.* New York: Viking, 1990.

Smith, James R. *From Plane to Spheroid.* Rancho Cordova, CA: Landmark Enterprises, 1986.

Trystram, Florence. *El proceso con las estrellas.* Quito: Libri Mundi Enrique Grosse—Lumern, 1999. Spanish translation from French edition, which was published in 1979.

Vera, Humberto. *Mitad del Mundo.* Quito: Graficas Iberia, 1997.

von Hagen, Victor Wolfgang. *South America Called Them.* New York: Alfred A. Knopf, 1945.

Wakefield, Celia. *Searching for Isabel Godin.* Chicago: Chicago Review Press, 1995.

Whitaker, Arthur. "Antonio de Ulloa." *The Hispanic American Historical Review* 15 (May 1935): 155–194.

Wolf, Howard, and Ralph Wolf. *Rubber.* New York: Covici Friede, 1936.

Zúñiga, Neptalí. *250 Años: Mision geodesica Francesa.* Quito: I. Municipio de Quito, 1986.

ISABEL GODIN AND JEAN GODIN

Arellano, Carlos Ortiz. *Una historia de amor.* Quito: Abya-yala Press, 2000.

Boyer, N. Entry on Jean Godin des Odonais. In *Nouvelle biographie generale* 20: 1914–1915.

Charcellet, Jacques. "Histoire fantastique de Jean et Isabelle Godin des Odonais." *Le Rotarien,* October 1986, 20–26.

Grandmaison y Bruno, Felix de. "Un drame inconnu: Voyage de Madame Godin des Odonnais" (1830). Unpublished manuscript. Felix was the son of Isabel Godin's nephew, Jean-Antoine Grandmaison.

La Condamine, Pierre de. "Les aventures extraordinaires de Jean et Isabelle Godin des Odonais." *Miroir de l'Histoire* 99 (1958): 1314–1322.

*Le Magasin Pittoresque.* "Adventures de Mme. Godin des Odonais." Vols. 22, 23 (1854): 371–374, 389–401.

Lemaire, Marc. *À la recherche de la famille d'Isabel Godin.* Berry, France: Berry-Chimborazo Friendship Association. Marc Lemaire is a descendant of Isabel Godin's nephew and has done extensive genealogical research on her family and on Jean Godin's family.

———. "Mais … qui etait Dona Isabelle Godin des Odonais?" Photocopied manuscript, nine pages.

———. "Qui etait Pedro Manuel Gramesón?" Photocopied manuscript, thirteen pages.

Touzel, Hélène. "Isabelle Godin, aventurière malgré elle." Photocopied manuscript, six pages.

Vannier, Bernard. "La fin d'une vie: Isabelle Godin et les débuts de la Révolution à Saint-Amand Montrond." *Bulletin de liaison Saint-Amand-Riobamba* 6: 18–25.


ECUADOR AND THE AUDIENCIA DE QUITO

Anhalzer, J. *The Andes of Ecuador.* Quito: Imprenta Mariscal, 2000.

Brain, Yossi. *Ecuador: A Climbing Guide.* Seattle, WA: Mountaineers Books, 2000.

Delavaud, Anne Collin. *Quito: The City and the Volcano.* Quito: Ediciones Libri Mundi Enrique Grosse-Luemern, 2001.

*Ecuador.* Barcelona: Lexus Editores, 1999.

*Ecuador: Insight Guide.* London: APA Publications, 1999.

*Encyclopedia del Ecuador.* Barcelona: Oceano, 1999.

Gómez, Nelson. *Nuevo Atlas del Ecuador.* Quito: Ediguías C. Ltda., 2001.

Mejía, Juan Carlos Morales. *Riobamba: La villa peregrina.* Riobamba: Editorial Pedagógica Freire, 1999.

Mora, Enrique Ayala. *Resumen de Historia Del Ecuador.* Quito: Corporación Editora Nacional, 2001.

*Origen de Los Puruhaes.* Riobamba: Editorial Pedagógica Freire, 1998.

Rachowiecki, Rob. *Climbing and Hiking in Ecuador.* Cambridge, MA: Bradt Publications, 1984.

*Riobamba: Pesonajes ilustres de la Colonia.* Riobamba: Editorial Pedagógica Freire, 1999.

*Riobamba.* Quito: Banco Central del Ecuador, 2002.

Tyrer, Robson Brines. *Historia Demografica y Economica de La Audiencia de Quito.* Quito: Banco Central del Ecuador, 1988.


## The Amazon

Canada, Chris, and Lou Jost. *Common Birds of Amazonian Ecuador.* Quito: Ediciones Libri Mundi Enrique Grosse-Luemern, 1997.

Castner, James. *Amazon Insects.* Gainesville, FL: Feline Press, 2000.

Causey, Don. *Killer Insects.* New York: Franklin Watts, 1979.

Cohen, J. M. *Journeys down the Amazon.* London: Charles Knight, 1975.

Emmons, Louise. *Neotropical Rainforest Mammals.* Chicago: University of Chicago Press, 1990.

Fletcher, Alan Mark. *The Land and People of the Guianas.* Philadelphia: J. B. Lippincott, 1966.

Forsyth, Adrian, and Kenneth Miyata. *Tropical Nature.* New York: Charles Scribner's Sons, 1984.

Furneaux, Robin. *The Amazon.* New York: G. P. Putnam's Sons, 1969.

Gheerbrant, Alain. *The Amazon: Past, Present, and Future.* New York: Harry Abrams, 1992.

Hanson, Earl Parker. *South from the Spanish Main.* New York: Delacorte Press, 1967.

Hemming, John. *Red Gold.* Cambridge, MA: Harvard University Press, 1978.

Honigsbaum, Mark. *The Fever Trail.* New York: Farrar, Straus, and Giroux, 2001.

Kane, Joe. *Running the Amazon.* New York: Vintage, 1990.

Kricher, John. *A Neotropical Companion.* Princeton: Princeton University Press, 1997.

Lathrap, Donald. *The Upper Amazon.* New York and Washington, DC: Praeger Publishers, 1970.

Medina, José Toribio. *The Discovery of the Amazon* (1894). New York: American Geographical Society, 1934.

O'Hanlon, Redmond. *In Trouble Again.* New York: Vintage, 1988.

Patzelt, Erwin. *Fauna del Ecuador.* Quito: Imprefepp, 2000.

Paymal, Noemi, and Catalina Sosa, eds. *Amazon World*. Quito: Sinchi Sacha Editions, 1993.

Robinson, Alex, and Gardênia Robinson. *The Amazon*. London: Cadogan Guides.

Spruce, Richard. *Notes of a Botanist on the Amazon and in the Andes* (1908). New York: Johnson Reprint Corporation, 1970.

Tirira, Diego, ed. *Libro rojo de los mamíferos del Ecuador*. Quito: SIM-BIOE/EcoCiencia/Ministerio del Ambiente/UICN, 2001.

Ure, John. *Trespassers on the Amazon*. London: Constable, 1986.

von Hagen, Victor. *Off with Their Heads*. New York: Macmillan, 1937.

Von Humboldt, Alexander. *Personal Narrative of a Journey to the Equinoctal Regions of the New Continent*. London and New York: Penguin Classics, 1995.

## STARVATION AND SURVIVAL

Keys, Ancel. *The Biology of Human Starvation*. Minneapolis: University of Minnesota Press, 1950.

King, Joseph. *Winter of Entrapment*. Toronto: P. D. Meany, 1992.

Leach, John. *Survival Psychology*. New York: Macmillan, 1994.

Noyce, Wilfrid. *They Survived: A Study of the Will to Live*. New York: E. P. Dutton, 1963.

Read, Piers Paul. *Alive*. Philadelphia: J. P. Lippincott, 1974.

Whitney, Eleanor, and Corinne Cataldo. *Understanding Normal and Clinical Nutrition*. St. Paul, MN: West Publishing, 1983.

# Acknowledgments

I AM DEEPLY GRATEFUL to a number of people, on three continents, who helped make this book possible.

To research French documents, I relied on two translators: Jennifer Yanco and Gabriela Ansari. Jennifer Yanco translated articles published in *Histoire et memoires de l'Académie Royale des Sciences* and the collection of letters published in 1895 by Henri Froidevaux, "Documents inédits sur Godin des Odonnais et son séjour à la Guyane." She also traveled to Saint Amand-Montrond to research and translate documents in the city's municipal library, which included Jean Godin's will and various articles by local historians. In Saint Amand, she was graciously assisted by the mayor's office and the town's librarians, Madame Alquier, Madame Richard, and Madame Hardy. Jean-Baptiste Baudon, head of the Berry-Chimborazo Friendship Society, also provided her with assistance and time, as did Alain Eclache, owner of the Chateau d'Igny, where there is a stained-glass window with a portrait of Isabel Godin.

Gabriela Ansari ably translated La Condamine's *Journal du voyage fait par ordre du roi à l'équateur* and various French letters published in LaFuente and Delgado's *La geometrizacion de la tierra*.

My trip down the Bobonaza River was made possible by Cary Kanoy, an American who has been guiding in Ecuador for about a decade and who now has a company called Core Expeditions. I approached a number of guides about making this journey, and he was the only one willing to tackle it. His wife Grace helped with planning the trip.

On that journey, Ricardo Alzamora, an Ecuadorian guide who works with Cary, proved to be a fount of information about the birds of the Amazon and other wildlife that we came upon. In the dugout canoe, I also had the distinct pleasure of sharing stories with Luis Hernandez. A former colonel in the Ecuadorian army, he helped smooth out several bumps we encountered in our trip. One of the lasting rewards of researching this book has been his friendship.

We were piloted down the Bobonaza by Tito Machoa and Marlon Santi, who are from Sarayacu, a traditional village on the upper section of the river. Their navigational skills and their knowledge of the surrounding forest were extraordinary, as was their generosity and grace. In Sarayacu, they put us up with their families, who provided us with food, chicha (a fermented drink), and a memorable evening of talk. I am also grateful to village leaders in Sarayacu who permitted us to continue our voyage downriver, in spite of their concerns about outsiders coming into this region to explore for oil. Finally, at the end of our voyage, near the Peruvian border, we were treated with much hospitality by the Ecuadorian military in their camp at Nuevo Ishpingo.

As Cary Kanoy and I bicycled from Riobamba to Puyo, we were assisted by Sebastián Ponce. On an earlier trip to Ecuador, Ricardo Alzamora and Maria Clara Espinosa arranged for a wonderful day trip to the top of Guagua Pichincha, the volcano climbed by Charles de La Condamine and Pierre Bouguer.

In Riobamba, I am particularly thankful to Adela Irene Moscoso Valarezo, director of the Colegio de Isabel Godin. In an interview, she provided much insight into how extraordinary it was for a woman of eighteenth-century Peru to make the journey that Isabel did and into why Isabel remains an inspiration to the school's students today. Finally, in Quito, the friendly staff at Casa Sol made the bed-and-breakfast feel like home while I did research there.

I owe a tremendous debt to Amanda Cook, my editor at Basic Books. At the outset, she helped me conceive of how to tell the story, and once I turned in a first draft, she improved it in innumerable ways. She also provided much-appreciated encouragement and guidance throughout the time I was working on the book. I am also grateful to Kathy Delfosse for the skillful copy-editing and to the many others at Perseus who make it such a wonderful house for writers. And as always, my agent Jane Dystel provided me with thoughtful advice and help throughout this lengthy process, starting with the shaping of the initial proposal.

Finally, I am thankful to my wife, Andrea, and my three children, Rabi, Zoey, and Dylan, for their continued love and support.

# Index

Acuña, Cristóbal de, 181, 184, 190, 193, 258
Aguirre, Lope de, 179
Almagro, Diego de, 171
Alsedo y Herrera, Dionesio de, 88, 95–96, 102, 112, 298
  and La Condamine, 99–102
  replacement of, 109–110
Altar volcano, 173–174
Altitude measurements, 68, 122
Amadís de Gaula, 36–37
Amazon River, 3, 164, 169, 175–193, 200, 206, 258, 279
  discovery of mouth of, 175
  maps of, 183(illus.), 185(illus.), 188, 193(illus.), 195(illus.)
  population decline along, 193
  See also Marañón River
Amazons (women warriors), 38, 40, 43–44, 44(illus.), 58, 175, 178, 182, 190
Andes mountains, 80, 88, 90–91, 118, 119, 164, 170, 175, 176, 195, 226, 124, 272
  Guanacas Pass, 158

Andoas (mission station), 231, 239, 240, 243, 251, 253, 262, 264, 274, 275–276
Animals. See Wildlife
Ants, 256–257, 258, 270
Aparia the Great, 177
Araujo y Río, Joseph de, 110, 111–113, 298
Aristotle, 9, 14
Armendáriz, José de (Marqués de Castelfuerte), 32, 33, 298
Atahualpa (Inca ruler), 40–41, 42, 43(illus.), 94, 124
Auschwitz survivors, 271–272
Aztecs, 39, 54
Azuays, 129–130, 131

Baños (town), 232, 234, 235, 237, 267
Barbasco root, 191
Barometers, 66, 68, 79, 115, 122, 129
Barry, David, 289
Bats, 240, 243, 250, 259
Belém do Pará, 179. See also Pará
Benalcázar, Sebastián de, 94
Benavides José, 102
Bernoulli, Johann, 26, 29, 126, 298

Birds, 234, 242, 248, 250, 259
Biscay, Acarete du, 59
Blechynden, Thomas, 113
Bobonaza River, 237, 238, 240–242,
    243–245, 249, 252(illus.), 254, 257,
    275
Bogé, Phelipe, 230, 244, 246, 262, 263
Botflies, 258, 274, 281
Bouguer, Pierre, 29, 47, 49–50, 49(illus.),
    51, 60, 64, 65, 66, 67, 68, 70–71, 77,
    78, 80–81, 82, 83, 89, 83, 96, 101,
    103, 109, 114, 115, 117, 120, 121,
    125–126, 128–129, 130, 142, 145,
    158, 162, 163, 164, 166
  death of, 287
  disparagement of La Condamine,
    196–197
Bourbon kings, 60, 61, 107
Brazil, 229
Bridges, 86–87, 90, 96, 186, 232, 235,
    236(illus.)
Bry, Theodore de, 55, 56(illus.)
Buffon, Georges Leclerc de, 208, 292,
    298–299
Bullfighting, 142–143, 174
Burnet, Thomas, 25
Burriel, Andres, 197

Canada, 220
Cañar (town), 130
Candiru fish, 249
Canelos (village), 231, 235, 237, 238–240
Cannibalism, 251
Caoutchouc, 163
Carib Indians, 67. 206
Carletti, Francesco, 56, 58–59
Carmelites, 193, 201
Cartagena, Peru, 71, 72–75, 99, 158, 159,
    199
Carvajal, Gaspar de, 44, 177, 178, 190
Cassini, Jean-Dominique, 18, 19–20, 25,
    26, 27, 28, 29, 102, 103, 126, 194, 299
  son of (Jacques), 19–20, 21, 102, 103,
    126, 194, 299
Caste system, 74, 140
Castillo, Bernal Díaz del, 39, 54
Cathedrals/churches, 94, 96, 171
Catholic Church, 21, 22, 36, 39

and child brides, 151
  *See also* Christianity; Jesuits; Virgin
    Mary
Cayambe, plain of, 103, 104
Cayenne, French Guiana, 194, 202, 206,
    208, 214, 215, 285
Celestial observations. *See* Latitude, and
    measuring altitude of sun or star
Censorship, 55–56
Chagres River, 77, 78, 79(illus.)
Chambo River, 231
Chapetones, 112
Charles II (King of Spain), 60, 69
Chastity, 37
*Chatas* (barges), 77–78
Châtelet, Gabrielle-Émilie du, 28
Children, 73, 74, 128, 151, 170. *See also*
    Convent schools
Choiseul, Étienne-François de, 220,
    220(n), 221, 222, 283, 284, 299
Choiseul-Praslin, Cesar-Gabriel de, 284,
    299
Christianity, 8, 11, 37, 174, 182, 218. *See*
    *also* Catholic Church; Huguenots
*Chronicle of Don Roderick*, 38
Chuchunga River, 186
Cinchona trees, 110–111, 186, 194, 195,
    212
Clairaut, Alexis-Claude, 27, 51, 126, 127,
    299
Clothing, 97–98, 98(illus.), 101, 102, 193,
    251, 254, 262, 276
Colbert, Jean-Baptiste, 16, 17
Columbus, Christopher, 13, 67
Compasses, 12–13, 189
Concubines, 45, 229
Condorcet, Jean, 50
Conquistadors, 38–43, 54, 82, 89, 176
  cruelty of, 55, 56(illus.)
Contraband, selling of, 112(n)
Convent schools, 34, 46, 108, 151, 217
Copernicus, Nicholas, 21
Corregidors, 33, 88, 138, 146, 217, 279
Cortés, Hernando, 38–40, 54
Couplet (expedition assistant), 52, 53, 79,
    98, 103–104, 287
Creoles, 32, 45, 112, 113, 140, 141, 151,
    157, 161

Crespo, Juan Jiménez, 136–137, 142, 143
Cuba, 38
Cuenca, Peru, 129, 131, 134, 135–137,
  142, 145, 146, 147, 149, 165, 185
Curare, 189
Cuzco region, 40, 42

Daniel, João, 182, 193
Davalos, Joseph, 128
Dehydration, 261, 270–271
Delille, Jacques, 197
Desaguliers, John Theophilus, 27
Descartes, René, 8, 22–23, 24, 27, 28, 299
D'Herouville (Count), 222, 225, 299
Diguja, Joseph, 265–266, 299
*Discourse on Method* (Descartes), 8, 22
*Discourses on Two Sciences* (Galileo), 22
*Discurso y reflexiones políticos sobre el*
  *estado presente de los reynos del Peru*
  (Ulloa), 289
Disease, 76–77, 182, 206. *See also*
  Malaria; Smallpox; Yellow fever
Donner Party, 261(n)
D'Oreasaval, Tristan, 225, 226, 277,
  284–285, 299
D'Orvilliers, Gilbert Guillouet, 202, 206,
  209, 211, 212, 214, 299
Dowries, 160, 172
Drake, Sir Francis, 72
Dunezat (commander of Cayenne),
  214–215
Dutch Guiana, 194

Earth
  circumference of, 9–10, 11, 13, 18, 20,
    24, 62, 102, 103
  rotation of, 194
  size/shape of, 7, 8–9, 11, 12, 14, 15, 20,
    21, 24, 25–26, 29, 30, 51, 61, 62, 70,
    102–103, 126, 162, 166, 194
Eclipses, 163
Eisenschmidt, Samuel, 25
El Cid, 35
El Dorado, 57, 58, 175, 176, 179, 190
Elites, 152, 172, 199, 218, 227. *See also*
  *under* Quito
Emeralds, 82–83, 101
Encomienda system, 39, 54, 137

England, 25, 26, 36, 54, 60, 179, 199, 220
  British Armada, 157, 159
  Royal Society of London, 27, 66, 197
Enlightenment movement, 7–8, 36, 122,
  142, 167, 190
*Entretiens sur la pluralisté des mondes*
  (Fontenelle), 23
Eratosthenes, 9
Escabo, Manuel de, 102
Esmeraldas/Esmeraldas River, 89, 93,
  163
Expedition to equator, 29–30, 47, 51–52,
  290
  end of, 169–170
  illness/deaths during, 68–69, 104, 115,
    125, 157, 198
  letters to, 125, 126
  members of, 52, 63, 287–288, 297
  money problems of, 100–101, 109, 125,
    158, 170
  scientific equipment for, 48, 52, 63,
    66–67, 76, 79, 90, 95, 115, 147
  Spanish conditions for, 62–63
  tensions among leaders of, 70–71, 78,
    80–81, 125, 157, 184
  voyage to Quito, 69(illus.)

Feijoo, Benito Jerónimo, 61
Ferdinand III (Castilian king), 35
Fernel, Jean, 14
Fiedmont (Governor), 219, 222–223, 224,
  283, 299–300
Fontenelle, Bernard Le Bovier de, 23, 26,
  27–28
Food(s), 78, 79, 90, 96, 161, 172, 177, 178,
  181, 232, 235, 243, 246, 250, 252,
  254, 275
  in rain forests, 258–260
Forsyth, Adrian, 256
Fort Curupa, 202, 281
France, 25, 26, 36, 54, 69, 108, 142, 160,
  175, 179, 206–207, 214, 219, 229
  arrival of Jean and Isabel Godin in,
    286
  Compagnie Royale de la Mer
    Pacifique, 60
  French Academy of Sciences, 7, 8,
    16–18, 20, 22, 25–26, 27, 28, 20, 47,

48, 66, 111, 119, 126, 194, 197, 198, 208, 287, 288, 292, 297
overseas empire of, 220
Paris, 8, 14, 18
Paris observatory, 18, 19(illus.)
*See also under* Maps
Franciscan monks, 180
French Guiana, 2, 3, 61, 202, 205–206, 292
colonists sent to, 220
*See also* Guiana; *individual towns*
Frezier, Amadée, 59
Frisius, Gemma, 14
Fritz, Samuel, 183–184, 194
Froidevaux, Henri, 209

Galelei, Galileo, 15–16. 18, 22
Games, 174
Gnomon, 189
Godin, Isabel, 2–3, 149
death of, 295
described, 4, 154, 281
illness of, 284
and Jean Rocha, 277–278, 279
journey to meet Jean Godin, 3–5, 229–242
letter concerning Joaquín's freedom, 279–280
maids of, 230, 252
members of traveling party, 298
nephew of, 294
pregnancies/children of, 161, 169, 170, 175, 200, 211, 215–216, 217, 218, 226. 298
properties owned by, 172, 217, 229
religious faith of, 218, 244, 271, 273, 278
reunion with Jean Godin, 281–282
statue of, 2
stranded on sandbars and in rain forest, 242–255, 257–258, 261–262, 269–271
*See also* Gramesón, Isabel
Godin, Jean, 2–3, 52–53, 64, 79, 86, 107, 108, 114, 149, 156, 157–161, 198, 253, 254, 266, 279
attempt to return to France, 199–203.
*See also* Godin Jean, passports for

brother of, 286
business ventures of, 170, 175, 219, 283, 284, 285, 292
death of, 294
inventory of Cayenne forests by, 208
and La Condamine, 169, 200, 201, 208, 210, 219–220,
286, 292–293, 295
marriage of, 160–161
as official geographer of expedition, 293
passports for, 202, 208, 209, 210, 211–212, 215, 219
proposal that France seize northern banks of the Amazon, 206–208, 212–214, 220–221
reunion with Isabel Godin, 281–282
as signal carrier, 118–120, 130, 158, 169
will of, 293–294
*See also under* La Condamine, Charles-Marie de
Godin, Louis, 29, 47–49, 51, 64, 65, 66, 70–71, 77, 78, 80–81, 95, 98, 100–101, 103, 109, 114, 147, 157, 158, 198, 287–288
death of, 287, 288
illness of, 125
Gold/silver, 39, 41, 42, 43, 54, 58–59. 93, 111, 124, 176, 190, 212
Gorjaô, Francis Mendoza, 201
Graham, George, 48, 147
Gramesón, Isabel, 30, 34, 46, 108
brothers/parents of, 4, 31–33, 174, 216, 217–218, 225, 229, 230, 238, 244, 245, 252, 253, 254, 257, 261, 269, 297–298. *See also* Gramesón y Bruno, Pedro Manuel
dowry of, 160, 217
engagement/marriage to Jean Godin, 160–161
sister of, 174–175, 229, 285–286
*See also* Godin, Isabel
Gramesón, Joaquín (slave), 226, 229–230, 244, 246, 262–266, 277, 280
release from prison, 285–286
Gramesón, Martin, 229, 253, 254, 257, 261

Gramesón y Bruno, Pedro Manuel,
    32–33, 107–108, 149, 160, 174, 217,
    238, 277, 280, 285
  death of, 293
Granada, 36, 155(n)
Grandmaison, Jean-Antoine, 294, 295
Gravity, 20, 21, 23, 24–25, 28, 48, 62, 115,
    127, 164, 194
  and altitude, 121–122
Greece (ancient), 8–9, 10, 15, 21
Guaranda (village), 88
Guayaquil, Peru, 32–33, 82, 84, 89, 154
Guerrero, Tomás, 102
Guiana, 57, 179, 190, 214. *See also*
    French Guiana; Dutch Guiana

Hadley, John, 66
Halley, Edmond, 48
Hapsburg kings, 60
Henriquez de Ribera, Francisca, 110
Hipparchus, 10
Hispaniola, 68, 69
Holland, 26, 36, 54, 179. *See also*
    Netherlands
Honor, 101
Hormaegui (Jesuit rector), 101
Howler monkeys, 239–240, 250
Huayna Capac (Inca ruler), 40, 94
Hugo (instrument maker), 52, 118, 147,
    155, 157, 161, 164, 169, 198, 287
Huguenots, 26–27
Humboldt, Alexander von, 234, 256
Huygens, Christiaan, 16, 17, 23, 26

Illness. *See* Disease; Expedition to equa-
    tor, illness/deaths during
Incas, 40, 94, 119, 170, 176
Indians, 45, 93–94, 116, 117, 120, 121,
    124, 148–149, 173, 177–178, 180,
    181, 209, 227, 258
  of Andoas, 263, 264, 279
  of Canelos, 238–239, 240, 242, 243,
    245, 251, 273–274
  exploitation/physical abuse of,
    137–140, 176, 229, 289
  Isabel's Indian rescuers, 273–274,
    275–276
  in Isabel's traveling group, 230, 232,

    235–236, 239, 240
  revolts of, 199, 218, 228
  traditional customs of, 192
  *See also individual Indian groups*
Indicopleustes, Cosmas, 11
Insecticides, 259
Insects, 75, 83, 86, 176, 205, 247, 250, 251,
    259, 260, 262, 275. *See also* Ants;
    Botflies; Mosquitoes; *under* Rain
    forest
Isabella and Ferdinand (Iberian rulers),
    36

Jaen, 184, 186
Jaguars, 248–249, 259
Jenkins, Robert, 157(n)
Jesuits, 99, 100, 101, 102, 128, 140, 145,
    166, 181, 182, 193, 209, 211, 225,
    226, 238
  expulsion from Peru, 228–229, 276
Jews, 35, 36
Jibaros Indians, 186–187, 187(n),
    191–192, 251, 258, 265
Joaquín. *See* Gramesón, Joaquín
*Journal du voyage fait par ordre du roi à*
    *l'équateur* (La Condamine), 291
Juan y Santacilia, Jorge, 71, 72, 73, 75, 76,
    77, 81, 84, 87, 96, 104, 105, 121, 137,
    138–139, 144, 227, 288
  and Araujo, 112–113
  dispute with La Condamine, 155–157
  return to Europe, 197, 289
Jupiter (planet), 20, 25
  moons of, 15–16, 18, 19, 188
Jussieu, Joseph de, 52, 67, 69, 71, 77, 78,
    79, 118, 129, 145, 157, 198–199
  return to Paris and death of, 288

Kepler, Johannes, 21, 24
Knights, 34, 35, 36–38, 39, 45, 59, 152
Kricher, John, 257

La Cerda, Commander, 210
La Condamine, Charles-Marie de, 47,
    50–51, 51(illus.), 51–52, 61, 63, 64,
    65, 66, 67, 70–71, 76, 77, 78, 79,
    80–81, 82, 83, 96, 103, 110, 113, 114,
    115, 120, 121, 128, 130, 136, 141,

148–149, 154, 155
dispute with Ulloa and Juan, 155–157,
165
eulogized, 292
final years, 290–292
illness of, 68–69
and Jean Godin. *See* Godin, Jean, and
La Condamine
and murder of Senièrgues, 144, 155,
165, 185
and Pardo de Figueroa, 107
publications by, 291
return to France, 194–197
and rubber/platinum/*quinquina*, 163,
191, 195
sale of personal belongings, 101–102
title page of book by, 196(illus.)
treatise on cinchona tree and leaves,
110–111
trip to Quito, 89–91, 98–100
trunk of curiosities of, 158–159
voyage down Amazon River, 184–193
Laguna del Colta, 170
Laguna Ishpingococha, 249
Lagunas (village), 183, 184, 188, 191, 225,
265, 276, 277, 284
Lake Parima, 58, 190
Langlois, Claude, 48, 117
Languages, 53, 79, 128, 154, 201, 216. *See
also* Quechua language
Lapland expedition, 70, 126, 127, 128,
162, 166, 167
Las Casas, Bartolomé de, 54
Latitude, 10, 11, 13, 14, 18. 19, 20–21, 29,
51, 70, 91, 102–103, 114, 126, 129
determining at sea, 66, 67
and measuring altitude of sun or star,
133, 147, 148, 149, 154, 155,
161–162, 189
*L'Aventure* (ship), 208, 209
Leach, John, 271, 272–273
Lemaire, Marc, 295
Lemoyne (deputy to d'Orvilliers), 212,
214
Leon, Diego de, 136, 146, 165, 186
León, Pedro Cieza de, 171
León Portocarrero, Pedro de, 59
Letters, 125, 126, 203, 208, 209–210, 211,

214(n), 214–215, 216, 219–220, 221,
222, 224, 225, 277, 278, 279–280,
283, 284, 286, 292, 295
Letters of credit, 100, 109, 110, 113
*Lettres philosophiques* (Voltaire), 28–29
Lima, Peru, 99, 110, 111–112, 128, 155,
184, 199
Liripamba (Inca town), 170–171
Loneliness, 125
Longitude, 10–11, 13, 15, 16, 18, 19, 70,
82, 89, 102–103, 114, 125, 147, 188.
*See also* Meridians
Loreto (mission station), 225, 226, 229,
230, 277, 279, 280
Los Colorados Indians, 90
Louisiana, 290
Louis XIV (King of France), 16, 19, 60,
300
Louis XV (King of France), 61–62, 292,
293, 300
Luis de León, Fray, 142
Lunar eclipse, 82

Machiparos Indians, 177
Maclaurin, Colin, 146
Magdalena River, 158
Magnetic attraction at poles, 163
Malaria, 77, 110, 183, 195
Maldonado, Pedro, 3, 89, 100, 101, 128,
163, 165, 171, 184, 188–189, 191,
192, 193, 194, 197–198, 209, 228, 300
death of, 198(n)
Maldonado, Ramon, 100, 101, 128
Manaos Indians, 190
Maps, 52, 62, 70, 77, 81, 89, 157, 195
Christian, 11, 12(illus.), 37
of colonial South America, 57–58, 82,
207(illus.)
of France, 18, 19, 21
of Henricus Martellus, 13(illus.)
Ptolemy's map of the world, 10(illus.),
13
of Quito, 97(illus.), 163
*See also under* Amazon River
Marañón River, 182(n), 186–187, 192,
276–277. *See also* Amazon River
Margarita (island), 179
Marriage, 149, 151–152, 153, 160–161,

171, 172, 291, 294
Martel (Captain), 281, 283
Martín, Luis, 153
Martinez, Juan, 57
Martinique, 67–68
Maupertuis, Pierre-Louis Moreau de, 27,
    29, 51, 70, 103, 126–127, 162, 166,
    194, 300
Maurepas, Jean-Frédéric Phélypeaux de
    (Count), 61, 100, 125, 300
Measurement standardization, 164,
    167(illus.), 291
*Mémoire sur differents bois dans l'ile de
    Cayenne* (J. Godin), 208
*Mémoire sur la navigation de l'Amazone*
    (J. Godin), 206
Mendoza, José de (Marqués de
    Villagarcía), 72, 99, 100, 109, 113,
    300
Meridians, 9, 18, 20, 25, 102, 119, 120,
    131, 133, 147, 154, 162, 166. *See also*
    Longitude
*Mesure des trois premiers degrés du méridi-
    en dans l'hémisphere austral* (La
    Condamine), 291
Meters, 164, 164(n)
Mexico, 38, 39, 179
Middle Ages, 11–12, 35, 36, 57, 142
Mission stations, 182–183, 192, 193, 200,
    201, 225, 229, 230
Mita labor service, 138–140, 218, 289
Montezuma, 39
Moors, 34–36, 45
Morainville (engineer and assistant), 52,
    118, 142, 156, 157, 169, 198, 287
Mosquitoes, 75, 76, 83, 84, 239, 248,
    255–256, 270–271
    laden with botfly eggs, 258
    *See also* Insects
Mount Chimborazo, 171, 173(illus.),
    173–174, 230
Mount Corazon, 122, 130
Mount Cotopaxi, 121
Mount Pelée, 67, 68
Mount Pichincha, 114–118, 122, 124, 164
Mount Sangay, 129, 130
Mount Tungurahua, 3, 184

Napo River, 176–177, 180
Netherlands, 60, 194. *See also* Holland
*New Discovery of the Great River of the
    Amazons* (Acuña), 181–182, 184
Newton, Sir Isaac, 21, 24–29, 51, 102,
    126, 127, 166, 194, 300
Neyra, Nicolás de, 143–144, 146, 165,
    186
Nono (village), 100
Norwood, Richard, 15, 24
*Noticias Americanas* (Ulloa), 290
*Noticias secretas de América* (Ulloa), 289
Noyce, Wilfrid, 271, 272–273

Observatories (astronomical), 134, 147,
    164, 166. *See also* France, Paris
    observatory
Octants, 66–67
Omaguas (town), 265
Omaguas Indians, 177, 179, 180, 181,
    183, 191, 192
Orellana, Francisco de, 43, 177, 178, 258
Oyapock, French Guiana, 219, 223, 281,
    282, 283

Palm cabbage, 260
Panama City, 78
Pará (town), 179, 180, 181, 184, 191, 194,
    201, 211, 214
Pardo de Figueroa, José Augustín
    (Marqués de Valleumbroso), 31, 32,
    107, 156, 165–166
Pardo de Figueroa, Josefa, 31, 32, 217
Pascal, Blaise, 68
Passports. *See under* Godin, Jean
Pastaza River, 231, 232, 235, 238, 255,
    275, 276
Pedro II (King of Portugal), 184
Pelletier family, 107–108, 160
Peña, Antonio, 265
Pendulum clocks, 16, 17(illus.), 19, 20,
    24, 26, 103, 115, 121, 127, 148(illus.).
    *See also* Seconds pendulum
Peru, 31, 45, 53, 54, 56, 62, 76, 128, 137,
    179
    accounts of Peruvian society, 58–59
    audiencias in, 88(n), 94, 95(illus.)
    corrupt clergy in, 140–141

expulsion of Jesuits from, 228–229, 276
Huancavelica province, 289—290
racial mixtures in, 73–74
Spaniards in, 32, 45, 141, 151
Viceroyalty of Peru in 1650, 95(illus.)
viceroy of. *See* Mendoza, José de (Marqués de Villagarcía)
*See also individual locations*
Philip III (King of Spain), 16
Philip IV (King of Spain), 60
Philip V (King of Spain), 60–61, 61–63, 72, 94, 300
*Philosophical Transactions* (Royal Society of London), 27
Picard, Jean, 18, 19–20, 24, 300
Picot, Magdeleine, 294, 295
Pintado, Manuel, 71
Pinzón, Vicente Yáñez, 175
Pirates, 54, 69, 72, 194,k 198
Pizarro, Francisco, 40–42, 53, 54–55, 94, 171, 176
Pizarro, Gonzalo, 43, 176–177, 178, 235
Platinum, 163, 195
Plumb lines, 147(n), 149
Poison arrows, 189
Poleni (Marquis), 66
Pongo de Manseriche, 182, 185, 187, 188(illus.)
*Portefaix* (ship), 63, 65, 69
Porto Bello, Peru, 76–77, 199
Portugal/Portuguese, 176, 179–180, 181, 184, 191, 194, 201, 202, 203, 206, 212, 214, 220, 223, 229, 280, 283
Posidonius, 9, 11
Potosí, Peru, 288, 288(n)
Poverty, 73
Prayer, 271, 272, 273
*Principia* (Newton), 24–25
*Principles of Philosophy* (Descartes), 22
Printing press, 36
Ptolemy, Claudius, 11, 14
Puruhás Indians, 94, 170
Pyramid markers, 120, 155–156, 156(illus.), 165

Quadrants, 48, 117, 149
Quechua language, 94, 119, 120, 175, 201, 208, 209, 239, 274, 293
Quesada, Manuela, 136, 143
*Quinquina*/quinine110, 163, 195
Quito, Peru, 81, 82, 88, 91, 93–98, 112, 113, 128, 141, 149, 154, 157, 160, 165–166, 170, 178, 180, 198, 211, 265, 267
daily life in, 96
elites in, 107, 137, 161
Quitus Indians, 93–94

Racial mixtures. *See under* Peru
Rafts, 186, 187, 252–253, 263
Rain, 76, 84, 90, 105, 130, 148, 176, 186, 205, 234, 235, 237, 241, 244, 250, 261. *See also* Weather
Rain forest, 234, 239, 242, 247–248, 254–262
insects in, 255–257, 258, 262
Raleigh, Sir Walter, 54, 57, 58
Rebello (boat captain), 222–223, 224, 277, 279, 280, 281, 300
Refraction studies, 83, 128
*Relacion historica del viage a la America Merídional* (Ulloa and Juan), 197, 289
*Relation abrégée d'un voyage fait dans l'intérieur de l'Amérique Méridionale* (La Condamine), 286, 291
*Requierimiento* (document), 41–42, 54
Richer, Jean, 20, 24, 26, 194, 300
Ricour (ship captain), 65, 67
Riobamba, Peru, 1–2, 3, 125, 127–128, 129, 141, 170–175, 198, 210, 218, 226, 229, 230, 266, 267, 279, 285
Jean Godin's attempt to return to, 211–215
local economy, 199, 217
Río Negro River, 178, 191, 193
Rocha, Jean, 230, 243, 245–246, 247, 251, 262, 263, 265, 277–278, 279
Romances of chivalry, 36, 37–38, 152–153
Romero, Nicolás, 265, 277, 278, 279, 300
Rotenone, 191
Rouillé, Antoine-Louis, 202, 206, 208, 209, 210, 211, 212, 300
Rubber, 163, 191, 195

Rumiñahui, 94
Russian Academy of Sciences, 27

*Sacred Theory of the Earth* (Burnet), 25
Saint Domingue, 68, 70, 75
*San Cristóbal* (ship), 80, 82
Santa Fe de Bogotá, 155, 155(n)
Science, 8, 15, 23, 26, 48, 62, 95, 115, 122,
    129, 190, 291
    development of, 195
    *See also* Expedition to equator, scien-
      tific equipment for
Seconds pendulum, 166, 167(illus.), 194.
    *See also* Pendulum clocks
Senièrgues, Jean, 52, 67, 69, 80–81,
    135–137, 142, 287
    murder of, 143–146, 148, 155, 185
Serrano, Sebastián, 136, 143–144, 146,
    165
Seven Years War, 219–220
Sexuality, 142, 151, 153–154
Shackleton, Ernest, 272
*Short Account of the Destruction of the*
    *Indies, A* (Las Casas), 54–55, 289
Shyri Nation, 94
Slavery/slaves, 45, 60, 63, 67, 76, 80, 89,
    175, 206, 212, 215, 226, 226(n), 229,
    244, 285
    enslavement of Indians, 140, 180, 182,
      193, 228
Smallpox, 40, 50, 191, 198, 226, 238, 244,
    291
Snakes, 227–228, 228(n), 242, 247, 248,
    251
Snell, Willebrord, 15, 24
Sound, speed of, 125, 163
Space, 22, 23(illus.)
Spain, 32, 34–38, 53–56, 60, 62, 69, 81, 94,
    99, 100, 107, 166(n), 176, 179, 180,
    181, 182, 199, 214, 229, 289, 290
    *Casa de Contratación*, 53
    labor legislation for colonies, 137–138.
      *See also* Mita labor service
    Spanish Inquisition, 55, 61, 72
Spruce, Richard, 237, 238, 241, 251,
    255–256
Starvation, 260–262. *See also*
    Dehydration

Stirling, James, 127
Strabo, 10, 11
Suarez, Antonio, 102
Suasti, Juan, 262, 263, 264–265, 275, 276,
    301

*Tapada,* 153
Tarabita, 122
Tarqui, plain of, 133, 147, 148, 164, 184
Taxes, 152, 170, 199, 217
Teixeira, Pedro, 180, 181
Telescopes, 188
Tequendama Falls, 158, 159(illus.)
Teresa de Jesus of Ávila, Saint, 153
Textiles, 170, 172, 199, 217
*They Survived: A Study of the Will to Live*
    (Noyce), 271
Tiira, Ensio, 272
Time, measurement of, 11. *See also*
    Pendulum clocks
*Tirant lo Blanch,* 36, 38
Topo River, 237
Torricelli, Evangelista, 68
Travelogues, 56, 60, 75
*Treatise of the Figure of the Earth*
    (Eisenschmidt), 25
Treaty of Ryswick, 69
Treaty of Tordesillas, 176
Treaty of Utrecht, 26, 60, 157(n)
Triangulation, 14. 19–20, 53, 62, 114,
    128, 129–130, 131–133
    baseline for, 103, 104–106, 117, 155,
      156(illus.), 166(n)
    second baseline for, 131, 133
    wooden pyramids and tents as mark-
      ers for, 120
*True History of the Conquest of New*
    *Spain* (del Castillo), 39
Tungurahua volcano, 173–174, 232
Tupac Yupanqui, 94

Ulloa, Antonio de, 71–72, 73, 75, 76, 77,
    78, 80, 81, 84, 87, 96, 97–98, 105,
    115, 116, 117, 122, 124, 137,
    138–139, 144, 152, 227, 288
    and Araujo, 112–113
    dispute with La Condamine, 155–157
    illness of, 125

post-expedition life and death of, 197, 289–290
Urquizu, Bruno de, 217
Ursúa, Pedro de, 179

*Vautour* (ship), 75, 76, 77
Velázquez, Diego, 38
Velvarde, Vincente de, 41, 42
Verguin, Jean, 52, 70, 77, 79, 103, 114, 118, 130, 156, 157, 163, 169, 198, 287
Vicuna, Gregorio, 142, 144
Villa Rica de Vera Cruz. 38
Violence, 137, 141, 142, 143–146
Virginity, 141, 152, 161
Virgin Mary, 174, 244
Visconti, Ignatius, 211, 225
Volcanoes, 115(n), 122, 129, 130, 131(illus.), 164, 171, 173–174, 232
Voltaire, François-Marie Arouet de, 7, 28–29, 51, 126, 194, 195–196, 301
Von Hagen, Victor, 259
Vrillière, Louis Phélypeaux de, 292, 301

War of Jenkins's Ear, 157(n), 166, 199
War of Spanish Succession, 20, 26, 60
Weather, 105–106, 116, 117, 119, 130, 135, 148, 171, 250, 270. *See also* Rain

West Indies, 67–68, 220
Whirlwinds, 106
Whiteness, 152, 154
Wildlife, 75, 78, 181, 189, 205, 234, 239, 242, 248–249, 251, 259
Women/girls, 34, 37, 229, 236–237
  child brides, 151
  Creole, 151–152
  elite, 172
  French, 160
  Indian, 193
  mulatto/mestizo, 153
  Peruvian, 59, 72–73, 97–98, 107, 108, 166, 202, 267
  sequestration of girls and women, 35, 45–46, 152, 153, 172
  *See also* Amazons; Virginity
Woods, 208, 209

Yaruqui, plain of, 104, 106(illus.), 114, 117, 164
Yellow fever, 68–69

Zabala, Antonio, 267, 285–286
Zapater, Domingo, 279
Zaruma (town), 185–186
Zenith sectors, 147, 148(illus.), 154–155, 157, 161, 162, 164, 166